RE...
for the
OTHER
SIDE

Dawn Hill was born in Launceston, Tasmania, and spent most of her childhood on King Island in Bass Strait. Although she began training as a nurse, circumstances prevented her finishing the course, and she now describes herself as a housewife. At the moment she is working on a second, more advanced guide to psychic development.

Dawn lives in Sydney with her husband Roland, son Darryl, and a large collection of animals.

REACHING
for the
OTHER
SIDE

Dawn Hill

Pan Books Sydney and London

for Roland

First published 1982 by Pan Books (Australia) Pty Limited
68 Moncur Street, Woollahra, Sydney
9 8 7 6 5 4 3
© Dawn Hill 1982

National Library of Australia
Cataloguing-in-Publication data
Hill, Dawn, 1946-
   Reaching for the other side.
   ISBN 0 330 27029 X.
   1. Psychical research. I. Title.
133.8'092'4

Printed and bound in Australia by
The Dominion Press–Hedges & Bell, Victoria

Contents

PART ONE

My Introduction to the Supernatural

CHAPTER ONE

What is happening to me?

I sat stiffly in my seat as the aircraft droned its way across Bass Strait towards Tasmania. It seemed incongruous to me that the other passengers and the cabin crew were able to carry on as though this flight were no different from countless others. The aura of impending disaster was so strong that I could not understand why my fellow travellers failed to notice it; yet it seemed that of them all, I was the only one who knew that the aircraft was doomed to crash. It was 11 a.m. on a beautiful sunny Sunday and I was only eighteen years old. I didn't want to die.

On the ground in Melbourne it had been fairly easy to tell myself that I was simply suffering from pre-flight jitters, even though I loved flying and hadn't been scared of aeroplanes since I was three years old. But now I could sense the aroma of death and the vision that had assailed me an hour before did not seem so ridiculous.

I didn't try to think about the incident but it kept forcing itself into my head. I grew weary of pushing it away and allowed my mind to back-track over the events that had taken place in the airport lounge, unnoticed by the teeming bustle of humanity that surrounded me.

As I idly watched the beehive of activity and awaited my flight call, I suddenly became aware of a feeling of disorientation. A grey mist seemed to grow up and enshroud me, shutting me off from my surroundings. I closed my eyes.

Immediately I felt myself hurtling downwards in a

dizzying fall. I heard the screeching sound of disinteg-rating metal, then suddenly it stopped and there was nothing but an eerie silence. I was totally disoriented—it was as though I had been transported into another dimension. Then, faintly at first, but with increasing volume, I became aware of the hubbub of voices around me. I opened my eyes and found that I was back in the airport lounge and my flight was being called.

I sat for a few moments, debating whether I should let the flight pass and get myself onto another plane. But I did not know if there would be another flight to my home town that day and my parents would certainly worry if I failed to arrive. Even if I rang them, what could I say? 'Sorry, folks, I've got the horrors and I'm too frightened to get onto the plane'?

Irritably, I told myself to be sensible: the airline had an impeccable safety record. Besides, if it were my fate to be killed in an airline disaster, it would be the plane I travelled on that crashed. I would not be able to escape my fate, no matter how often I changed my booking. I gathered up my bag and my courage and headed for the embarkation gate. The roar of aircraft engines on the tarmac made me think of hungy lions awaiting the first course of Christians. . .

I kept repeating to myself the admonition that I had heard so often as a child: 'Get hold of yourself girl! You're letting your imagination run away with you!' Yes, I thought glumly as I buckled my seat belt, and how many times had my imaginative fancies proven to be correct? Far too often for my present comfort.

I struggled to regain my composure but I could not dispel the leaden feeling of approaching doom. 'Any moment now,' I thought. I closed my eyes and leaned wearily back in my seat, waiting in resignation for the sudden, sickening lurch and plummeting fall. The tension built up inside me. My nerves jangled raw edged as the moment drew closer. I could feel it coming, the moment in time that would kill.

I looked around in a near-panic: there was no escape . . . here it comes . . . *now*! I felt it. I knew it. I saw it. Then it was gone. I sat shaking as the powerful engines pulled the aircraft smoothly through clear, sunny skies. Soon the patchwork pattern of neatly tended farms slid beneath us as the plane dipped gracefully into its landing approach.

'Silly girl!' I smiled to myself as we taxied along the runway. 'You've spoiled your whole flight on account of that stupid daydream.'

The horror of that stupid daydream hit hard when I was told that at approximately 11 a.m. that morning, my favourite cousin Ray had been killed. He was a passenger in a car which had hurtled over a two-hundred foot cliff and smashed into the valley floor below.

My chief reaction to the news was utter astonishment. My mind simply failed to comprehend. I was so shocked that I could not even feel pain—or if I did, it was a pain so new to my experience that I was incapable of recognizing it. I felt as though I were sitting in the eye of an emotional cyclone. Around me swirled a torrent of violent and unfamiliar emotions; within I felt anaesthetised, unable to think or feel anything.

So blank was my response that at first my mother thought I had no feelings at all and she chided me for my callousness. I tried to explain my feelings, stammering with shock and, bless her, she understood. She simply left me alone with my thoughts until the reality penetrated, then she was there with warm, comforting arms and gentle words of consolation as I broke under the fury of the emotional storm.

There was a sense of unreality about the whole situation that had me bewildered. Ray was my junior by about eighteen months, tall, handsome and always smiling. I could not believe that such a lively soul could be snuffed out and simply cease to be. Although my conscious mind understood that he had been killed, my inner feelings were violently opposed to the idea. Logic told me to fight my emotions but I found myself clinging absurdly to the childlike notion, 'He isn't dead, he's just gone away'.

Inevitably, however, the finality of my cousin's journey swept over me and I realised at last that I was never to see him alive again. Then the tears came, and the anguished, heart-rending pain.

Hardest of all for me to bear was the realisation of the true meaning of my airport vision. I now understood that

9

some intangible force had been trying to alert me to the approaching tragedy an hour before it happened. If only I had been capable of interpreting my premonition correctly, it might have been possible for me to telephone Ray and warn him to stay at home that day. I felt that my ignorance had betrayed us both and I could not have been more responsible if I had been driving the car.

That is when I began to feel fear. If it were possible for me to have a premonition of tragedy once, it might happen again. I didn't want to know. As far as I was concerned, premonitions should only happen to seasoned psychics and occultists who knew how to cope with them. It never occurred to me that they all had to begin learning at some time.

I was only a teenager; I had never possessed any outstanding abilities before and I did not wish to start being different now, especially in such a horrifying way. The everyday world presented enough problems as it was; I neither wanted nor needed the added complication of visions that came unbidden, throwing my life and emotions into uncontrollable chaos. It frightened me.

I also felt a crushing burden of guilt. It was as though by receiving that premonition, I had been a party to my cousin's death. I felt like a murderess. I could not handle these dire thoughts alone and I took my distress to my mother. I really expected her to banish my fancies with a no-nonsense admonition and it would have been a vast relief for me if she had done so. But she listened quietly to my story and when I had finished, she placed a reassuring arm around my shoulders.

'Dawn, you have always had an uncanny sort of perception that has told you things you could not ordinarily have known. I don't think you ever fully realised what you were doing before but you have sometimes stopped me in my tracks with that insight of yours. I think it was inevitable that something like this would happen to you one day and I also think you are going to have to face the possibility that it will happen again. It's some sort of clairvoyance I suppose, but you are no more responsible for it than you are for the colour of your hair. You mustn't feel guilty.'

'How can I help it?' I cried. 'Heaven only knows what

I'm likely to do next. Whatever this ability is, I wish it would go away. I don't want to know when awful things are going to happen!'

Mum shook her head with obvious regret.

'I don't think you can just wish it away, dear. I don't know much about these things but I have an idea that once they start to happen, they keep on happening. You are going to have to get used to it somehow.'

I stared at her, horror-struck.

'Get *used* to it? How? It will drive me mad first!'

Again, she shook her head.

'Perhaps it won't if you learn to understand it. Just think, if you could find out how to interpret these premonitions properly, you might be able to warn people in time to stop these things from happening to them.'

I felt as though she had deserted me. I could not argue with her quiet common sense but my emotions were in rebellion. I retreated into a corner and subsided in moody contemplation. Whatever this strange ability was, it did nothing but upset me and I fully intended to do my utmost to drive it out. I was full of indignation at whatever unseen force had caused all of these complications and I resented the fact that I seemed to have little choice in the matter.

'My mind belongs to me,' I muttered sulkily. 'I won't have it invaded.'

My reaction might have been vastly different if I had been able to forecast good fortune instead of tragedy, for I was not in the least sceptical about psychic phenomena. Ghost stories were among my favourite forms of literature and I found the supernatural a fascinating subject. Whilst still in high school, I had written a horror story which gave my English master a few cold chills and caused him to inform me quite seriously that if I did not pursue a literary career when I left school, he would personally come back and haunt me. But my understanding of the subject was largely confined to fiction and I did not know that what I was experiencing was quite normal as far as psychic development is concerned. It is always easier to pick up vibrations which presage disaster, because the force behind them is stronger than the subtle emanations of pleasurable events.

I had no idea of how to go about learning to develop my gifts, even if I had wanted to do so. There was no one in my circle of acquaintances who knew anything about the subject and professional clairvoyants were generally regarded as little more than clever charlatans. I had no choice but to live one day at a time and hope that my unwelcome gift would subside into inactivity, at least as far as tragedies were concerned.

For a time, it seemed as though my wish had been fulfilled. I still had an uncanny instinct for predicting things, but it was confined to small matters, like knowing that the phone was about to ring or thinking about someone a few minutes before they knocked on the door. However, these things were easy to accept, particularly as I had always been able to do them and I regarded such events as a normal part of life. When other people seemed surprised about it I was slightly taken aback because I really believed it was an ability that everyone possessed to some extent. It didn't really occur to me to think that I was being psychic.

Two years passed and I moved to Sydney and married a young sailor. The wedding bells had hardly stopped ringing when I had another premonition, this time about my husband. I was watching him pack his sea bag in preparation for a trip, when I felt an irresistible urge to warn him to take care. He looked at me in surprise and asked for an explanation.

'I have a feeling that you might have a fall,' I answered hesitantly. 'Not a serious one, but enough to stun you. You should be careful of the number four and the colour green. There's another man involved—a fair-haired person. I keep thinking of the name Scott.'

Dennis patted me on the head with amusement.

'Imagination,' he assured me. 'Nothing will happen, you'll see.'

I believed it was more than likely that Dennis would prove to be correct. In retrospect, my impulse seemed silly and I decided to forget about it. Dennis was away for three weeks and the incident was totally forgotten by the time he returned, so I was quite unprepared for his actions. Dumping his bag on the floor, he eyed me speculatively.

'Do me a favour?' he asked. 'If you get any more premonitions about me, keep them to yourself.'

It was unnerving to hear that my premonition had been correct in almost every detail. He had been taking a shower after finishing his shift in the engine room when the ship pitched suddenly and he lost his balance. He fell heavily, stunning himself, and a shipmate came quickly to his aid. As he staggered to his feet, he noticed that the slippery floor of the shower recess was green. The time was four in the afternoon and the fair-haired mate who helped him to his feet was of Scottish descent—I shivered!

Far from being impressed by my ability to forecast the future, Dennis was alarmed by it. He was suspicious of anything that lay outside the boundaries of three-dimensional reality and he preferred to live his life within limits that he could see and understand.

My precognitive abilities subsided and I carried on once again with the business of day-to-day living, but from that time onwards a series of supernatural events began to occur around me. Strangely enough, I was often unaware of them. Only occasionally did I perceive anything unusual; it was more likely that the people with me would speak of something strange that was happening at the time.

Dennis and I had set up house in a tiny flat near Kings Cross. The apartment building was an old rabbit warren of a place, tucked away in an unfashionable back street. Our flat was a bit decrepit but it was all that we could afford and we were quite happy there. When a couple of inexplicable incidents happened, I cheerfully decided that the old place must have a resident ghost, an idea that only added to its atmosphere as far as I was concerned.

We were in the habit of allowing our clock to run down at weekends, so that we could spend our time unguided by anything other than our own whims. Despite this, we often heard a clock ticking loudly in the bedroom at night. I lost count of the number of times that Dennis picked up our clock and shook it as though he suspected it of playing tricks on us. But even when he had satisfied himself that the clock was silent, the steady ticking continued.

One night, I decided mischievously that I would challenge our phantom ticker.

'If there's anyone here, make something move,' I giggled. The windows and doors were closed but the curtains began to silently billow out into the room as though driven by some unseen breath of wind. Several times they lifted out horizontally, yet we could feel no breeze.

I shivered and cuddled closer to Dennis, who was staring at the curtains in disbelief.

'That will do, thank you,' I squeaked politely. 'You can leave the curtains alone now.' Obediently the curtains dropped and remained still. Dennis favoured me with a long, searching stare.

'Know something?' he murmured. 'You are really weird!'

I was quite undismayed by the presence of a supernatural being. In fact, when I became pregnant and gave up work, I often chatted to the ghost during the long, lonely days that I spent by myself while Dennis was at sea. It didn't matter that the conversations were all one-sided; I *felt* that the presence was listening in friendly silence.

After Darryl was born, the Navy allocated a service flat to us and we moved away from Kings Cross. Our new home was in a modern, high-rise apartment block and was twice the size of our previous flat. I thought that we had bidden farewell to our amiable ghost, but I was soon to decide that he had taken a liking to our company, for the supernatural events followed us to our new residence. Now, however, they did not make themselves so apparent to me.

It was Dennis who complained of hearing footsteps crossing the living-room floor and pacing up the passage in the middle of the night. He also mentioned hearing the bathroom door opening and closing. I heard none of this and, to be honest, I felt a little peeved because I was being left out.

As if to compensate, our ghostly visitor finally made his presence known to me. Dennis and I were lying in bed one night when there came a series of sharp knocks on the bedroom door.

14

'Did you hear what I heard?' I asked Dennis. He nodded and we both eyed the door, which stood innocently ajar. Almost immediately, the knocks were repeated, this time on the door of our bedroom cupboard, on the opposite side of the room. Dennis burrowed under the covers.

'Don't talk about it!' came his muffled request. 'I'm asleep. Can't hear a thing!'

As far as I was concerned, these inexplicable events only served to make life more interesting, but Dennis held quite the opposite point of view. Our ghost overstepped my boundaries only once while we were living in that flat and I truly believe it was unintentional on his part.

I was awakened one night by terrified screams from Darryl, who was at that time about two years old. Thinking he was having a nightmare, I hurried into his room, to find him backed up in the farthest corner of his cot, wide-eyed and panic-stricken. He flung himself into my arms and kept sobbing the same thing over and over:

'Go 'way, Man! Go 'way!'

'What man? Where?' I asked the terrified child. Hiding his face against my breast, he pointed to a corner of the room. I turned to look. To my eyes, the corner was empty.

'What is the man doing?'

'Nuffin!' whimpered Darryl. 'Just lookin'. Make him go 'way, Mummy.'

This placed me in a quandary. How to banish the spectre from Darryl's view? I could not just tell him that there was no man there, since he was obviously seeing one. For him to be reassured, he needed to see me take some action that impelled his unwanted visitor to leave.

I turned to face the corner, still cuddling Darryl against me.

'Listen, Man,' I began, feeling slightly ridiculous, 'you can't go around scaring babies. I know you don't mean any harm, but you are frightening Darryl. Go away now, and leave him in peace.'

'Has he gone now?' I asked Darryl. He peeped timidly over my shoulder, then nodded. I settled him back into bed and stayed with him until he fell asleep. As I trailed

15

back to bed, I muttered a few scolding words at the intruder:

'Dumb spook! Don't do that again!'

Supernatural visitations were not a subject that I cared to discuss with friends over a cup of coffee. Most of my acquaintances were other naval wives whose interest lay in more mundane directions. I was already aware that most of them regarded me as an idealistic dreamer, somewhat out of touch with reality, and instinct told me that any attempt to discuss the paranormal with them would not do my reputation for sanity any good.

However, there was one friend with whom I felt that I could discuss the subject. Her name was Christine and her outlook on life was similar to mine in many ways. After some judicious probing on my part, which revealed that she was not unsympathetic to the subject, I told her about our visitations. If I expected to surprise her, I was in for a disappointment. It was Christine who startled me.

'Your flat isn't haunted,' she announced. '*You* are!'

I almost choked on my coffee. 'What do you mean by that?' I spluttered.

'Precisely what I said,' was her matter-of-fact reply. 'Your ghost follows you around. I've felt it. When you walk past me, I feel a slight breeze. A few seconds later, there is always another breeze that follows you. The two are quite distinct.'

I was all ears as Christine explained her impressions. She had not seen or heard anything, she had only felt the breezes, but her intuition told her that the spirit was attached to me in some way and that its intentions were not hostile. She was the first person who had ever accepted my psychic experiences as normal and I was gratified to have found such acceptance. I was also intrigued by her attitude: I had always thought of supernatural events as arising outside myself. The idea that they might be directly connected *with* me was one I had never thought about.

There was more to come. Christine suspected that the psychic events which had been trailing me were all caused by this one spirit.

'I think it's trying to get your attention,' she said.

'Well, if that is the case, it has succeeded,' I commented.

16

'But why go to so much trouble?'

Christine shrugged. 'How should I know? Maybe it wants your help.'

'To do what?'

'Am I a clairvoyant?' she grinned wickedly. 'Why don't you try to learn more about it and find out for yourself?'

Back to square one! Here I was, several years after the event that had forced me to face the supernatural, still being told to find out more about it. My basically lazy mind protested vehemently: it's hopeless—like a dog chasing its tail—why not just forget about it? But a feeling was beginning to grow inside me and it argued softly that, deep down, it was my wish to understand. Besides, I told myself, it seemed unlikely that I would be allowed to drop the matter. Whoever or whatever wanted my attention, they had a persistent way of asking for it at the most unexpected times. And after all, had my unseen companion ever done me any harm? Could he or she (or it) be held responsible for the flaws in my perception of the attempted warnings that had come to me?

The idea that a spirit might be seeking my help was provocative. I am the kind of person who will stand in the street at 3 a.m., barefooted and clad in a nightgown, earnestly coaxing a stranded cat out of a tree. An appeal for help, particularly if it comes from a waif, is guaranteed to home in on my most sensitive spots. I had a sudden mental impression of a lost and lonely wraith, begging me not to turn it away. Ah yes, argued my logic, but what if it is a sinister creature, bent on ensnaring you for who knows what nefarious purpose?

Alas for logic, a mystery tantalises me only marginally less than an appeal for help. I was certainly not prepared to throw myself heedlessly into a pursuit of occult knowledge but neither could I ignore it. Whatever the arguments on either side, one central fact remained: the supernatural was not going to go away, even if I chose to deny it. Psychic events had happened to me, they were still happening and there was no reason to suppose that they would not continue to happen.

I no longer felt that I was being forced to undergo events over which I had no control. It seemed that I was being *asked* to become involved. It was apparent that I had

17

some degree of competency, or else the curtains would not have moved at my command, nor would I have been able to banish Darryl's nocturnal visitor. As to the extent of my abilities and their purpose, the answer was still shrouded in mystery. I had no idea of where I was heading, but I was beginning to have some notions as to how I should proceed.

Knowledge was the key. Somehow, I would have to find out all about the supernatural. Only when I understood the subject could I have any idea of my own role in relation to it. Reason told me that if a person has something to offer in the way of knowledge, chances are that he will write a book about it, so I could start by reading up on the subject.

I also felt that the churches might be able to help, since they are largely concerned with the hereafter. But which church? And whose books?

I have always had a deep love for the teachings of Christ, but I had rejected the religious faith in which I had been raised when, at the age of thirteen, I heard the minister defending war on the basis that our side always fights in the name of God. Even at that age, my own intelligence told me that violence of any kind is totally in opposition to the views presented by Jesus. I decided that the Saviour knew more about the will of God than our pompous reverend did, and from that time forward, I stubbornly resisted my mother's attempts to cajole me into returning to Sunday School.

However, my native faith was not the only church available. I decided to investigate some of the others. I visited numerous members of the clergy and listened to their views. Then I asked about the supernatural.

'Imagination!' scoffed one.

'The work of Satan!' squealed another.

'Have you ever had psychiatric treatment?' asked someone else.

I was quite alarmed by the idea that my experiences might be the work of the devil. If that were so, I wanted to be cleansed from all such influences. I prayed hard and often for the psychic gift to be taken from me if it originated from any source other than God. Yet it remained. If anything, my flashes of intuition increased,

18

but they were still confined to small, coincidental experiences. I comforted myself with the assurance that God would never ignore a prayer for spiritual guidance.

Nor was I to be disappointed. Several clergymen gave serious attention to my story and I was advised to continue my search until I felt in my own heart that I had found an answer that I could accept.

'It doesn't matter whether you find it in this church or in another,' said one. 'If you want to be reached, God will find a way to reach you. Don't lose heart—seek and ye shall find.'

One minister went even further.

'I believe that God has already reached you where it counts,' he told me. 'You seek Him so earnestly and you only want to use your gifts to help others—there is no selfishness in your search. Don't be afraid. God has His hand on you and I am sure that the answer you seek will not be long in coming.'

I was comforted and reassured. I had begun to have faith in the unknown force that guided my footsteps. Whoever it was and whatever it wanted, I felt that there might be love in its motives, for I was gradually becoming more steady on my feet. God's reassurance had come to me in several ways: the acceptance of the clergymen, the continuance of my psychic perception and a small but warm light within me that illuminated my path, step by step.

I was no longer floundering in a maze of incomprehensible and frightening events. I had learned very little about the supernatural so far but I had discovered within myself the single, most important factor in my development: wholehearted trust in God. I was not alone any more, nor had I any need to be afraid. I realised, however, that I could not sit back and expect God to drop everything into my lap. If I wanted understanding I would have to search for it. If I expected protection it was only reasonable for me to use caution. It was at that time that I first heard and adopted as my own a motto that I have since quoted to countless other searchers: God will work *with* you, but not *for* you.

CHAPTER TWO

I find a teacher

Dennis and I had moved from our flat to a rented house in the outer western suburbs of Sydney. I had become deeply engrossed in my search for spiritual enlightenment, much to his disgust. He discounted it as a load of superstitious rubbish and he told me often that I had embarked on a fool's errand. I was hurt, not only by his ridicule but because I could see a rift growing between us. If it had only been the spiritual matters that divided us, I could have overcome the problem, for I sensed that his attitude arose from a deep-seated fear of the unknown rather than blind scepticism. But the psychic issue was only one of an increasing burden of marital pressures. Our marriage was beginning to fray around the edges and I knew it; but I was determined to see it through until it either dissolved completely or the difficulties were reconciled. Neither of us wanted to part; Dennis tried as hard as I to heal the breach, but it was a task of ever-increasing complexity.

My marital problems were heavy on my mind one afternoon as I was driving home from work. I was focusing automatically on my driving but at the back of my mind there was a gnawing pressure that would not go away.

As I approached an intersection, I mentally noted a small truck which was converging on the same point, from a street on my right. I eased my foot off the accelerator and prepared to give away.

Suddenly, I found myself parked on the side of the road, still some distance away from the intersection. I had no recollection of pulling over, nor could I understand why I should have done so when it was only necessary for me to stop at the junction and allow the other vehicle to pass by. I shook my head and restarted the engine.

From out of nowhere, there came a screech of brakes and a whooshing sound as a huge petrol tanker sped past me, the driver frantically trying to bring his vehicle to a halt before it reached the intersection. He succeeded in the nick of time: there was a distance of a couple of feet between the two trucks when they met at the crossroads.

A horrifying realisation dawned on me. At the crucial point, there had not been enough space to allow a car to fit between the trucks. If I hadn't pulled my car off the road, I would have been crushed between the two, and one of those trucks was carrying a load of petrol! I felt sick with relief. Someone had seen that petrol tanker coming and I had been carefully guarded against harm. I drove home in a state of joyous exhilaration.

I now owed my life to my invisible friend and I was even more eager to find out as much as I could. Progress was slow, however. I had been reading everything I could lay hands on, but so far I had been disappointed. Some of the books that I read explained the occult in terms of witchcraft—usually purporting to be white, but I was highly sceptical. It occurred to me that only the most blatant practitioners would admit to practising black witchcraft. The dividing line between black and white was too diffuse for a novice like me. I preferred to stay within boundaries that I had some chance of understanding.

I was more attracted by the books that presented a spiritual outlook, but most of these were also disappointing. They gave a great deal of attention to the life histories of well-known psychics, but explained very little about what I wanted to know—the principles of psychic development.

Then I found a book which gave me a reference point. It was called *How to Develop Your ESP Potential* and was written by a woman named Jane Roberts. In it, she told how her own gifts had been awakened and, like me, she had begun with no knowledge at all. Her process of development had also provided her with a source of instruction.

She had begun by using a ouija board and had managed to contact a spirit entity named Seth, who proceeded to teach her about the realms which lie outside the physical world. As her knowledge increased, her psychic gifts developed smoothly and naturally. It seems that Seth had always been with her, patiently awaiting the time when she would give him an avenue of communication.

I was elated. What Jane Roberts had achieved, I could attempt. If, as Christine had suggested, my spirit friend was indeed trying to contact me, I could provide a ouija board as the channel. I was hesitant to try it alone, so I discussed the idea with a friend named Lyn, who was also interested in the paranormal. She was enthusiastic and we decided to give it a try.

Lyn's husband made a board for us and we sat down eagerly to try it out. The first few attempts were frustrating for me, as the communications were bland, ambiguous, and mainly addressed to Lyn. Still, we persevered in the hope that something specific might come through for me. When it came, I received a shock that froze me to my chair.

The sitting commenced normally enough and when we asked if any spirits were present, the planchette slid smoothly to the word 'Yes'.

'What is your name?' asked Lyn.

'CELIA.'

'Do you have a message for someone here?'

'YES. DAWN.'

I leaned forward eagerly. Perhaps this was the long-awaited communication. I asked the spirit to define her purpose.

'I WAS SENT TO PROTECT YOU,' replied the board.

'By whom?'

'THE PURIFIER.'

'Is this protection spiritual or do you also protect me physically?' I ventured.

'DO YOU NORMALLY PULL OFF THE ROAD TO GIVE WAY?'

Now I was intrigued, but not convinced. Lyn knew about the incident in the car and either one of us could be subconsciously influencing the movement of the planchette. I decided to try another approach.

'Are you my teacher?'

'NO I AM HERE TO PROTECT YOU. YOUR TEACHER WILL COME WHEN YOU ARE READY.'

'How long have you been with me?'

'EVER SINCE YOU TOOK A WALK IN A BEAUTIFUL GARDEN.'

I gasped and jerked my hand away from the board. My

flesh was icy cold and for a few moments I was unable to speak. Lyn was eyeing me with concern but it was some time before I was able to explain my actions.

When I was seven years old, I caught the measles. As a secondary complication, I contracted what my grandmother called 'brain fever'—probably encephalitis. This is a serious condition and can prove fatal, so my family was understandably very worried. We lived in a remote rural community and it was not advisable to take a risk on transporting me the long distance by air to a hospital, so my mother shouldered the burden of nursing me through the disease.

I remember very little about the illness but I have a vivid recollection of an experience that I later recalled as a dream. I had been sleeping and I opened my eyes to see a beautiful lady standing at the foot of my bed. She wore a white dress and had flaxen hair, arranged in a plaited coronet around her head. She held out her hand and smilingly invited me to go for a walk with her.

My next memory is of being in a beautiful garden, playing with a group of laughing children and a collection of placid animals. My lovely companion stood by while I frolicked joyfully on the soft grass for what seemed like hours. Suddenly, a long way away in the distance, I heard my mother calling my name.

'I have to go home now,' I told my new friends. They looked at me somewhat blankly and one of them said, 'You can't go home. You're dead. Didn't you know?'

I gazed at the speaker in horror, then ran screaming to my lady friend.

'I don't want to be dead!' I sobbed as she gathered me into her arms. 'I want to go home!'

Suddenly everything was hushed and I felt that I was again lying down, yet I could still feel a woman's soft arms holding me close. I spiralled up to the surface and opened my eyes, to see that it was my mother who held me and I was back in my bedroom.

'It's all right Mummy,' I murmured sleepily. 'I came back.'

For years I believed that experience to be nothing more than a dream. When I grew up, I mentioned it to Mum during a conversation about dreams. She looked pensive and told me that there was something strange about it, for she also remembered an incident that had happened during my illness.

She told me that I had been delirious for several days, constantly muttering or crying out and tossing restlessly in my bed. One morning, while she was occupied in another part of the house, she became aware that I had fallen silent. She came into my room to check. I was lying completely still. Too still! She grabbed my wrist and felt for my pulse. There was nothing and my hand flopped limply in her grasp. In panic, she seized me to her, frantically calling my name. A few seconds later, my eyelids fluttered open and I spoke to her, saying the words that I remember speaking at the end of my dream: 'It's all right Mummy, I came back'.

After hearing Mum's story, I had mentally filed the experience away as a strange coincidence. Yet here was a spirit referring to it as though it had really happened! At Lyn's urging, I decided to try for more information.

'Did I really die?' I asked.

'IN YOUR TERMS YES. YOU LEFT THE PHYSICAL WORLD.'

'Then why did I return?'

'YOU WERE NOT MEANT TO STAY THEN. YOU WERE TIRED AND NEEDED A REST.'

'Dying is a pretty dramatic way of taking a rest,' I remarked.

'DEATH IS NOT FINAL. YOU WILL UNDERSTAND MORE LATER.'

'How much later?'

'DEPENDS ON YOU. YOU MUST LEARN MORE,' was the enigmatic reply.

'Here we go again,' I thought. Life was becoming a conundrum. Just when I began to think that knowledge was within my grasp, it eluded me and once again I was told to learn. But how could I, if no one would teach me? One thing seemed certain—*somebody* wanted me to make a continuing effort and it seemed that whoever it may be, there was to be no hand-feeding. I failed to see why the process should be so difficult but I resigned myself to plodding along steadfastly until I reached my goal— whatever and wherever it might prove to be.

Without realising it, I was making progress. I had

24

begun to seek specific understanding from one direction. I wanted to know more about spirit teachers. I felt that if I were to learn about the supernatural, it might be best to seek information from a supernatural source. It did not occur to me that I was being steadily guided in that direction; indeed it seemed to me that I was groping blindly through a thick fog. I only knew that what I felt inside was a steadily mounting desire to find and communicate with my own spirit teacher.

It was around this time that I conceived the idea of taking up a more rewarding career. Office work was beginning to bore me to tears; I needed to do something more challenging. I decided that I would like to take up nursing and promptly had myself enrolled as a student nurse at the local district hospital. The work was hard, the salary much less than I had been accustomed to and there were long hours of study but I felt my mind coming alive. I gained high marks in Anatomy and Physiology because I was fascinated by the intricacies of the human body and the interplay between the life systems. I had never thought of myself as the Florence Nightingale type but I was surprised to discover that many of my patients seemed to see me in that light. We were expected to maintain our professional decorum and only use our surnames whilst on duty, but one dear old lady christened me 'Nurse Sunshine' and the title stuck.

In everyday life, I had very little self-confidence and usually hid my inner feelings behind an outwardly carefree facade. As a nurse, I discovered that I could relate to other people in a way that I had never managed before and many of the patients saw through my facade as well.

'Oh Nurse!' sighed one woman when I arrived at her bedside to do her dressing. 'Thank God it's you, you're so gentle.'

'Isn't everyone?' I asked in mild surprise.

'Not like you. You really care about people.'

'Shucks!' I grinned. 'It wasn't supposed to show.'

I had expected to be upset when I encountered death but I was rather dismayed to discover that it hardly affected me at all. I never saw a death that was not preceded by intense pain and suffering; my attitude was

25

usually one of relief for the patient who had been released from this distress. Most of my peers were awed by death and at times I wondered if I was being hardhearted but I could not generate an emotion that I did not feel.

I was much more affected by the sight of human pain and distress. Many times I wished that I could wave a magic wand and drive people's troubles away. I wanted to see them healed, not suffering.

Someone had once told me that my spiritual faith would take a nosedive when I was confronted with the realities of nursing but this proved to be incorrect. If anything my faith was reinforced. The delicately balanced machinery of the human body was evidence to me of a Master Designer. I had an innate belief that disease was not part of the design but something that we humans impose upon ourselves. I couldn't believe that sickness and death were God's punishment for original sin. My concept of God was one of a loving and concerned Father who wished no harm to his children. I found nothing in nursing to dispel this belief.

I was still hotly pursuing an understanding of psychic development and my quest was beginning to show some promise. I had discovered another book—*The Teachings of Silver Birch*. I later discovered that this book is virtually a classic in Spiritualism but at the time I was simply overwhelmed by the beauty of its contents.

Silver Birch is a spirit teacher who spoke through a young trance medium named Maurice Barbanell in the 1930s. The exquisite simplicity and wisdom of this spirit's teachings were as alive and vital to me in 1974 as they must have been to the people who had first received them.

The guide's words were gentle but profound. He spoke of spirit worlds beyond our own, to which we will all progress when the barrier of death is passed. Human beings, he said, are spirits who are learning and growing in a physical environment but spiritual gifts are inherent in all of us. It is natural for those above us in the spiritual spheres to do all they can to assist us on our path of development.

What a breath of fresh air and oh, how I wished that I

26

could have a guide such as Silver Birch! Not that I seriously believed it could ever happen—I tended to think that I was far from being worthy of such a singular honour. Even if such an elevated being were to notice me squirming around in the dust, what could he possibly do with me? I wasn't especially talented; I had learned enough to know that there were a great many psychics with more startling abilities than mine. I would be satisfied to have my questions answered, if I could ever figure out what questions I was supposed to be asking.

I had borrowed the Silver Birch book from a library and there was an additional bonus in it. Stamped on the flyleaf was the name and address of a bookshop that specialises in psychic literature. I could scarcely wait to explore the place! As soon as I had some free time, I headed for the shop to see what I could find. I was amazed by the scope and quantity of books on display. They covered every subject from Astral Travel to Zen Buddhism. I could cheerfully have camped there and worked my way through the lot, but instead I headed for the section on Spiritualism.

Of all the philosophies that I had encountered thus far, Spiritualism seemed the most promising and it explained the supernatural in terms that I could accept. Spiritualists believe that death is not an end to life but one step in the process of spiritual evolution. Outside the physical is the spirit world, where souls continue to learn and grow until they reach the point of ultimate perfection. If a soul fails at one lesson, he must keep repeating it until he succeeds, for only then can he pass on to a higher level of development.

As a child, I had been taught that there was a blissful Heaven (to which I, a mere sinner, could hardly dare to aspire) and a gruesome Hell (which I fervently hoped to avoid). If during my span of life, which could be cut short at any time, I managed to achieve a state of Christ-like perfection, I might just manage to squeeze through the Pearly Gates—as long as St Peter looked the other way. Should I fail, I was to be cast into the fiery depths of Hell, where gloating demons would torment me forevermore. As a consequence of those teachings, I tried very hard not to think about the hereafter at all.

Spiritualism made more sense. It presented the concept of a just and reasonable Creator who expects no more of us than we are capable of giving. To achieve a state of perfection, one simply keeps working towards it. It certainly improved on the concept of shovelling coal and being jabbed with pitchforks for all eternity!

I found another book called *This is Spiritualism* written by Maurice Barbanell. I was interested to learn from it that the Spiritualist movement has its own churches. I was eager to locate one, for I wanted to speak with the members. I felt sure that they could offer the kind of guidance that I was seeking.

It was several weeks before I found a church in my area and I looked forward to my first visit with eagerness. Surely I would be able to find someone who would be willing to advise me.

When the great day came I felt miserable. I had a pounding headache and I was certain that I would be unable to last through the service, much less carry on an intelligent discussion afterwards. Nevertheless I went and managed to survive the proceedings without falling from my chair in a dead faint. Afterwards I approached the medium who had conducted the service and explained my quest. She was polite and helpful but when I told her that I had been using a ouija board she was horrified.

'Don't touch it again,' was her advice. 'You might be lucky enough to communicate with a good spirit but there are nasty ones as well. If you get one of those, it may refuse to leave and it could create havoc. You aren't experienced enough to cope with such a situation, so don't take the risk. Leave the board alone and keep trying to increase your understanding in other ways.'

Then she gave me a penetrating look.

'You are very pale,' she commented. 'Do you feel unwell?'

I admitted that I did and told her about the headache.

'Why didn't you mention it?' she asked. 'We have a medium here who does healing. She might be able to help you. Wait here.'

She returned a few moments later with a plump, dark-haired lady whom she introduced as Mary Pound.

'Got a headache?' Mary spoke with a pronounced English accent. 'Right, sit down here and I'll have a go at it.'

I perched gingerly on the chair and Mary went to work. She placed her hands on my head and I noticed that they were very warm. For several minutes she made sweeping movements over my head, shaking her hands at the end of each pass as though trying to flick something away from her fingers. I felt the pain ease, then disappear. I was so impressed that I peppered her with questions. She answered a few, then smilingly motioned me to hush.

'You've got more questions than I've got time to answer,' she laughed. 'Where do you live?'

I told her and she nodded.

'Not far from me. Want to call on me when I've got more time to talk?'

I accepted eagerly and we arranged to meet on my next day off. I was thrilled at the prospect of finding some answers and also happy to have met someone who was so willing to help. I could hardly believe my luck.

I did not know it then, but I had also met my first teacher.

CHAPTER THREE
The Psychic makes friends

Mary was quite the most fascinating person I had ever met. Her physical appearance was unremarkable except for a pair of velvety brown eyes that sparkled with wit and humour, and a smile that could eclipse a rainbow. Her life had never been easy but she had no regrets and often remarked that an easy life built very little character. She had been psychic for as long as she could remember and her gifts were outstanding. In addition to her healing abilities, she was clairvoyant, clairaudient, and a trance medium but it was not in her nature to find anything remarkable about herself. She accepted her gifts as a normal part of life. Although she gave her services readily whenever they were needed, she refused to charge a fee.

'Taking money for what I do would be a crime,' she told me. 'My gifts were given to me free of charge and it would be wrong for me to charge a fee for sharing them. Bear that in mind, my girl: there's far too little sharing in this world and it's a sad place because of it. Too many people sitting on the blessings that the Good Lord intended for everyone, raking in a fortune for selling what isn't theirs to people who have a right to it. Take what you need out of life and no more. Leave the rest for those who need it too.'

'How can I start developing my spiritual gifts?' I asked. She looked at me in mild amazement.

'What do you think you've been doing all your life—playing hopscotch? You wouldn't be here if you weren't developing.'

'But I don't understand anything,' I protested. 'I want to know all about it. You are so far ahead of me. How do I get to where you are?'

Mary paused before she answered. She appeared to be sizing me up.

'Would you believe me if I told you that you're already ahead of me?' she asked.

'Of course not!'

'Didn't think you would. Never mind, I'll tell you this much: the day will come when you will be teaching people like me, and it isn't far off.'

To say that I was sceptical would be putting things mildly. I failed to see how it could be possible for me to teach something that I did not understand. My knowledge was scanty and my psychic gifts minimal. I could not trance or see and hear spirits. What could I possibly offer as a teacher?

'You already have the knowledge, you've just forgotten it,' remarked Mary. 'But it will be triggered off soon enough, mark my words. Then you'll be looking back and telling me to hurry up.'

'What makes you so sure of all this?'

'Let's just say a little bird told me. You don't have to believe me now, just wait and see. Time will tell.'

Mary was right about so many things that it was only reasonable to expect that she would be wrong occasionally. After all, she was only human and even psychics can

30

have their off days. For the present, I wanted to learn: the future would undoubtedly take care of itself, but I could not believe that it held a career in store for me as a spiritual teacher. Mary knew I did not believe her prediction and she wasn't the slightest bit concerned.

'I can only tell you what I know myself,' she said in a placid voice. 'If I'm wrong, you can always laugh at me later.'

'I would never laugh at you,' I hastened to assure her. 'I just think that your ambitions for me are a wee bit beyond my capabilities.'

'I have no ambitions for you,' was her reply. 'Your life is your own and it's no concern of mine. I'm only here to teach you the things that I know. What you do with that knowledge is for you to decide.'

Talking with Mary was like taking a bath in a clear, cold stream. I always came away feeling clean and refreshed. No sooner had she answered one question than a dozen more would pop into my head: there was so much I wanted to know. I admired her greatly and visited her as often as I could, which was roughly once a week, depending on my nursing schedule.

I found myself thinking about her words most of the time and my awareness of a spiritual existence was growing. I wondered if it might be possible for me to use psychic understanding to help me develop better as a nurse. While I might never be a great psychic, perhaps I could use nursing as a means of helping people with their problems, using the added insight imbued in me by psychic understanding.

One morning I walked into one of the rooms on my ward to find a patient writhing with pain. This woman had originally had her appendix removed and all had gone well for a few days afterwards. Then she developed diverticulitis, which necessitated another operation. Post-operative pain was severe for her but on this occasion I could do little to help. She had already had an injection and the next was not due for over an hour. We could not overdose her. She understood, but this did nothing to ease her pain.

'Just stay here for a while,' she pleaded. 'Let me hang onto your hand. It's worse when I'm alone.'

I took her hand between both of mine and sat by her bedside, furiously wishing that I were not so powerless to help. After a few minutes, she relaxed a little.

'Your hands feel very warm,' she commented. 'It feels good. Soothing.'

A few minutes later, she sighed and opened her eyes.

'I don't know what you did, Nurse, but the pain has gone. Thank you.'

I looked at her with amazement.

'I didn't do anything!' I exclaimed.

'Oh yes, you did,' she insisted. 'I felt the warmth from your hands going right through me and then the pain went away. You're the psychic one, aren't you?'

'How did you know that?' I asked in surprise.

'People talk, and I've been here for a while,' she smiled. 'You don't have to admit that you did something if you don't want to. I won't tell anyone anyway.'

'Thank you!' was all I could say.

I was bemused as I left the ward. I had not realised that my interest in the supernatural was so widely known. I had never tried to conceal it, but neither did I advertise it. A few people had noticed me reading books on the subject at lunch time and some had asked questions, but I was surprised to discover that it was a matter for open discussion.

More surprising was my patient's evident belief that I had used some mysterious ability to relieve her pain. I had very good reasons for not wanting her to discuss the matter with other people. I thought it more likely that her pain had been a spasmodic thing that had eased of its own accord and it had merely been coincidental that I had been with her at the time. The last thing I needed was a reputation as a miracle-worker, especially since it was unfounded. I could imagine the kind of talk it would cause and the hospital authorities might frown severely on a nurse who filled her patients' heads with such unprofessional ideas. The incident worried me and I discussed it with Mary.

'It's quite possible that you did ease the woman's pain,' she argued. 'You have a lot of blue in your aura, which indicates a natural affinity for healing and you're working in an environment that's likely to bring it out.

32

That is probably what attracted you to nursing in the first place.'

'But that kind of talk could ruin my future!' I protested.

'As what? A nurse or a healer? You don't know what the future has in store. Anyway, you didn't claim to have healing abilities, it was your patient who decided that. She's probably psychic herself, or else she wouldn't have recognised it. Don't worry, she has promised not to talk about it, so it can't do your precious career any harm.'

Mary advised me to continue acting the way I had thus far, neither concealing nor advertising my psychic interests. To make an attempt at hiding the truth might cause people to wonder what dark secrets I had to protect. On the other hand, vigorous efforts to explain myself might be seen as a bid for admiring attention.

'Just be yourself and let people say what they like,' said Mary. 'It is not your place to govern their thoughts or their actions. Everyone has free will. You would protest violently if someone tried to stop you from being interested in psychic development, wouldn't you?'

'Of course I would! My private life is nobody else's business.'

'And their thoughts are none of yours,' was the firm reply.

'But we aren't speaking about thoughts,' I argued. 'People are talking about me, in a way that could hurt my career. Surely that gives me some rights!'

'You can only fight gossip by holding yourself above it, if gossip is what we are discussing. People may only be talking about you because you interest them. They might be discussing you in glowing terms. Have you thought of that?'

'Knowing human nature, I doubt it,' I said morosely.

I had my ear to the ground after that, trying to be as unobtrusive as possible whilst finding out just what was being said about me. I found that the opinions of the other staff members varied a great deal. Most regarded it as an individual idiosyncrasy on my part. They did not believe in the supernatural themselves, but saw no harm in my indulging myself with it if I wanted to. A few were intrigued, and when they realised that I was not unwilling to discuss the matter, they ventured some questions. Some were disapproving but the general concensus of opinion here was that if I chose to take risks with my own sanity, that was my prerogative, so long as I didn't try to force my ideas onto other people.

Then I learned about a rumour that had begun to circulate. I had been seen, it was said, making voodoo dolls and sticking pins into them. The story was so ridiculous that I should have laughed, but instead I grew angry. I had a fairly good idea about who had originated the story and I wished it was possible to confront her openly but this could not be done without proof.

'I hope she falls down and breaks her neck!' I fumed to Mary.

'Don't say such things!' she answered sharply. 'You don't know what you might be setting into motion.'

'Oh, come on! Surely you aren't telling me that I could actually cause her to have an accident?'

'That is precisely what I *am* saying,' said Mary. 'You don't know much about the power of thought and it's about time you learned. If you focus harmful thoughts on another person, you can set up an imbalance in her aura. It can cause harm to both her and you. When you do things like that, a law of nature says that the negative energy you send out will eventually return and affect you.'

I began to feel defensive. 'Maybe I'm just returning the negative energy she is focusing on me. Heaven knows, she deserves to get it back.'

'Heaven may well know, but you don't,' admonished Mary. 'It isn't your place to judge others. Leave that to the powers who possess all the facts.'

'Mary, I was just letting off steam! What am I supposed to do when someone makes me angry—just let it fester away inside me?'

'Don't let it build up in the first place. Imagine what a miserable life that girl must be leading, to have so much bitterness inside her. You should pity her.'

'It isn't my fault if her life is miserable,' I grumbled. 'I can't wave a magic wand and make it better.'

'Right,' she agreed. 'So don't make it worse. When someone annoys you, I want you to say "God Bless You".

You can say it in your head if you like, but say it.'

I was beginning to be amused. I had a mental image of myself saying 'God Bless You' as I emptied the contents of a brimming bedpan over the girl's head. Mary was unimpressed by my sense of humour.

'You can laugh if you like, but if you build up anger in your aura, you'll hold back your psychic development. Is your enemy worth that much?'

That was a sobering thought! Psychic development had become an important issue for me and I was determined to allow nothing to stand in my way. Retaliating on an enemy certainly wasn't worth the price. I decided that I could spare a few blessings for the sake of enlightenment.

I was now working in the Children's Ward, which I had privately christened 'The Hall of Howling Horrors'. Not that I dislike children; I have one of my own and in general I find them quite endearing and full of vim. But illness often brings out the worst in human nature and children are human. Also, having so much energy and imagination, they can find more ways of getting into mischief than a harassed nurse can circumvent. Children's Ward was nothing if not full of action!

There always seems to be one child who is determined to set the whole hospital on its ear, and this time it was little Jason, a three-year-old who was not at all happy about being admitted. He had so far registered his disapproval by dumping his bedclothes onto the floor, upending his dinner on top of them and letting forth a continuous wail that made an ambulance siren sound like a mouse with laryngitis. My attempts to give him a consoling cuddle had almost resulted in a black eye. Reasoning with him was impossible, since his screams must have deafened everyone within a five-mile radius—including himself.

I was becoming annoyed and I decided that the moment was as good as any for trying out Mary's advice. There seemed precious little else that I could do anyhow.

'God bless you, you little cherub!' I groaned, casting my eyes hopefully heavenwards.

Jason stopped screaming, popped his finger into his mouth and stared at me with wide-eyed innocence. I stared back, stupefied. The difference in him was

35

magical. I don't know if Jason felt surprised, but *I* certainly did!

Mary often saw spirit forms around me. To her, they appeared as solid as flesh and blood. She cheerfully described them to me and sometimes passed on messages from them. She said that she could see Celia and the description she gave me tallied with that of the woman I saw when I was seven. There was a distinguished-looking Indian gentleman (from India, not the United States), who stayed quietly in the background but appeared to be immensely pleased whenever my conversation displayed that I was making progress. And there was a jaunty Irishman who referred to me as his 'little darlin'' and fiercely declared that anyone who tried to harm me would first have to contend with him.

They sounded like a fascinating group of people and I bitterly regretted my inability to see them.

'All things will come in time,' soothed Mary. 'Don't worry, your friends will wait.'

One afternoon while we were talking, I noticed that Mary appeared to be uncomfortable. She kept rubbing at her left eye as though it were bothering her.

'Do you know an elderly gentleman who has passed over and had something wrong with his eye?' she asked at last.

'My grandfather. He lost his eye during the First World War.'

'Yes, that seems to be right, he's nodding,' she said. 'I think he wants to tell you something. Hang on while I tune in.'

She perched in her chair, head cocked to the side as though listening to something.

'He says he'll be popping in on you from time to time,' she said. 'And you aren't to worry about your psychic development. He says you always did try to start everything from the top.'

That made me laugh. I remembered a conversation that I had with Grandad when I was in my early teens. I had decided that I was going to be a famous actress when I grew up. No behind-the-scenes work for me: instant stardom would burst forth and carry me to the dizzying heights of fame and fortune. . .

'I know the perfect job for you,' Grandad said, 'digging graves.'

When I asked why, he replied 'It's the only job I know where you can start from the top and work down!'

Mary suggested that my abilities might develop more readily if I sat for five minutes in meditation each day.

'You can sit or lie down,' she said, 'somewhere quiet, where you won't be disturbed. Always begin with a prayer for protection and ask for your guides to be sent to you. It may be a while before you receive any impressions, but keep it up, it should be worth the effort.'

I did it faithfully each day for weeks, without results. Eventually I grew tired of the blankness and one evening as I meditated I thought 'If you guys are really there, why don't you do something to make your presence felt?'

Immediately, the doorknob rattled in a slow turn and the door swung silently open, all by itself.

'Okay, okay!' I gasped hastily. 'Just don't close it, for Heaven's sake.'

Shortly after that, I began to feel feather-light touches on my face and the top of my head. The feeling was like a whisper of wind on my skin. It happened several times each day, sometimes while I was sitting quietly at home, but also at work, when I might be busily engaged in doing something. The sensation was quite distinct and I asked Mary if I might be beginning to imagine things.

'No,' was her reply. 'I've seen your friends touching you many times. You are just becoming aware of it, that's all. They just want you to know that they are with you.'

It was all very encouraging but hardly spectacular. The more involved I became in my study of the supernatural, the more I wanted to be able to do the things that Mary did. I would dearly have loved to be able to see spirits and talk with them but as far as psychic senses were concerned, I seemed to be deaf and blind. I may have been gaining in theoretical knowledge but I was denied any practical experience and I couldn't understand why. When I did demonstrate psychic ability, it happened at unexpected times and was always of a light and superficial nature. It was not very satisfying for me.

As I walked into a small room on my ward one morning, a name suddenly popped into my head. It was a

37

woman's name and quite an unusual one, and on impulse, I asked the two occupants of the room if either of them recognized it. One of them replied that she had a friend by that name, and I had an immediate mental picture of a small blue car. Did her friend own such a car? I asked the patient. The reply was affirmative and the patient was now looking at me with great curiosity.

'I sometimes get little psychic flashes,' I explained. 'Would you ask your friend to have her brakes checked? I have a feeling that there is something faulty there and it might cause an accident.'

My patient looked rather startled, but she agreed to pass on my message to her friend. A few days later, when I was again working in that room, I found the lady in a state of eager excitement. When she saw me, she could hardly contain herself.

'My friend had her brakes checked, like you said,' she told me.

'Oh? What was the result?'

'Nothing wrong with the brakes, but the kingpin was damaged. The mechanic said that if he hadn't found it, it might have broken and caused an accident.'

I suppose it was too much to hope that word of this exploit of mine would not circulate the hospital, and sure enough, a few of my friends mentioned having heard something about it and asked me for details. I tried not to make a big deal out of it and pointed out that many psychics could do much better than I. As far as clairvoyance is concerned, it was a very minor example. Nevertheless, it was encouraging for me to know that my gifts, small as they were, had been put to good use in helping someone to avoid a misfortune.

Two of my workmates were particularly interested in my psychic activities. One is still my dearest friend. Her name is Helen Iddon and her attitude was quite down-to-earth. Psychic phenomena did not deeply concern her, but she was quite prepared to believe that it could happen.

'I'm sure it must be very exciting,' she commented one day, 'but be careful not to let yourself get carried away. We wouldn't want you to go off the rails, would we?'

Rhonda Behan was a Sister with whom I worked fairly

often and we had established an easy camaraderie. She, too, was very interested, but admitted that the subject made her nervous.

'I could never get involved in it,' she would say, 'I like to hear about it, but if I had anything to do with it, I'd never get to sleep at night. You must be quite fearless.'

I walked into the locker room after work one day to find Rhonda halfway through changing into her street clothes. As I started to unbutton my uniform, I had another mental flash. I turned and looked at her with curiosity.

'Are you going away on holiday soon?' I asked her. She froze and eyed me suspiciously.

'Who told you about it?'

'You did. It was on your mind when I walked into the room, wasn't it?'

'Okay, Smarty,' she chuckled, 'if you're so psychic, tell me where I'm going.'

'The Gold Coast?'

'Wrong! I'm going to Mackay.'

I shrugged. 'Both places are in Queensland. Two out of three ain't bad.'

About a week later, at a staff party, I felt a tap on my shoulder and turned to see Rhonda grinning at me.

'You and your darned ESP!' was her greeting.

'What about it?'

'By a strange coincidence, I now find myself going to the Gold Coast instead of Mackay, that's what.'

She told me that she had visited a travel agent that morning to arrange her booking. When the clerk learned that she planned to visit Mackay, he suggested that the Gold Coast offered more facilities at the same cost. After discussing the matter with him, she had decided that the Gold Coast was a better proposition after all. It was not until she was halfway home that she remembered my prediction.

The incident was amusing and I mentally filed it away with my other experiences, but as a demonstration of psychic ability it was inconclusive. Without realising it, Rhonda could have been subconsciously influenced by my suggestion that she would go to the Gold Coast. I decided not to base any suppositions on it.

Considering his attitude to the supernatural, I never expected Dennis to provide me with an opportunity to practise my abilities but, surprisingly enough, he did. In bed one night, his restless tossing and turning kept me awake and I asked him what was wrong.

'Headache,' he muttered. 'I've taken a couple of aspirins but they're not working.'

'Here, let me see if I can help,' I offered impulsively, stretching out my hands.

I placed one hand on his forehead and the other at the nape of his neck. After they had been resting there for a few moments, I felt a warm, tingling sensation in the palm of my right hand. When the feeling subsided, I took my hands away.

'Does that feel better?'

'Yeah.' Dennis gave me a wondering look. 'What did you do? The headache's gone.'

'Just tried some psychic healing,' I replied, feeling quite pleased with myself. Dennis looked appalled and edged away from me.

'I don't think I like that idea,' he said.

'Why ever not? It fixed your pain, didn't it?'

'Yes, but if you can take pain away, you could cause it. How do I know you're not a witch?'

'I give up!' I growled and pulled the covers over my head.

CHAPTER FOUR

Roland: an odd introduction

My marital situation had degenerated to the stage where I realised that it was useless to keep trying. The rift between Dennis and I had widened to the point where we no longer had anything in common and all avenues of communication were closed. My feelings towards him were dominated by irritation and impatience. I knew that my love had finally withered. To allow the situation to remain as it was would have been risking a lot of bitterness and ill-feeling. I decided that a clean break was necessary and I told Dennis of my decision to end our marriage.

After the initial shock had subsided, Dennis admitted that he, too, had been finding the situation intolerable. We wished each other no harm but it was obvious to both of us that we could not continue as man and wife. I offered to take Darryl and move into a flat, but Dennis demurred.

'Don't make any hasty decisions,' he said. 'I can live on the ship for a while and we are going away shortly anyway. We will be away for about six months; that should give you time to get yourself sorted out. There's no point in disturbing Darryl any more than you have to.'

I was touched by his offer. I had expected unpleasant scenes and my chief area of concern had been for Darryl, who could have been hurt, caught in the middle as he was. It was a relief to know that he would have time to adjust to the separation before being uprooted.

I promised Dennis that I would remain in the house to discourage burglary until just before he returned from overseas. As the weeks passed, I began to regret that decision, for I found the house gloomy and oppressive. During the years that I spent there with Dennis, I had been told by a number of people that there seemed to be a sinister presence in the house but I had not experienced anything that I could classify as supernatural. I simply felt depressed by the place and I had put that down to my marital troubles.

Since it was I who was deeply interested in the supernatural, I would have expected to be the one who sensed any psychic activity that might be present. In practice it was always other people who told me about it. I grew accustomed to the guests who commented that they had heard footsteps walking up the concrete steps which led to the front door. I never heard the sounds, nor did I ever hear the steps that Dennis claimed to hear at night, pacing back and forth on the path outside, under our bedroom window.

My sister Amanda had stayed with us for several months and during that time she had always insisted on sleeping with the bedroom light on. She said that she felt a brooding presence which seemed to grow more active in

41

the dark. Whatever it may have been, she was terrified of it.

I seemed to live in a cocoon that shut out these manifestations and I wasn't terribly pleased about it. I would have been quite interested in doing some ghost-hunting but it is impossible to track down something you have no way of perceiving. It might have been standing right in front of me all the time but I could not see it. I saw this as evidence of my deplorable lack of psychic ability but Mary had other ideas.

'Has it occurred to you that you might actually be protected from it?' she asked. 'Whatever it is, it doesn't sound pleasant to me. I'd be grateful that you can't be affected by it, if I were you. It sounds like an earthbound spirit of some kind and it might even be malicious.'

'Why don't you try to track it down?' I suggested.

Mary shuddered and shook her head emphatically. 'No thanks! I don't get involved with that side of things if I can help it.'

It seemed as though the ghostly intruder would forever remain a mystery but I was not too concerned about the situation. I had other mysteries to deal with. For one thing, my ability to psychometrize objects was being blocked. This had been one psychic function that I was able to perform fairly well and I often amused my friends by holding an object that belonged to someone else and forming impressions from it. In this way, I could tell the owner things about herself that only she had known. It was a good way to exercise and develop my abilities but lately I had found that I had been having difficulty with it.

I seemed to have developed a fixation on green cars with faulty brakes. Whenever I attempted to tune in on psychometry, I would get an impression of a motor vehicle accident which involved a green car with faulty brakes. I couldn't understand it.

'You have a green car,' said someone.

'I've thought of that,' I replied, 'but this car has something wrong with its brakes and mine hasn't. I've only recently had the brakes relined and a new power brake unit fitted. They work perfectly, so it can't be my car that I'm seeing.'

42

There was something else that had me mystified. I had suddenly developed a fear of heights. It had manifested itself when I climbed a ladder in the ward to hang some Christmas decorations from the ceiling. Without warning I had been overcome by the sickening fear that I was going to fall. I had never been afraid of such a thing before and at first I thought that the incident was just an isolated dizzy spell. But as time wore on, I discovered that the fear continued and I could not even stand on a chair without clutching at something solid for support. I was deeply perplexed and it was to be several years before the riddle was solved.

Life was not all mysteries and depression however. I had made a new friend, a man named Keith Rowe who worked as a control operator at Radio 2UE. He was bright, breezy and affectionate and he knew how to be a good friend without placing expectations on the relationship. I christened him my 'Big Brother' and both of us enjoyed the easy-going fondness that had sprung up between us.

On the morning of 28 December 1975 my thoughts were partially on Keith as I drove home after finishing my shift on night duty. I was looking forward to three nights off and Keith had arranged to take me out that evening. I would have to arrange a babysitter for Darryl. Amanda had been staying with me over Christmas but she had to return to her flat that morning. I had promised to drive her home but I was now wishing that I hadn't. I was tired and only wanted to sleep.

I debated the idea of giving Mandy some money for a cab fare but it seemed like a copout. She had been minding Darryl while I worked night duty and she deserved some consideration. I decided to drive her home straight away so that there would be no need for my sleep to be disturbed later.

It had been raining and the roads were wet but our spirits were high as we set off for Mandy's place. If this was to be the day that changed my life, there was nothing that gave me an inkling about it.

I was taking a short cut through a side street when it happened. I was about to enter an intersection when I suddenly spotted a stop sign that had been obscured behind an overhanging tree. Reflex made me stamp on the brake pedal and my efficient power-brake system came into action, locking the wheels so that I had no control over the car. But we didn't stop. The car aquaplaned on the wet surface, sliding past the stop sign and into the path of an oncoming car. I tried to accelerate out of the way but it was too late. The other car slammed into us and I felt a bump against my side as my door caved in.

My car spun across the road and mounted the footpath. Mandy was screaming in terror long after we skidded to a halt. I sat stunned for a while, then remembered to turn off the ignition. I had to get out of my car and see whether anyone had been hurt, I decided. Stupidly, I struggled with my door for a minute, wondering why it would not open. When I realised that the twisted metal would not move, I scrambled over Mandy's sobbing figure after first checking to see that she was all right. Then I looked into the back seat and saw Darryl.

He sat motionless, eyes staring blankly ahead. Blood was pouring from his forehead and the front of his shirt was stained red. He didn't move. My knees buckled and I leaned weakly against the side of the car. 'Oh God!' I thought, 'I've killed my son.'

I reached out and gently touched his face and he swung his head to face me, wide-eyed with fear. Then he screamed. It was at once the most dreadful and beautiful sound that I had ever heard. I held him against me, sobbing into his hair.

'I'm sorry, Baby. I'm sorry.'

We were all taken by ambulance to the nearest hospital. The staff seemed most concerned about me, but I kept assuring them that I was unhurt. I was not making an effort to be brave; I simply didn't feel any pain. All I felt was overwhelming remorse and the horrifying knowledge that my moment of inattention might easily have killed someone. Darryl's injury was only a scalp wound—the blood on his shirt had come from that and not from any other injury, thank heaven. Mandy needed treatment for a few cuts and bruises and she was trembling with shock. I felt a bit as though the situation was unreal and I was walking in a nightmare from which I could not awaken. I wandered off to find a telephone and ring Keith.

'I can't meet you tonight,' I said when he answered. 'My car is out of action.'

'What's wrong with it?' he asked.

'I had a crash.'

'*What*? Are you all right?'

I started to cry. 'I'm all right but Darryl has a cut on his head. The car is wrecked and. . .'

'Damn the car! Where are you?'

'W-western Suburbs Hospital,' I sniffled.

'I'll be right over,' he said, and hung up.

Keith walked into the hospital waiting room about twenty minutes later while I was being interviewed by a sympathetic policeman. I must have looked a mess: my stockings were torn, my dress was grubby and my face was streaked with dirt and tears. Keith didn't even appear to notice, he just sat beside me on the seat and pulled my head down onto his shoulder with a protective gesture that said 'Relax, I'll take over'.

When the policeman had all the information he wanted, I turned to Keith.

'What a way to meet a woman,' I mumbled. 'Look at me, torn stockings, dirty face—I'm a mess.'

Keith threw back his head and roared with laughter. 'If that isn't typically female!' he grinned. 'You come through an accident that wrecked your car and might easily have killed you and all you can worry about is torn stockings. Women! They're wonderful.'

He shepherded us all into his car and took Mandy home first. She invited us in for a cup of coffee and I accepted gratefully. I was beginning to feel as though I needed some refreshment. While we were sipping our drinks and discussing the accident, I noticed an uncomfortable sensation on the side of my leg. I pulled up my skirt to look. There was a huge, purple swelling.

'A haematoma,' I remarked. 'Look at that. I did get a bump after all!'

A slight frown puckered Keith's brow.

'What part of your car took most of the impact?' he asked me.

45

'The driver's door. Why?'

'It seems odd that the driver doesn't have a few more injuries,' was his reply. I pulled a face.

'Don't wish them on me. Losing my car hurts badly enough.'

Our coffee finished, we set off for my place. I chattered nonstop and Keith drove steadily, submerged in his own thoughts. All of a sudden, I felt a sharp pain in my wrist. Looking down, I was startled to see it visibly swelling. Then my leg started to hurt, and my side. I sank backwards in the seat, all at once overcome by waves of pain. Keith glanced at me and nodded.

'Thought you were in shock,' he said. 'Starting to feel it now, aren't you? I'll take you to another hospital and, this time, let them take a look at you.'

I didn't have the strength or will to argue.

No serious damage had been done, but I was a mass of sprains and bruises and the doctor ordered me off work for a month.

So it had, after all, been my car to which the premonition had referred. I knew also that the accident would mean the end of my nursing career. I could not afford to buy another car and the public transport in our area did not cater for people who did shift work. Without my own transport I was finished as a nurse. I would have to seek office work when my injuries healed. Knowing that I had to stop nursing hurt me most of all.

For some time I was restless and full of pain and often could not sleep at night. I felt lonely and deserted and I drifted into the habit of ringing Keith. He was working a midnight to dawn shift at the radio station and there were long periods when he had little to do. He never seemed to mind talking to me and his cheerful conversation eased my loneliness. He called to see me each day, to bring me anything I might need and to rub a soothing salve into the mess of bruises on my back. Our relationship remained platonic but he was more supportive and solicitous than any lover I had ever known.

I forget when it was that the name Roland Hill entered his conversation but he mentioned it quite often, in a tone which implied that they were friends.

'Who is this Roland Hill?' I asked him.

46

'Another control operator. You wouldn't want to know him,' he replied with a satirical grin. 'He's not your type. Mad sex fiend.'

I laughed. 'According to you, *everyone* is a sex fiend!'

'Of course!' Keith wore an air of injured innocence but his eyes sparkled with mirth. 'Everyone but me. I'm the only one with a pure heart.'

'Pure drivel!' I mocked.

A few nights later, I couldn't sleep. Pain had been tormenting me for some time, so I called the doctor. When he arrived he administered a pain-killing injection. It took the pain away but it also made me feel giggly and lightheaded. I decided to ring Keith and talk to him until I settled down. When I rang 2UE, a strange voice told me that Keith wasn't there.

'Roland Hill speaking,' said the voice. 'Can I help you?'

'Ooh, no,' I giggled. 'You're the mad sex fiend I'm not allowed to talk to.'

The following afternoon, Keith rang.

'I'm coming over there to rub your back with sandpaper,' he vowed. I was rather surprised until he reminded me about my conversation with Roland. My memory was misty but when he quoted it to me it came flooding back and I remembered it clearly.

'Oh no!' I wailed. 'What must he think of me?'

'To tell the truth,' chuckled Keith, 'he's rather amused. I've told him about you and he thinks you sound agreeably scatterbrained.'

'Thanks heaps,' I groaned.

I never had a very clear idea of how Keith's shifts operated and the next time I rang, the strange voice answered again.

'Is Keith there?' I asked.

'No,' came the reply. 'This is the sex fiend you're not allowed to talk to. How are your bumps and bruises?'

'Oh—Roland,' I stammered. 'I am sorry about that. You see, I had this injection and. . .'

'Don't explain,' he laughed. 'I was rather enjoying my newfound image.'

Before I realised what I was doing, I had settled down to a friendly conversation with Roland. His voice was warm and attractive and it felt good to talk with him.

47

While I was talking, Darryl wandered sleepily into the room and asked if he could watch television. I said no, but called him to me for a cuddle.

'Who is on the phone?' he asked.

'A nice man named Roland,' I replied.

'Can I talk to him?'

I asked Roland if he would care to converse with my son and he accepted with good humour.

I listened with amusement to Darryl's end of the conversation.

'Why are you talking to my Mum? . . . Where do you work? . . . Have you got any kids? . . . Our cat had kittens and Mum says now we've got six million cats . . . Yes we have . . . have so! . . . we have so too!'

Darryl dissolved into helpless giggles and I took the receiver from him.

'He sounds delightful,' said Roland.

'Oh, he has his moments,' I replied, trying not to show too much motherly pride.

I spoke with Roland several times after that, and as our friendship grew, we decided that we would like to meet each other.

'Just call me Cupid,' grinned Keith when I told him.

'Shut up. Cupid is the last person I need. I'm only meeting Roland because he sounds like a nice man and I like him.'

'Romance will rear its head,' promised Keith. 'You're not the only one who can make predictions.' Then he ducked to avoid an airborne cushion.

Roland was working an evening shift which ended at 11 p.m. and we arranged to meet in town after he finished work. It was decided that we would meet at a nightclub which I liked because it featured a good Country and Western band. After I had arrived there, I was to ring Roland and tell him where I was sitting so that he would be able to locate me in the crowd.

'I'd better tell you what I look like,' he said when I rang.

'I already know. Tall and dark-haired.'

'Lots of men fit that description. Want to know what I'm wearing?'

'No need. I'll know you when I see you. I'm psychic, remember?'

Roland chuckled and there was a note of challenge in his voice.

'Okay, we'll see how good you are.'

By coincidence, Roland's relief arrived at the studio an hour late and when Roland finally arrived at the nightclub he was not at all sure that I would still be waiting. A cluster of people were lounging in the doorway, several more were pushing their way out and some others were trying to work their way in. Roland mingled with the crowd, thinking that it would be a miracle if I managed to spot him.

As he entered, I looked directly at him and called his name. He did a swift double-take and came to me.

'How did you do that?' he asked.

'Do what?'

'Pick me out in that crowd.'

'I told you,' I grinned. 'I'm psychic.'

As the evening drew to a close, I asked Roland if he would mind driving me home.

'That depends,' he said, with a wicked grin. 'Do I get invited in for coffee?'

'As long as you understand that coffee is all you get,' I answered, mentally calculating the cost of a cab fare. He smiled.

'Under those conditions, fair damsel, I would be happy to drive you home. Your carriage awaits.' With a courtly bow, he took my arm and led me into the street.

I was not romantically attracted to Roland, but I liked him a great deal. He was intelligent, kind and perceptive and he treated me with gentle courtesy. I enjoyed his company and believed that I had found another big brother.

For his part, Roland's interest was definitely romantic but he was far too clever to reveal it. He sensed that I was afraid of romantic involvement, preferring the relaxed security of friendship. He decided to stay around until I overcame my fear and in the meantime he gave me the undemanding friendship that I desired.

Although he had always been sceptical about psychic phenomena, he decided that it was acceptable in connection with me. It seemed to be quite in character with my personality, which he found endearingly

49

scatterbrained. To him, I was the kind of girl who found daffodils where other people saw only dandelions. If I seemed to live in a world of flying saucers, pixies and amiable spooks, it only lent me an aura of delicious vulnerability that stirred his protective masculine instincts.

However, it bore no relation to the world that he had inhabited for thirty-one years. He saw my belief in the supernatural as a beautiful, fragile bubble and he could not bring himself to imagine what would happen to me if that bubble should ever burst. He developed a consuming desire to place himself as a shield between me and the harsh realities of life. He believed that I would surely break if I were left to endure the onslaughts of a merciless world alone.

If it occurred to him that I had managed to survive those onslaughts quite well so far, he put it down to an accident of luck rather than any inner strength of my own. As long as he was around, he decided, nothing would ever hurt me again.

He had himself come to terms with the pain that can be inflicted on those who look for fulfilment in this life. He had loved and married a warm, tender woman and he had been filled with glowing dreams about the wonderful life they would live together. But she had succumbed to a painful terminal illness. She died eight months after their wedding. A couple of years later, he married again but the relationship failed to work. It lasted for three years, after which he resigned himself to the idea that lasting happiness in marriage was not meant for him.

If he saw me as a helpless scrap of femininity, I saw in him a wistful and romantic soul who deserved much better than the raw deal he had received so far. I wished that I could comfort him with the beliefs from which I drew my own strength but he could not believe that the supernatural held any place for him. As far as he was concerned, psychic events were things that happened to other people.

He liked to draw in his spare time and he once showed me a picture in which a man sits, pensively strumming a guitar while in the background the silhouetted figure of a woman stands quietly waiting. The man resembled

50

Roland and the female figure bore a resemblance to me. The outline of the woman's gown was very similar to the dress I had been wearing when I first met Roland. I was struck by the similarity and I asked Roland when he had drawn the picture. He replied that it had been done two months before we met.

'The resemblance is uncanny,' I commented. 'Has it ever occurred to you that you might be psychic?'

'No. It's just coincidence.'

'A lot of people use that word to explain away the things that they don't understand,' I said. 'To quote Taylor Caldwell, men give a mystery a name and then think they have solved it. There are people known as psychic artists, who draw or paint the impressions they receive from the spirit world.'

'Well I'm not one of them,' he insisted, 'I drew that picture using exactly the same method that I have used in all of my drawings.'

I had caught a whiff of the supernatural and I decided to question him further.

'What method do you use?'

'I just sit and stare at a blank sheet of paper until I see a picture form on it. It's rather like watching a photograph come up in developing fluid. Then I just trace over the picture that I see. It's that simple.'

'Simple, is it!' I declared. 'The man is psychic and doesn't even know it.'

'Coincidence,' he insisted. 'I am not a person who has psychic experiences.'

I gave him a knowing smile. 'Aren't you? Take another look at the picture.'

I didn't press the issue after that. I had no desire to force my own beliefs on someone who had no wish to accept them. Roland had a right to make his own decisions about what he wanted to believe. If he really possessed any remarkable abilities they would no doubt surface of their own accord when the time was right.

Just how soon those abilities would surface and what their effect was to be was something that would have rocked me back on my heels if I had been able to foresee it.

CHAPTER FIVE
David makes contact

Roland and I were talking on the phone. He was midway through his evening shift at 2UE and I was resting at home. We had been chatting for some time when Roland came up with a crazy idea.

'Hey, psychic lady, I'm feeling tense. How about sending me some soothing vibes down the telephone?'

'Don't be silly,' I chuckled, 'it would never work.'

'What's the matter, you afraid of a failure?'

'Of course not. I simply don't think I could do such a thing.'

'Try it and see,' he challenged.

I decided to play along with his game and told him to lean back and close his eyes. Then I pictured him being overcome by a feeling of total relaxation. I heard his breathing becoming deep and rhythmic and I giggled.

'Any minute now, you'll start snoring.'

There was no answer. The heavy breathing continued for several minutes and I grew impatient.

'A joke's a joke,' I said irritably, 'but this has gone on for long enough. Cut it out.'

No reply, just more heavy breathing.

I thought for a while that he was pretending to go into a trance, because his breathing was characteristic of an oncoming trance state. But then a chilling realization hit me. Roland had never experienced psychic phenomena of any kind. He would not know how to imitate a trance medium because he had never seen one. Fear clenched at the pit of my stomach.

'Roland!' I called, with breathless urgency. The only response was a loud clatter. The receiver had tumbled from his hand. Frantically I tried to disconnect the call so that I could ring the studio on another number and have someone come to his aid. But he had called me and the connection could not be broken at my end.

I waited an agonizing length of time and eventually

heard scuffling noises as Roland recovered his wits and picked up the phone. Finally he spoke and his voice was unsteady.

'Dawn, what did you do to me?'

I was appalled. 'I didn't do anything!' I protested.

'Don't give me that!' his voice was harsh with an emotion I could not name.

'Roland, you asked me to relax you. I only sat and imagined that you were feeling relaxed.'

'You're a witch!' he snarled. 'You did something else.'

'Roland, please . . .'

I heard a mumble of voices. Someone else had come into the control room. I could not hear the conversation, as Roland had laid the phone down on his desk, but now and then he raised his voice and I thought I could detect a note of panic. Then the receiver was picked up and a new voice spoke to me.

'Dawn? Brian Wilshire here. Roland is in quite a state. Can you tell me what happened?' I almost sobbed with relief. Brian was the newsreader and a rational, intelligent man. If anyone could calm Roland down, it would be Brian. I now had some idea as to what had taken place and I sketched in the details of the preceding events, adding my theory to the explanation.

'I think Roland has some latent psychic ability and when he tried to tune himself in to my mind, he opened his channels. Some force hanging around him has caused him to trance. Brian, I have to see him—tonight if possible. I need to analyse what has happened in case there's an unpleasant spirit involved.'

Brian relayed my message to Roland and I heard his panicky response.

'No way! This is the twentieth century . . . no one believes that evil spirits can take over a person's mind. Woman's a witch! *She* did something.'

'Roland,' Brian's voice was patient, but firm. 'In the twentieth century, by your reasoning, witches don't cast spells either. Now, Dawn seems to think she knows what has happened and since the whole thing was your idea in the first place, I think you owe her a chance to explain it to you.'

Brian's calm reason won through and Roland reluctantly agreed to call on me when he finished work. But there was a condition: Brian must come with him. He would not face me alone. If I had not been so concerned, the idea of a six-foot-three male being afraid of being alone with me would have been amusing.

I was certain that the explanation for the evening's events lay in Roland's own abilities rather than any mysterious and hitherto untapped powers that I might possess. My problem lay in convincing Roland. It was easy to see that he was unwilling to accept the idea that he had psychic tendencies of his own, yet I could not allow him to think that I had set these events in motion. I thought it quite likely that his friendship for me had been irreparably damaged but I was more concerned for him. Somehow I would have to find out what had caused him to trance and that meant convincing him that his co-operation was necessary, for his own peace of mind. My task was not going to be easy.

I scoured my memory for everything that I knew about the kind of entities who might force someone to trance. My knowledge was scanty and I could think of little that was very encouraging.

The most comforting idea I could summon was that Roland might have a guide who was trying to reach him by stimulating his psychic abilities, as mine had done just over a decade before. But would Roland accept the idea? And could I handle the situation if it proved that the entity responsible was an undesirable one?

I could no longer call on Mary for help, as she had moved to the country several weeks before my car accident. I was quite alone with my dilemma and could only pray that I would be capable of dealing with it. I hoped too that I would be able to convince Roland that I had not been responsible for what had happened. I valued his friendship and didn't want to lose it. I was very nervous about the coming confrontation, on all of those counts, but I had to keep my uncertainty hidden from Roland. If he thought that I couldn't cope with the situation he would be doubly afraid. To give him confidence, I would have to display some.

When the men arrived, I was relieved to see that Roland seemed to have calmed down. He gave me a hesitant little smile and apologised for flying off the handle.

'It was fear', he explained. 'It is a horrible feeling when you know that you are not in control of your own body. For a while, I panicked.'

'He sure did,' added Brian. 'When I walked into the control room I thought at first that he was having a stroke. His face was grey, the veins were standing out in his forehead like cords and he was bathed in sweat. The expression on his face was ghastly.'

'I can imagine,' I replied. 'Roland, I can explain what happened to you but you may not accept it. That's up to you, but please believe me when I say that I did nothing to cause the incident to happen as it did.'

Roland nodded and I went on to explain my understanding of the evening's events.

'Mediums are people who have an ability to bridge the gap between our world and the realms of spiritual existence. Whatever you may think now, the ability is natural although it is not common. I believe that you possess that ability but up until now it has been dormant. Tonight, for some unknown reason, it was triggered off.'

I explained as well as I could the function of a trance medium but I was aware that my information was woefully inadequate. All I really knew was that when a medium trances, the body is used by spirits who wish to communicate with the physical world. Roland was noticeably lacking in enthusiasm.

'What would these spirits want from me?' he asked.

'I don't know. The only way to find out would be to hold a controlled sitting, allow them to come through, and ask them.'

'Are you kidding? What person in his right mind would volunteer for what I went through tonight?'

'It doesn't have to be like that,' I argued. 'Your reaction was caused by shock and fear. Under controlled conditions, trancing is no more difficult than falling asleep.'

Roland seemed dubious and I couldn't blame him. He had suffered a severe shock and his mind must have been struggling to assimilate the information I had given him.

'I thought you'd be able to help me stop it from

happening,' he said hopefully. I shook my head, remembering the time when I had voiced the same hope to my mother.

'You have to understand that this is a natural ability which has awoken in you. Now that it's functioning, the odds are that it will continue to do so and unless you learn to control it, you can trance at any time, whenever you are near a spirit that wants to communicate. And please remember that not all spirits are pleasant.'

'Could it happen while I'm driving the car?' asked Roland. I nodded, 'Yes.' He looked deeply thoughtful.

'Unless you control it and get yourself under the protection of your own guide, anything can happen.'

'This is heavy news!' he breathed. 'It's going to take a while for everything to sink in. Can I have time to think about it?'

I shrugged. What could I tell him?

'If the decision were in my hands, I would give you as much time as you want but I have no control over the matter. This is something inside yourself. Who knows when it might happen again?'

Roland did not entirely agree with me. Whilst he no longer believed that I had deliberately caused him to trance, he felt quite strongly that I had influenced the events somehow, even if it was unconscious on my part. He had a couple of good reasons for holding that attitude: he had never had any experiences with psychic phenomena until he met me, and my involvement in the field may have created some influences around me, without my being consciously aware of them. It was much too coincidental, he said, that he should suddenly begin to have psychic experiences just after he became acquainted with an active psychic.

I could not dispute his logic. If I had learned anything in my research so far, it was that the untapped potential in the supernatural is limitless. It is not possible to set down a marker at any selected point and say 'Here is where the supernatural begins'. Anything is possible and the unexpected can happen with almost tedious frequency. There is no such word as impossible and a flexible mind is practically a necessity. Although I did not want to be responsible for frightening Roland so badly, I had to admit the possibility that I had exerted some unconscious influence.

With Roland's experience that evening, I could see a new corridor opening and I would dearly have loved to start exploring it to see where it might lead. But I had to hold my enthusiasm in check, for that decision was not mine to make. It was Roland who was directly affected and even if he were prepared to go along with any suggestions I might make, he needed time to adjust. It would have been grossly unfair to put pressure on him, even though I thought that he was going to be forced to face the issue squarely sooner or later.

I could not hide the fact that I was highly impressed. Without even trying, Roland had succeeded in doing something that I badly wanted to do, but couldn't. For all of my interest and efforts, I had never succeeded at such an impressive level. I was full of admiration and a little envious about what I saw as his good fortune. With a lopsided grin, he told me that if I really wanted to experience that particular brand of luck, I was welcome to it. He was totally unimpressed by the fact that many experienced psychics might have given their eye teeth to possess his ability. I had to make an effort to remember that this experience was alien to him. He didn't understand it and he saw no particular value in it. I would have to be satisfied with the assurance that he no longer blamed me and I still had his friendship. Under the circumstances, I considered that I had ample cause to be grateful.

I also suspected that Roland's first psychic exploit was unlikely to be his last. There had to be a reason for the sudden awakening of his talents and I strongly doubted that it had been purely accidental. I hadn't deliberately triggered it; he certainly couldn't, so that left another possibility—another mind, not known to either of us. Some unseen intelligence might wish to communicate through him and if that were the case, it would no doubt continue its efforts until the communication was made. I wondered when the next attempt would be.

It came a couple of days later, again during a telephone conversation. Roland felt it coming and this time he didn't panic, although he sounded alarmed.

'Dawn, I feel strange. What will I do?'

'Stay calm,' I urged. 'You will come out of it safely, I assure you. Relax and let it happen.'

'Don't go away,' his voice held a plaintive note.

'I won't, don't worry.'

I heard his breathing alter, and I waited. He seemed to be making an effort to speak but it was some time before his words were clear and then his voice sounded oddly weak.

'D. . .David will contact you. . .in. . .two day's. . .time.'

'David who?' I asked, but the only answer was his laboured breathing.

When he had returned to normal, Roland was intrigued.

'I didn't lose consciousness that time, but my voice seemed to come from a long way off and I don't know what the message means. Do you know anyone named David?'

'No, do you?'

'Uh-uh! Anyway, I get the idea that you are the one who will be contacted.'

Now my curiosity was off and running. What could the message mean? If I were to meet someone named David, what importance was attached to the meeting? Would this mysterious man be aware that the meeting was predestined? I wondered how I would react if I opened the door to a smiling stranger who said: 'Hi, I'm David. I believe you're expecting me'. Even my fertile imagination found that possibility rather remote.

It occurred to me that the whole thing might be a hoax. I couldn't imagine Roland playing such a trick, but he could have fallen victim to a mischievous entity that used him as a means of having fun with some gullible mortals. In any case, I had two days to wait before I could learn anything further. I wondered if I would burst with impatience in the interim.

There were a number of times when I wondered what I would do if the promised contact failed to eventuate and I had to admit that it would be a disappointment. Whilst Roland had mixed feelings, my desires were clear. The more I discovered about psychic phenomena, the more I wanted to know. I was beginning to realise that I would

58

never have enough knowledge. As quickly as one set of questions were answered, I could dream up twice as many more.

On the second day, Roland rang me. His voice sounded hesitant and held a note of embarrassment.

'I have a note for you,' he said. 'And by some coincidence, it seems to have been signed by someone named David.'

I was overcome with eagerness. 'What does it say? How did you get it?'

'Well. . .I'd rather not discuss it over the phone. It's rather unusual. . .can I come and see you?'

'Try doing anything else! I'm dying of suspense.' I could hardly wait for him to arrive and when he came I flung the door open and all but dragged him into the room.

'Where's this mysterious note?' I demanded. 'How did you come by it?'

Roland cleared his throat and looked embarrassed. 'I'd rather tell you how I got it before you see it. It was delivered in a rather unorthodox way—I don't understand it, but maybe you will. You see, when I get to work on the night shift, I have a little routine. I have a chat with the other operator and after he leaves, I make myself a cup of coffee. Then I sit down and sign the log book. All of that usually takes about fifteen minutes, all told. Last night I did everything as usual. I put my coffee on the console and sat down and signed the logbook . . .

'After that, I picked up my coffee to take a sip and it was stone cold. Not only that, but the clock on the wall was showing midnight when by my reasoning it should only have been a little after eleven fifteen. It was a few minutes before I noticed that my writing pad was covered with writing. That's where this note came from. I hope it all makes sense to you, because it certainly has me confounded.'

He drew a folded sheet of paper from his pocket and handed it to me. I examined it eagerly. The first half of the page was covered with meaningless scribble which looked as though someone had been practising with the pen. Then followed the note: 'Dawn you must teach Roland for it is only through you that he can be reached.

The triad will be formed. You will be joined. David.'

'Well?' said Roland, after I had read and reread the note several times.

'Yes, it's all very interesting,' I answered slowly, 'I can explain the method to you, and the first part of the note. The last two sentences have me a bit puzzled though.'

'Then tell me what you can.'

'The method is fairly simple to explain. It's a process called automatic writing. Similar to trance communication as far as origin is concerned; that is, a spirit uses the medium as a channel. The words are written instead of spoken and the medium usually doesn't lose consciousness.'

'And the message?' prompted Roland.

'It would seem that David is your spirit guide and he is apparently trying to reach you. He wants me to teach you—obviously he wants you to understand the phenomenon so that you won't resist his efforts to contact you. As for the other parts, I know nothing about the reference to a triad, beyond the fact that a triad is a group of three. The part about us being joined is anybody's guess—it could mean that we will be working as a team.'

'It could also mean something else,' said Roland, a devilish glint dancing in his eyes.

'Well it doesn't, and get your mind cleaned out!' was my retort. 'The spirits wouldn't be interested in that kind of thing.'

'You've got a terribly suspicious nature,' he grinned. 'What makes you think that I don't have honourable intentions?'

'You're a man! Besides, I'm psychic. Anyway, if your David has any ideas about managing my love life he can go peddle his pitchfork somewhere else!'

I expected Roland to baulk at the idea of studying psychic phenomena but to my surprise he was quite agreeable.

'I don't promise to believe anything you tell me,' he warned, 'but I see no harm in listening to what you have to say. I don't understand anything about the things that are happening to me and even though I may not accept your explanations, you at least have some theories to offer. As long as you understand that you will find my scepticism hard to budge, you can teach to your little heart's content.'

Under those conditions, I accepted the challenge. Roland continued to tease me a little about the prophecy that we would be joined but I took it as his way of having a joke. At the time, it would not have occurred to me to think anything else.

My friendship with Roland deepened as the weeks passed and before long he was visiting more often than Keith. I felt comfortable and secure with both men and wasted no time in sighing over lost loves. My experiences with love had proven to be painful and I was much more at ease with my two friends. Roland and Keith liked me as I was and in the company of either one I could relax and be myself.

Keith was indulgent and treated me like a cute and funny kid sister. Roland was more attuned to my inner self. He treated me with gentle understanding and chivalry; at times he made me feel like a delicate hothouse bloom in the solicitous care of a dedicated gardener.

I felt more free than I had ever felt before. I went out once or twice a week, sometimes alone but more often with Roland. It was on one of my solitary nights out that the thunderbolt hit me. I was bored with the nightlife and irritated because one or two men had seen me alone and interpreted that as meaning I was available. But I didn't want to go home just yet. I knew that Roland was working so I decided to call and ask him if I could visit him at the studio.

It was against the rules but he told me to call in and he would drive me home when he finished work. It was plain that he didn't relish the idea of me wandering Sydney alone at night. I began to feel quite special and protected!

I was fascinated by the control room at the radio station. The array of knobs, dials and switches was mind-boggling and I was highly impressed by Roland's calm efficiency. This was a side of his personality that I had never seen before. I felt admiration growing inside me.

Then the phone rang and Roland bent to answer it. As he spoke into the receiver, he turned to face me, seated opposite. He gazed steadily at me, smiling slightly to let me know that I hadn't been forgotten. All of a sudden, I was drowning in his eyes. I felt them drawing me to him and I was powerless to resist. I didn't fall in love with him then, I simply realised that I had loved him for a long time without knowing it. I wanted to reach out and touch him but I dared not move.

Roland finished the phone call and replaced the receiver. Then he turned to face me. Cupping his chin in his hand, he very deliberately returned my gaze.

'Gotcha!' he said softly, and there was quiet satisfaction in his voice.

CHAPTER SIX
A challenge is laid

Being in love with Roland gave my life a whole new sense of depth and perspective. If I had felt free before, I now felt as though I had come home. I belonged with him and we both knew it, although being the cleverer of the two, he had been aware of it for a long time before I had woken up.

Becoming his lover was the most natural thing I had ever done in my life. While he assured me that he had every intention of marrying me when we were free, we were in no hurry. We already had each other and to be honest, the fact that we were unwed lent some piquancy to the relationship.

Darryl was happy too. He and Roland had become friends from the moment of their first meeting. Darryl showed no signs of resenting a stranger who had usurped his mother's affections; he was welcoming a dear friend into his life and he showed it.

Even David had his say. One evening, as I was resting luxuriously with my head on Roland's lap, he tranced and David spoke to me.

'Dawn, I am David. You have been joined. I am well pleased.'

At least he didn't say, 'I told you so'!

Keith was another matter. He practically crowed with delight when he heard the news.

'See? I told you,' he said to me, 'I said romance would rear its head. Don't tell me I don't know a thing or two!'

'Just for that, Smartypants, you can give the bride away when we get married,' I laughed.

'I would be delighted,' vowed Keith. And he was, too.

There was only one cloud on my horizon. In all conscience, I could not remain in Dennis's house. His ship was due to return in a couple of weeks and I would have to vacate the house before then. If I had been alone it might have been different but I would not think of allowing him to live in the cramped quarters of a ship and let me have the house now that I had formed a relationship with someone else. I was now only fulfilling my promise to take care of the place in his absence. Yet how could I move out, now that I had lost my job? I could not afford my own accommodation and the only option that I could see would be to live with my family in Tasmania, but that would mean leaving Roland.

Roland had another alternative to offer: 'Live with me. I'll find a house for the three of us. I want you and Darryl to be my family. Why should you go out to work when I want to take care of you?'

And so we went to live in a rambling old semi-detached house at Lavender Bay, overlooking Sydney Harbour. It was a little rundown but spacious and full of character and I loved it from the moment I first saw it. It was within walking distance of the radio station and I enjoyed knowing that Roland was always near at hand. As a 'coming home' present, I bought him a silver cross on a chain, to wear around his neck.

A few nights after we moved in, we had a hair-raising adventure. We had retired to bed and I noticed the altered breathing that told me Roland was entering a trance. I began to get alarmed when instead of hearing David's calm, measured tones, I noticed that Roland seemed to be in distress. He began to moan and arch his back and I wondered if he were in the grip of an unpleasant entity. When his fingers clutched at the cross around his neck and he made as if to jerk it away, I was certain.

If the cross was preventing something nasty from getting hold of Roland, it must stay in place. I flung myself across him and seized the cross, holding it flat against his chest. He struggled violently for a few seconds, then lay still.

Then a gasping, distressed voice spoke to me.

'Cross evil. Cross evil.'

'Oh, no you don't!' I thought, 'I won't be fooled like that.'

'Cross evil,' repeated the voice. 'In the name of Christ. Cross evil.'

I froze. I had been taught that evil entities do not call on the name of Christ because its power and authority brings strong spirits of light into the vicinity. I moved away from Roland. His hand came up and clutched the cross. With a jerk, the chain was snapped and the cross went flying across the room.

'Dawn.' It was David's voice, still gentle but filled with urgency. 'The cross has absorbed unwholesome vibrations. Rid yourself of it.'

'How?' I asked helplessly.

'Throw it out of the window. Do it now.'

I rushed across the room and bent to pick up the cross.

'No!' came David's command. 'My daughter, protect yourself before you touch it.'

I whispered a rapid prayer for protection, then picked up the cross and flung it quickly out of the window. I crept back to bed, fingering the delicate gold cross around my neck.

'Would my cross protect Roland?' I asked.

'It would. Place it around his neck,' was the reply.

I was filled with confusion. I had been told that a cross is good protection for those who are involved with the supernatural and I had given the cross to Roland with the best of intentions. I began to cry.

'I didn't know there was anything wrong with the cross when I bought it,' I sobbed.

'Comfort yourself, Child,' said David. 'There was nothing wrong with it. It was neutral. A cross can be used for one of two purposes. It can be used for protection or for cleansing. This house had absorbed unwholesome vibrations from previous tenants. To cleanse the house, I drew these emanations into the cross. It became contaminated, but the house is now safe and clear.

Purchase another cross and I shall imbue it with my own vibrations so that it may fulfil the function that you desire.'

Roland awoke a few minutes later and looked at my tear-stained cheeks with curiosity. I told him what had happened.

'Sounds a bit far-fetched to me,' he said. 'How long did all of this take?'

'I don't know . . . it seemed like a long time.'

Roland glanced at the illuminated dial of the clock. 'Couldn't have been,' he decided. 'We came to bed at ten forty-five It's only five past eleven now.'

'Then the clock has stopped. My watch says eleven thirty-five.'

'Don't be silly. The clock is electric—how could it stop when the dial is still lit up?'

'Look at the sweep hand. It isn't moving.'

Roland stared disbelievingly at the clock. 'It *has* stopped. There must be something wrong with it. You watch, I'll reset it and it will stop again.' After he had reset the clock, we both watched for several minutes as the sweep hand moved smoothly around the dial. Roland's face showed his consternation. 'What kind of force could stop an electric clock without cutting off the power?' he breathed. 'I hope this David of yours never gets annoyed with me.'

Out of curiosity, Roland searched the area below our bedroom window the following morning, before anyone else could be up and about. Although he gave the area a thorough scrutiny, he could find no trace of the cross. It had completely disappeared. After this incident, I found myself rethinking the things that I had learned. I could not explain the disappearance of the cross but I had some understanding about the cleansing of the house. I knew that it is possible for inanimate objects to absorb vibrations from people; it was on that principle that I had been able to register impressions from articles of jewellery whilst performing psychometry for my friends.

It had never occurred to me that the principle could be projected onto a wider scale. The idea that houses could actually absorb vibrations from their tenants was new to me, but the more I considered it, the more sense it made.

I had noticed different 'atmospheres' in houses that I had visited from time to time. Some felt cheerful and inviting; others sombre and depressing, whilst new houses made very little impression on me at all.

I had even commented to Roland that our house felt as though it was glad to have someone living in it. It had stood empty for some time and was quite grimy when we moved in. When I got busy with pails of hot soapy water, I had the whimsical impression that it was gratefully holding up its face to be washed. It was a very old house and must have sheltered many people in its time. I could imagine the number of human dramas that might have been played out within its walls, each leaving an imprint therein. Just as I had cleaned away the physical grime, David had cleansed the place of its psychic residue. It made sense to me.

Roland wasn't so sure. The idea sounded like good storybook material to him but he could not accept it as a workable reality. I decided that the best way to help him understand would be to teach him how to perform psychometry. If he could experience for himself the effect of vibrations from objects that had been worn by other people, he would find it easier to understand the principle.

'Hold the object in your hands. Press it against your forehead if you want to,' I told him, 'then relax your mind and let it form impressions. You may get mental images or you might think of certain words. Whatever sensations you get, quote them to the owner even if they don't make sense to you. They might mean something to the other person.'

He was dubious at first, but he tried it. When he found that his impressions were being confirmed, he became quite enthusiastic. His ability soon surpassed mine and from that time on, whenever I wanted someone to see a display of psychometry, I asked Roland to do it because his impressions are always clearer and more comprehensive than mine.

It may seem as though Roland slipped quite easily into an acceptance of psychic phenomena, but that is not really the case. Once he entered a trance state, he was to all intents and purposes asleep and his mind was blank.

No matter what took place during his trance, he knew nothing of it. I would repeat it to him when he awoke but to him it was like hearing about the activities of a stranger: he was unable to relate it to himself. Under those circumstances, he was not easy to teach for he maintained that unless he could see something and touch it, it didn't exist. No matter what gems of psychic wisdom David might present to me, he held to his attitude that nothing had been proven. It was this attitude that was to lead to our first real argument. I had been trying to explain some facet of David's teachings and he persisted in meeting my explanations with a wall of scepticism. I could see that the difficulty lay in his inability to accept the fact that another being really was making use of his physical body.

'Roland, this is where the difficulty arises,' I said. 'You are having trouble accepting your own level of psychic ability because you have never learned to recognize it for what it is. I realise that it's all very new to you and it has happened very suddenly, but if you let me explain . . .'

'You've been trying to explain it,' he interrupted, 'and it just keeps getting more and more complicated. I'm not saying that your arguments don't make sense. It's quite obvious that you have devoted a great deal of time and intelligence to your research. You are, nevertheless, postulating a theory. A well thought out theory, to be sure, but I don't see how I can accept it as fact unless you can offer some kind of conclusive proof.'

'Isn't your experience proof enough?' I demanded. 'You drew a woman that you yourself identify as me, and it was drawn two months before you met me. I correctly identified you in a crowd of people, even though I had never seen you before. If that isn't enough, consider your trances. You accept that something beyond either your control or your comprehension is responsible for these, and that something even gave me a message, in writing, without any conscious contribution from you.

'I could understand your attitude if that message had been written while you were with me,' I continued. 'I can't see that I would blame you if you thought I had written it myself, as a practical joke. But you weren't with me, you were twenty miles away, at work. No one there would have seen any significance in the name of David and even if they did, it would be awfully hard for a prankster to arrange for you to conveniently fall into a trance, wouldn't it?'

'I agree, but you are missing the point,' said Roland. 'I can't deny that these things are happening. What I'm trying to say is that there may be an explanation other than the one you propose. For instance, it could be a submerged facet of my own personality that is doing these things.'

'That idea doesn't hold water; there are gaping holes in it. How could any part of your personality, submerged or otherwise, have known what I look like, two months before you laid eyes on me? For that matter, how could it have known that you were going to meet me? Does your split personality idea also account for my immediate recognition of you? Honestly Roland, what kind of proof do you need?'

'It would have to be something that could not be explained by any physical means or attributed to coincidence. And it would have to be indisputable. So far, I've experienced some unusual occurrences that may or may not be psychic, as you suggest. But the rest of the world tells me that such things do not happen. How am I to know that I am not imagining things? It is even possible that I might be insane. You could be insane too, for that matter. I've heard that lunatics can often present an argument with devastating logic. Do I have any particular justification for believing that you are right and the rest of the world is wrong?'

My self control evaporated in a wave of furious indignation.

'You are beyond a doubt the most obtuse man I have ever met!' I stormed. 'It is easier for you to doubt my sanity than to accept that your own rigid sense of logic might be based on nothing more solid than hidebound tradition! You sit there, smugly inferring that I'm a candidate for a funny-farm, when by your own admission you are unable to come up with anything that makes more sense! Use your logic Roland. Offer me an alternative explanation. You say that nothing like this has ever happened to you before. What I propose makes sense. You cannot offer a "logical" explanation for your trances; by your own admission you could offer no explanation for the note that came from David, and you cannot explain the lady in the picture, yet you know it's me. Now use your head! Psychic phenomena exists. It's too well documented not to. Now how else are you going to explain these things?'

He sat there silently.

'There is another alternative,' I suggested, with less than a hint of subtlety. 'That you might have been trying to win favour by producing "evidence" of psychic occurrences around yourself to hold my interest for motives other than altruistic.'

He exploded. 'Why, you arrogant, self-opinionated female! Of all the gall!' he roared. 'What makes you think that you warrant such an elaborate and utterly impractical subterfuge? I have never in all my born days heard of such a conceited, high-handed attitude! If it weren't for the fact that you are a woman . . .'

'Then what will it take to convince you?' I shouted. 'Do you want your arm healed? Will that do it?'

An icy calm swept the room and crystallised the moment. When next he spoke, his voice was dangerously controlled. 'All right. Do it!'

I wanted to bite my tongue, for Roland's right forearm was crippled. He had fallen from an upstairs window at the age of two, fracturing his skull. He was left with partial paralysis of his right side. Neurosurgery was performed when he was thirteen but nothing could be done to restore feeling or movement to his arm and it had been totally nerveless ever since. It was not in my nature to make capital out of another person's misfortune, but I had done it. No matter how bitterly I might regret speaking those words, nothing would recall them. The gauntlet had been thrown and accepted.

I could not back down: the only course open to me was to make the attempt. I placed my hands on either side of Roland's arm, near his elbow, and slowly passed them down towards his hand. As I did so, I created a mental image of a tightly fitting glove, peeling away from the arm under my touch. While my hands moved, I prayed for healing energy to be directed into the damaged area of Roland's body.

Nothing happened. No dramatic thunderclap or bolt of lightening—nothing. Roland's arm remained as nerveless as ever. I bit my lip and tried not to cry.

The white-hot flood of emotion had ebbed away from both of us. Roland's face was soft with compassion.

'Don't be upset,' he said gently, 'I know you meant well, but you asked for something that was a task too great for the best neurosurgeons in the country. Perhaps your spirit friends will find another way to convince me, who knows?'

But I was filled with shame. It wasn't just that I had lashed out at Roland's handicap, although that was bad enough. I had also made an unreasonable demand on David, simply because my ego had been wounded. Not for the first time, I cursed my flashing temper and the things that it caused me to say. Would I ever learn to keep my impulses harnessed and cultivate a little patience and understanding? Judging by my current performance record, I doubted it very much.

CHAPTER SEVEN
The Teacher speaks

Three weeks had passed since our argument. In accordance with an unspoken agreement, neither of us had mentioned it in that time, but it still played heavily on my conscience. I had decided to back off; Roland had a right to hold his own counsel and it was not my place to force change upon him. At least he accepted my interest in the supernatural without scorn or criticism and he was perfectly willing to go into trances and allow me to talk with David. He listened attentively when I recounted David's words to him but he passed no judgements. To be sure, David had asked me to teach Roland and I was doing my best, but I avoided debating the issue and so did he. If he chose to disagree, it was his privilege to do so.

I was preparing tea while Roland practised guitar in the dining room. I really admired his determination and the ingenious ways in which he overcame his disability whenever it got in the way of something he wanted to do.

The guitar was an example. As a teenager he had conceived a desire to play the guitar but his useless right hand was a major impediment. He solved the problem by using his left hand to finger the chords and strumming the instrument with a plectrum wedged between the fingers of his right hand.

The method had its disadvantages. The plectrum frequently slipped from his fingers and the music would have to be interrupted while he repositioned it. Naturally he was unable to pick individual notes with his fingers but he played very well with a complicated strumming style and had built up a considerable repertoire. His music made pleasant listening and I hummed along with it as I worked in the kitchen.

The melody stopped suddenly and I assumed that the plectrum had slipped again, but then I heard him give a startled exclamation. I went to investigate and found him staring in stupefaction at his hand. He noticed me standing there.

'The plectrum slipped,' he said.

'It often does, doesn't it?'

'Yes. But this time, I *felt* it.'

The significance of this took a few moments to sink in and I must have looked puzzled because Roland explained carefully:

'I hold the plectrum in my right hand. I cannot feel with my right hand, remember? But I felt the plectrum when it slipped.'

'Are you sure?' was all I could say.

'Of course I am. I've tested it. What's more, I can move my fingers—look!'

He held up his hand and wiggled his fingers, then flexed each one individually, something which had hitherto been impossible.

I didn't know what to say. Whilst he had seldom complained, I knew that his right hand had been a continuing source of frustration for him. I could only guess at the emotions that must have been surging through him then. He was like a child with a new toy. He picked up a cigarette lighter and flicked it repeatedly, opened a matchbox and extracted the matches one by one. True, he fumbled a lot and these actions are things

71

that the rest of us would take for granted, but they were things that he had never been able to do with his right hand before. Imagine how you would feel if you suddenly discovered that you were able to fly. His face was transfigured: he wore an expression of enraptured wonder and I rejoiced with him.

'Well,' he said, when the first flush of excitement had paled, 'I suppose I have to accept that you know what you're talking about. You chose the proof and you got it, even though I thought it was impossible. I can't promise never to question what you say, but it's apparent that you know something that's worth listening to.'

'That is what I hoped for,' I said softly.

When I gave David my enthusiastic thanks his reply was guarded.

'I do not require thanks. What was needed is being done, but remember this: some of the nerves have been damaged beyond repair. It will not be possible to return the hand to full normality but it will continue to improve for some time.'

Roland's right hand is now as useful to him as my left hand is to me. That in itself is a matter of no small significance. As Roland says, any improvement, no matter how slight, is infinitely preferable to a limb that is about as useful as a lump of wood.

When David first entered our lives, I thought that I knew a fair amount about psychic phenomena. I knew at least as much as the next enthusiast and maybe a little more than some, but I was to discover very quickly that my knowledge was only basic and very patchy in a number of areas.

I knew a little about earthbound entities, but not nearly enough. I was to learn very quickly and I soon realised that we would need to take conclusive action if we were not to be regularly aggravated by such beings.

My first brush with a troublesome entity came, as might be expected, while Roland was in trance. I had expected a pleasant conversation with David but instead I received a stream of invective and indecent suggestions.

'Who are you?' I demanded.

'Who's askin'?' replied the coarse voice.

'The wife of the man whose body you are controlling.'

'Well now, ain't we fine and proper? And why is he stupid enough to let me in, then?'

'We weren't expecting you.'

The entity laughed, an unpleasant grating sound.

'Well, I'm here, ain't I? I might just decide to stay, too.'

'You can't.'

'And how are you going to stop me? There's nothing you can do to make me go away.'

Alarming as this experience was, the entity's words were beginning to sound like a lot of bluster and scare tactics. I suspected that it was not nearly as cocksure as it seemed. While I knew very little about how to handle earthbound spirits, I did know something about dealing with bluff.

'Maybe I can't force you to leave,' I admitted tranquilly, 'but if you stay you are going to be very bored, because as long as you are here, I'll find other things to occupy myself with.'

My show of unconcern was pure bravado, for inwardly I was quaking, but I managed to turn my back and, with an outward appearance of calm, I started to sing the Twenty-Third Psalm. The entity seemed to be allergic to religious occupations, for my song sent him off into a tirade of shouted threats and abuse.

'All right,' I said evenly, 'if you don't like listening to the song, I'll sing it in my head. Now I'm not going to talk to you any more.'

I was nowhere near as placid as I tried to pretend. I had no idea of how to get rid of this unwanted intruder, how powerful it might be or what it might be capable of doing. All I could think of was that Roland's body was at its mercy. I could not risk antagonising it too much but neither could I encourage it. Its manner indicated that it liked the idea of frightening me, so the best course seemed to lie in depriving it of that satisfaction. I did my best to draw comfort and strength from the words of the psalm and at the same time I prayed that some powerful spirit might come to our rescue.

My tormentor fell silent. I waited, still silently reciting my precious psalm. I was afraid to move lest the entity pounce on the opportunity to begin harassing me afresh.

'Dawn, I am David,' the voice startled me and my heart

73

bounded in my throat. 'Be not afraid,' continued the calm voice. 'It is truly I. The one who perplexed you has been removed.'

'Well, how did it get here in the first place?' I demanded, somewhat ungraciously.

'The door was open,' was the simple reply.

'I don't understand.'

'In your terms, this man is a medium. To us, he is a channel, a door through which we can enter into your level of existence. When he experiences that which you call trance, the door is open.'

'But you're a guide. Aren't you supposed to keep those other entities out?'

'I have not been asked.'

'Well, I'm asking you.'

'My daughter, it is not yours to ask this,' replied David gently. 'You are not the doorway. It is for this man to ask, if it is what he desires.'

'What happens if he doesn't ask?'

'Then the door is left open for all. This man has free will: I may not impose upon him something that he does not wish to have.'

'And if he asks?'

'If he wishes it, I shall guard the door and all who seek entry must do so through me.'

I relayed this information to Roland. He was concerned to hear of my experience, but rather sceptical about David's formula for protection.

'It sounds a bit like mumbo-jumbo to me,' he remarked. 'Still, we can't have bogey-men frightening you in the middle of the night and if David says it will work, we may as well give it a try. Tell him I don't mind if he plays doorkeepers.'

I couched Roland's message in slightly different terms when I passed it on to David and he answered with a slight smile.

'I am already aware. It is done,' he said.

David established a pattern of visiting me about three times a week, usually after Roland and I had retired to bed but sometimes our conversations would take place in the evening comfort of the lounge room. No matter where the talks took place, they satisfied a deep hunger in me, for they answered the questions that I had been asking for so long. I felt privileged that Roland's guide was willing to devote so much time to my spiritual education.

'For some time, my daughter, you have been under a misapprehension,' said David one evening. 'It is time that you were given the correct understanding.'

'What have I misunderstood?' I asked.

'It is your belief that I am this man's spirit guide. That is not so. I am yours.'

Although I was thrilled to hear this piece of information, I was a little confused.

'You speak through Roland. Why do you do that if you are not his guide? Why not speak to me direct?'

'Would you be able to hear me? I speak through this man in order that you will be able to hear. You are not yet sufficiently developed to perceive my words, should I address you in any other way. The time will come when I may speak directly to your mind, but that time is not yet. This man is attuned to you and he gives himself as an instrument, that I might reach you.'

'Isn't Roland being left out in the cold? He misses out on hearing what you have to say,' I remarked.

'My daughter, it is your desire to learn. His is to see that you are fulfilled. He feels no loss. He is happy to see that your desires are being satisfied: that is his reward. He shall also learn, but at his own pace, for do you not repeat to him the lessons I have given to you?'

'It makes sense,' said Roland when I told him the news. 'You are the one who was looking for a spirit teacher and I'm happy that you have found him through me. I did find it a bit odd that David was supposed to be my guide when it was you he talked to. This is a lot more logical.'

I was ecstatic. I had finally found what I had been seeking; my very own teacher. Yet I was aware that this was not an end but a beginning. A new phase was about to unfold for me: now I could really start to learn.

'How did you come to be with me, David?' I asked. 'Was I led to you or were you sent to me?'

'I have never left you, my daughter. I have been with you ever since you were.'

'Since I was what?'

'Since you . . . *were*. I have been with you since your inception, and by that I do not mean *con*ception.'

'Are you telling me that you have been with me through every life I have ever lived?'

'In my terms, my daughter, you have only one life,' smiled the guide, 'but you may have a number of physical incarnations within that life. I have been with you ever since you first came into being in my terms.'

Under David's gentle tuition I began to understand myself in terms of spirituality. My existence as a spirit had seemed unreal to me before: a spirit was something that I would become when I died. Now I could understand that I had always been a spirit. The contrast was subtle but it completely altered the perspective in my outlook on life. Whatever I am in this life or may have been in others, David knows me as a composite being, the end product which incorporates all of those forgotten experiences. In that respect, he knows me far better than I know myself.

He told me once that my first incarnation had been in Egypt, long before the time of the Pharoahs, in an era which is now recalled only in the misty pages of legend.

'Was I an Egyptian princess?' I asked, half joking.

'You were not.'

'Oh, just an ordinary Egyptian, huh?'

'My daughter,' the guide's voice rippled with mirth and his face was creased with suppressed laughter, 'I have been with you throughout every one of your physical lives. In that time, you have been many things—"ordinary" is not one of them.'

I was eager to know details about my previous lives but David would never reveal a great deal about them. Each life had contained its own set of lessons and experiences, he said, but those had already been learned. To spend a lot of time discussing them would only be exploring territory that I had already covered. Far better to apply myself to learning the lessons that this life entails. He assured me that if there was anything in a past life that was pertinent to a lesson I might currently be learning, he would see to it that I knew about it when the time was right.

David's method of teaching was a new experience for me. I began by assuming that he would deliver lectures on topics chosen by himself and it would be my place to accept his choice of subject matter. This was not the case. David waited for me to ask questions, which he answered in meticulous detail. I asked him why he had chosen this method.

'By the questions that you ask and the manner in which you phrase them, I am able to assess your level of understanding and structure your lessons to suit that level. Were I to choose our topics and you merely to listen, you might receive a lecture upon a matter that you cannot yet understand. Our efforts would be wasted. Better for you to choose those matters which you yourself wish to understand.'

'But how am I to know which questions I should be asking?'

'My daughter, if you do not know the questions, how can you hope to comprehend the answers? The questions are within you: they will arise when you are ready to hear the answers.'

Whenever David had explained something to me, he always asked if I had understood. If I said no, he would explain again, using slightly different words and examples to make the subject clearer for me. If my answer was yes, he would ask me to repeat the lesson in my own words. In this way he often picked up areas where I had misconstrued the meaning of his words and he would once again explain the subject to me. This might happen several times before he was satisfied that my answers demonstrated a clear understanding of the subject.

In the beginning, this procedure was repeated so often that I began to think I would never learn.

'I'm a complete dunderhead!' I remarked gloomily after David had finished explaining something for the umpteenth time. 'I don't know how you manage to be so patient when I'm so stupid.'

'My daughter, you are not stupid. If a student does not learn, the teacher is at fault, for he has neither correctly assessed the student's level of development nor delivered the lesson in the appropriate way. If something is explained to you properly, you will understand it. Therefore if you do not learn, you are not a poor student: I am a poor teacher.'

What a change there would be for children if our educational systems were to adopt that philosophy!

David was unfailingly patient, kind and understanding and I regarded him as much more than a teacher. If I had a problem, I would approach him for advice. He would never give me the solution outright and he always reminded me that he was a spiritual teacher, not a solver of physical problems. But he would discuss the problem with me and help me to analyse it objectively. The added insight this induced in me was sufficient to enable me to find a solution by myself.

'A problem is only a problem because it presents a set of circumstances that you do not fully comprehend,' he said. 'Understanding is the key to all things. If you understand a situation, you can see for yourself the course of action the circumstances require. Then it does not become a problem, for you know what to do. Were I merely to give you the solution, you would be equally perplexed by that problem when next it arose. If instead I help you to understand, then the knowledge is within you and you will not need to consult me should that situation confront you again. My purpose is not to solve problems for you but to give you understanding so that you may solve them for yourself.'

In those days I had no idea of where I was heading but I had implicit faith in David's ability to lead me. I accepted everything he said and I was somewhat taken aback when he told me that I should question him closely and put his words to the test thoroughly and often.

'But David,' I protested, 'you don't have to prove yourself. I believe what you tell me.'

'My daughter, I do not ask for blind faith. I am a teacher and you will learn more thoroughly if you test and examine the things that I tell you. You must not merely believe; it is necessary that you *know*, and you will know only if you prove things for yourself.'

I was beginning to understand the purpose behind my long, slow search for a teacher. In the beginning, I had not known that it was a teacher I was seeking, nor did I know what it was that I wanted to learn. Only when I had discovered these things for myself was it time for David to make himself known to me. He had waited for me to develop both the desire and the capacity to understand. His timing was impeccable and I could see how my footsteps had been guided inexorably towards him. I began to wonder if any of the events in my life had been chance occurrences or whether each tiny step had been charted in advance on an unseen master plan.

CHAPTER EIGHT
Learning the basics

David commenced the practice of identifying himself at the beginning of each sitting. This, I guessed, was done so that I would be less likely to be deluded by any spirit which might pretend to be my guide. However, I soon noticed a variation in his mode of introduction. Usually he would simply say 'I am David' but there were times when I would hear 'You know me as David'. On those occasions I also noticed slight differences in speech patterns and voice modulation.

I asked David for an explanation and he told me that there were other spirits working with him in order to learn under his guidance. It was not always necessary for David himself to answer my questions; several of his 'students' were equal to the task and since they needed to practise working through a medium, David allowed them the opportunity to do so. It was not necessary for me to know their individual names and indeed it might have been confusing if each had identified separately. Also, it was preferable that I be assured that I was not being misled so all of these entities identified themselves by their association with David, to let me know that they visited me with his approval.

Everything I learned was of the utmost interest to me, as I was beginning to understand something of the faultless efficiency of the spiritual world. David told me however, that they sometimes encounter problems whilst working in the physical, chiefly because human beings are highly unpredictable and often unwittingly interrupt the sequence in a well-laid plan, forcing the spirits to reorganize. Another factor which must be considered by the spirits is individual right to free will. David impressed on me time and again the importance of allowing other souls to make their own decisions. Never must one soul impede the free will of another, even though it might be considered to be in the best interests of the other person. Saying to oneself 'It's for his own good' is no justification. Even though we may see another person making mistakes that will cause problems for him, we may not interfere. It may be that the person needs to experience the results of his mistakes in order to learn from them.

This does not mean that we should keep silent when we see wrongs being done to other human souls. If, for example, you object to the use of napalm bombs in warfare, you have every right to make your views known, but you cannot fire-bomb the home of some high-ranking military nabob in order to get your point across! On a less spectacular level, you might give your opinion if you are asked for it, but to insist on your advice being followed might constitute interference with the other person's free will. By the same token, if your free will is being stifled, it is up to you to insist on the right to live by your own choices.

David was scrupulous in his adherence to this maxim. If I asked him to advise me, he pointed out the various factors involved in the situation, then discussed the possible results of any particular course of action. I was left to choose which course I found most appropriate to the situation. If I asked him to tell me which was the right choice, I would receive an answer like this: 'There is no right. There is no wrong. There is only free will and the consequences of it. The answer you seek is within yourself: look within and you shall find it'.

At first I found this concept frustrating. I wanted to be sure of doing the right thing and I trusted David's wisdom much more than my own. But in that wisdom, David was aware of what I had yet to learn: if I could use him as a crutch, I would never develop my own strength and perception. It might have seemed easier from my point of view to have David make all my decisions for me, but it would have robbed me of the opportunity to grow and develop. Since David's purpose was to teach me how to use my own abilities, it would have been self-defeating to relieve me of that responsibility.

I frequently champed at the bit and complained that I was not developing quickly enough. David patiently maintained that all things would come in time.

'My daughter, it is within you to grow at your own pace. It would benefit you nought if I were to carry you beyond your capabilities. Far better that you proceed steadily, learning all there is to know at each step. To skim across the surface would not bring you the depth of understanding that you desire and which is yours to have.'

'But I can't *do* anything!' I wailed. 'I want to be able to see you as you are, for instance.'

'It will come in time,' repeated David. 'Were you to see us before you are ready, you might be startled and afraid.'

I found that very difficult to believe, in view of my eagerness to produce some effective results, but as is always the case, David proved to be correct. Several months after that conversation took place, I did see a spirit. I was lying in bed and I had an impulse to open my eyes. When I did so, I saw what appeared to be a cloud of blue-white mist, about two feet in diameter, hovering above the bed. At the centre of the mist I could distinctly see the features of a human face. I squeaked with fright and dived under the bedclothes! When I ventured out a minute or so later, the mist had disappeared.

David later told me that the apparition had been one of the spirits who worked with him. He was not surprised to learn that I had reacted just as he had foreseen, but I was quite disgusted with myself.

'My first chance and I blew it!' I muttered disconsolately.

Despite his comparative lack of experience, Roland's reactions to psychic manifestations seemed more calm and objective than mine. He saw a misty female form standing in an archway near our bedroom window one evening. His reaction was to stand quite still and gaze steadily at it until it disappeared. He was not alarmed at all, only intrigued and curious to know why the figure had appeared to him. When I asked David about it, he replied simply that such things will be seen if we happen

81

to be attuned to them. He reminded me that we are always surrounded by those who have chosen to work with us. It is only to be expected that we would occasionally catch a glimpse of them.

By now we were growing accustomed to the knowledge that we were constantly surrounded by spirit beings but we could always be certain that sooner or later we were bound to be surprised again. Unexpected things became anticipated events in our lives and we often wondered aloud what new development would arise to set us thinking next.

One night Darryl was ill with asthma. For several hours he coughed and wheezed terribly. His sleep was fitful because severe coughing fits kept waking him up and Roland and I took it in turns to get out of bed and settle him down. We were both very tired and when we heard him working up to another crescendo of coughing we sat up wearily, wondering if the asthma attack would ever end. Roland was on the verge of stumbling out of bed for the umpteenth time when we were both frozen by the sound of a clear, silvery female voice coming from Darryl's room.

'It's all right Darryl, go to sleep.'

'Did you hear that?' breathed Roland. 'There's someone in Darryl's room.'

We bounded out of bed and rushed into Darryl's bedroom but there was no intruder to be seen. Darryl slept soundly, tendrils of hair clinging to his damp forehead. Roland and I stared at each other in bewilderment, then went back to bed. For the rest of the night, we all slept peacefully; there were no more coughing fits from Darryl. In the morning, his asthma had subsided. He was fascinated to hear our account of the mysterious voice but he had been aware of nothing out of the ordinary.

'Her name is Giselle,' said David, when I asked him about the incident. 'She is with your son as I am with you.'

'In other words, Giselle is Darryl's guide?'

'That is correct.'

At this stage in our lives we had attracted a circle of young friends who were interested in our activities as psychics. They ranged in age from about nineteen to twenty-one and among the enthusiasts were one or two people who weren't sure that they could believe all that they were told. One of these was a young nurse named Sue, who became the unwitting catalyst for a startling display of psychic energy.

There were about half a dozen people present in our lounge room one evening, as usual holding a relaxed discussion and waiting for David to arrive. We had adopted the practice of burning a candle in the centre of the room, because Roland had discovered that the bright overhead lights made it difficult for him to relax sufficiently for a comfortable trance. David duly arrived and there ensued a pleasant conversation, during which Sue commented that she had difficulty in accepting David at face value.

'What is it that causes you concern?' enquired the guide.

'I can't really accept that you are a separate being from some spirit world,' said Sue. 'Don't get me wrong—I'd like to believe it, but I'm the kind of person who needs physical proof. Now, if you could do something that Roland couldn't possibly do . . .'

David smiled. 'Would you have me extinguish your candle?' he asked mildly.

Sue shuddered. 'Please don't! I wouldn't like to be plunged into darkness and besides, it wouldn't really be proof. I could always argue that a stray draught had done it.'

'Very well,' said David, 'keep your eyes on the candle.'

We all gazed expectantly at the dancing flame, wondering what David was planning to do. I didn't bother to essay any guesses; I knew well enough that David always had a few surprises tucked up his ethereal sleeve. We waited—and the candle continued to flicker brightly in the middle of the room. Then it changed. The flame sputtered a couple of times, then suddenly surged upwards, growing to a height of some three or four inches. It burned steadily at that height for a while, then its orange colour changed and the flame became completely blue. As if that was not enough, the flame then decided to defy whatever law says that all flames should burn upwards. It tilted sideways and began to burn downwards, towards the floor, licking at the side of the candle as it did so.

No one moved or spoke. We were all completely spellbound. Before our flabbergasted gaze, the flame righted itself and returned to its normal size and colour. Roland awoke shortly afterwards and was immediately assailed by a chorus of excited voices as everyone clamoured to tell him all the details at once. He looked at us askance and made rude noises about people who tell tall stories. Then he picked up the candle and his attitude altered dramatically.

One side of the candle had partially melted away where the flame had been burning against it and the blackened wick was bent over into an inverted u. This evidence was sufficient to convince Roland that we had been telling him the truth.

There has only been one other occasion when I have seen David perform what I call parlour tricks; that is, a display of phenomena that has no particular purpose other than to demonstrate that it can be done. As a rule he does not bother with these performances, not because he frowns on them but simply because he usually comes with another purpose in mind. As he has repeatedly told me, his purpose is to teach. Perhaps his occasional lapses into some harmless fun and games only serve to emphasize that a good teacher sees no harm in occasionally providing his students with a little light relief.

For all his profound wisdom, David is by no means a pedantic lecturer. If it is possible for him to lighten our discussions by introducing a little humour, he cheerfully does so. His humour is usually dry and witty but never hurtful and it usually forms a part of my learning experience. It also helps to prevent me from becoming too awed by David's superior intelligence.

I have occasionally pestered David to tell me details about my future but this is something he is reluctant to do. His reasons can best be expressed by the well-worn adage: 'Don't cross your bridges before you come to them'. That may be a reasonable attitude, but it didn't always prevent me from trying to wangle some information out of him.

'My daughter, I am a teacher,' he reminded me one

evening, after I had unsuccessfully tried to prise a prediction from him. 'To tell the future, you need a prophet.'

'Ah, but the teacher must know what is in the curriculum,' I argued.

'That is so.'

'Then he *could* give his student a hint about what she might be doing next year?'

'. . . Which she would not understand, because she has not yet absorbed this year's material.'

'How is it possible to plan future events so that they work out as intended?' I asked.

'You would not understand if I were to tell you in precise detail,' said David, 'so I shall answer you this way: imagine that we have a gigantic chessboard. On it are pieces which represent all the influences with which you may come into contact. We know, for instance, that your purpose is to meet your teacher; but the teacher is in the school and you are at home. We must plan the moves and counter-moves that will get you to where you wish to be.

'Along comes a being we shall call the Bus Driver. It is his task to get you to your destination. You get onto his bus and he drives off, but when he reaches the school he discovers that you have already alighted, so back he goes to fetch you. Next time, when the journey ends, you are still on the bus—but the bus is seven blocks away from where it should be.

'The Bus Driver repeats his journey again and again, until finally he knows before he sets out that you will be delivered safely to your destination. And now he discovers that he is no longer needed for the *bus* knows where it has to go.'

'Aha!' I said, thinking that I had managed to catch David off guard, 'and I suppose it is the prophets who do all this planning?'

'No,' smiled the guide. 'They are just the blabber-mouths who run off and tell everyone before we are ready!'

CHAPTER NINE
Hair-raising encounters!

If it had been left for me to decide when I would begin to put my acquired knowledge into practice, I would probably still be content to sit at David's feet, soaking up information. The more I learn about spiritual existence, the greater becomes my conviction that I am merely paddling in the shallows of a sea of infinite possibilities. I would happily listen to David in endless discussions on the nature of those things that I have yet to experience for myself, but he maintains that second-hand information is no substitute for first-hand experience.

His method of teaching is simple. He supplies me with the information I seek and in carefully graded stages he allows me to be confronted by situations in which I must put my knowledge into practice. I am aware that he is always on hand to prevent serious mishaps from arising out of any mistakes that I might make, but it is for me to keep my senses alert and try to win my way through without making any mistakes. When I succeed, my reward is further education. If this sounds like an endless spiral, it is nevertheless the course I have chosen to pursue and nothing gives me greater pleasure than the knowledge that I have successfully negotiated one phase of development and am ready to commence upon another.

A basic principle in spiritual development lies in helping others. It is not merely a moral requirement, it is an active way of putting your knowledge into practice and seeing the results. Of what use is knowledge unless you can do something with it? It also affords an opportunity for further learning, because experience itself is a great teacher. In addition, it reinforces the sensation of belonging, for an awareness of having some value in a masterfully-designed system must arise when you are daily provided with opportunities to make your own unique contribution. There is something to be learned from each and every soul you help, whether they be ahead of you on the path of development or following along behind. Spiritual knowledge is never static: if it is to grow, it must be passed on.

It is possible to help higher beings by assisting them in the work they wish to carry out on levels close to ours. Just as David's spirit students helped him to teach me, we can do the same with people who are seeking the answers we have already been given. Every time Roland trances, he is giving himself as a channel so that David can reach directly into the physical.

We can also offer our guidance to any soul who may be a little way behind us in development, so long as we remember that they have a right to choose whether or not they wish to accept the help we are offering. We must also remember not to overstep our capabilities: if we are asked a question and we do not know the answer, an attempt at guessing might seriously mislead the enquirer. It is much better to admit that we do not know and seek counsel from David.

The souls that we can help are not only to be found in the physical world. There are many who wander the lower levels of spiritual existence, seeking a guiding light that will lead them to higher and happier spheres. In closest proximity to our level of existence are the earthbound spirits; these are souls who have ended one physical life but have remained within the physical sphere instead of graduating to a level in the spirit world.

The reasons why these spirits become enmeshed in the physical are as individual as the personalities themselves, but usually there is some lack of spiritual awareness, often caused by emotional trauma. This inhibits their ability to see where they are going, so they drift around helplessly until some stimulus can free the spiritual blockage for them. Some are malevolent but most are simply lost.

My first active experience with one of these souls came when we were least expecting anything of the kind. We had retired to bed and I fell asleep almost instantly but Roland sat up, reading a book. He became aware of some sounds of activity which sounded like shuffling footsteps in the passageway. He crept out of bed, armed himself with a shoe and ventured forth to confront the intruder. Although he searched the house high and low, he could find nothing amiss. He decided that his hearing must have been playing tricks on him, and made his way back to bed.

No sooner had he settled beneath the covers than the noises started up again and this time, they were quite distinct. There were three heavy footsteps on the stairs, then a solid *thud!* What followed was a sound that made Roland's blood curdle—the slow creaking of a weighted, swinging rope.

Even the most courageous of men need moral support sometimes, and Roland decided that it was time for me to wake up. While I blearily rubbed the sleep out of my eyes, he explained what had been happening.

'Something spooky is going on out there,' he said. 'You're the one who knows about these things—what do you think it is?'

'I don't know,' I answered, 'I wasn't the one who heard it. Let's investigate, shall we?' Roland bravely (if hesitantly) led the way, with me following close behind. I wondered how I would react if I actually saw a macabre vision in the stairwell and a fluttery feeling in the pit of my stomach hinted that I might well resort to inglorious flight. But the stairwell was deserted and the house silent and still. Although the night was warm, something made me shiver and I took Roland's hand as we went back to bed.

He closed his eyes as soon as his head touched the pillow and his heavy, rhythmic breathing signalled his withdrawal from the conscious world. I watched him carefully: he had switched off rather too quickly to have fallen asleep normally and his breathing pattern indicated that he was entering a trance. I waited. His respirations grew heavier, then something went wrong! He seemed to be having difficulty with his breathing. He arched his back and struggled for air, making gurgling sounds in the back of his throat, as though he were choking. His eyes flew open, bulging and filled with panic and foam flecked the corners of his mouth. I dared not touch him, so I called his name sharply several times, trying to bring him out of the trance.

There was no response. His struggles grew more frenzied. His legs jerked convulsively and his tortured body bucked and rolled in a desperate struggle for breath. When his hands came up and began to claw at his throat, I realised what was happening. This was a spirit who had died by strangulation and it was reliving the last, desperate moments it had spent in this world.

I didn't stop to think about the reasons why this was happening; my only instinct was to put an end to the ghastly panic. I couldn't bear to see a soul suffering such anguish.

'Listen to me!' I called. 'Listen! The rope has gone. Understand, there is no rope. What you are feeling is a memory, an imprint on your mind. The rope has gone. You can breathe. Stop remembering. Stop thinking about the rope. It has gone. Hear me, you can breathe.'

I cannot recall how long I stood there, repeating my theme over and again in as many ways as I could summon, trying to find the words that would penetrate the nightmare and reach the tormented soul on the bed. It seemed an eternity before Roland's body stopped threshing and lay still, gulping down life-giving air in huge, shuddering gasps. The eyes were now fixed on me and I read within them a pathetic gratitude combined with mute appeal. I had released the spirit from its struggles but not from its earthbound condition. It didn't know what to do next and it was looking to me for guidance.

I knew that there was little I could do to lead the spirit away from the physical world. I would have to call on the assistance of a spirit for that. I mentally radioed David to come and help, then I spoke again to the figure on the bed. I told it to look around, explaining that there was someone present who would lead it to a place where it could find rest. I watched the eyes as they flickered around the room, coming to rest at a point just over my shoulder. A faint smile touched the lips, then there came a deep sigh and Roland's body relaxed.

When Roland awoke, he had no recollection of the tumultuous events that had taken place during his trance, nor did he feel any ill effects. He listened in open-mouthed wonder as I recounted our adventure and when I had finished he gave a low, admiring whistle.

'You've got more pluck than me,' he commented. 'I

think I'd run a country mile if I saw something like that. Rather you than me!'

'What was I supposed to do, leave you to choke?' I enquired. 'Besides, from where I stood, it seemed as though you were going through a pretty hair-raising experience yourself.'

'Ah, but I don't remember it. Just as well too, otherwise I might be too scared to fall asleep at night.'

I had plenty of questions to ask David when he next arrived, and he was prepared for them. He told me that the spirit had been attracted by the strength of our vibrations, which functioned like a beacon on the level from which it had come. David had allowed it through because he judged me to be ready to cope with the situation and it was time for me to begin putting my studies into practice. I had acquitted myself quite well, he said, considering that it was the first time I had carried out such an operation.

'The *first* time?' I queried. 'Do you mean this kind of thing is going to happen again?'

'You are being requested to perform this work. You are free to refuse and if you do so, you will not suffer. I shall continue to teach you and you will find other ways of using your abilities. The choice is yours.'

I shrugged. 'What the heck? The work needs to be done and if I can do it, I suppose I might as well be of some use. Just don't get too far away from me, huh?'

'I shall not leave you alone,' he assured me.

'You've got rocks in your head!' was Roland's reaction when I told him about my agreement with David. 'You mean you actually enjoy getting involved with things that rattle chains and go into death throes in the middle of the night?'

'I didn't say I enjoyed it. It's work that needs doing and there is some satisfaction in being useful. How would you feel if it were someone dear to you who came to us lost and looking for help?'

'I see your point, but I still admire your spirit of adventure. You wouldn't find me doing something like that for worlds.'

Being tossed into the deep end seemed to be the order of the day, for our next encounter with an earthbound spirit was even more startling than the first. We had taken Darryl to visit his father for the weekend, and Dennis invited us to stay for coffee. Within minutes of entering the house, I began to feel lethargic and it became an effort for me to follow the conversation between the two men. Roland kept glancing at me and I noticed hazily that his forehead was creased with concern. As soon as it was politely possible, he cut short our visit and led me to the car, holding me firmly by the arm as though he were afraid that I might fall.

'There is something unhealthy in that house,' he said, once we were on our way.

'A lot of people have said that,' I remarked tiredly.

'I had to get you out of there,' Roland continued, 'I could feel something, like the walls were closing in on me. But it's you it was after. I could see you wilting.'

'Perhaps I'm just a little tired.'

'Maybe, but I think it's more than that.'

By the time we got home, I had recovered my vitality and I chattered gaily to Roland as he slipped the key into our front door. As it swung open, he reeled back against the wall, looking both horrified and nauseated.

'It followed us!' he gasped. 'It's in there now, waiting for us.'

'Well then, we'd better go and meet it,' I suggested. 'We can't camp on the doorstep forever.'

Trying to make light of the situation, I stepped past Roland and entered the house.

'Whoever you are,' I called, 'you have no business scaring people. I'm not afraid of you, so there.'

'Neither am I,' said Roland, just behind me. 'I'm all right now. I don't know what came over me just then.'

He passed me and walked into the lounge room. Half-way across the floor, he came to a standstill. His shoulders hunched forward and he spun slowly to face me.

Glittering eyes met mine and I looked into the distorted features of a face that was no longer Roland's. Clawed hands stretched out towards me. I disintegrated into a mass of terror and fled shrieking for the door. Outside, I stopped to catch my breath and looked back fearfully, expecting to see a lumbering form in hot pursuit. Nothing happened.

91

For a few moments I stood there, full of indecision. Then I considered Roland's plight. I had left him alone, in the grip of who knew what? I couldn't just desert him like that; I had to brave the house again and try to banish the entity that had taken control of him. My knees were shaking and my heart felt as though it had migrated to my throat as I wobbled uncertainly into the house, expecting a maniacal figure to pounce on me at any moment.

The house was hushed. I peeked into the lounge room and saw him slumped in a chair in an attitude of utter dejection. Huge tears welled up in his eyes and coursed down his cheeks. My fear was gone and in its place surged a wave of compassion. The poor creature had not been threatening me; it had reached out in an appeal for help and I had responded by flinging myself away from it in terror. I felt as though I had kicked an injured puppy.

I crept across the floor and knelt in front of the seated figure, taking its hands in mine.

'I'm sorry,' I whispered, 'I didn't mean to reject you. You just startled me, that's all. I'm here now and I want to help. Please forgive my stupidity.'

The tear-filled eyes gazed sadly into mine. No word was spoken but I felt a sensation of wistful searching and poignant loss. I could find no words of comfort, I could only look back into those drenched eyes and try my hardest to communicate my sympathy. Eventually the eyes closed and the head drooped forward. There was a pause, and then the figure spoke.

'My daughter, I am David. That one is now in our care.'

'Thank you,' I breathed fervently.

A few nights later, I received another surprising visitor. Roland had tranced normally and I was expecting to hear David's voice. What I got was quite another matter.

'Me little Eileen!' crooned a distinctly Irish voice.

'What? Who are you?' I asked in surprise.

'Me name's David . . . David Michael O'shea.'

'Are you a teacher?'

'Aye, a teacher is what I was, and a drunkard besides,' he replied, with a wicked chuckle.

Here we go again, I thought.

'You're lost, aren't you?' I remarked.

92

'No me darlin', I know where I'm at. I'm with you, is where.'

'Do you realise that you are no longer in the physical world?'

'Why, me love, of course I do. Didn't I leave it five hundred years ago, now, and you as well?'

'You. . .left me?' I asked in a weak voice.

'Aye, me darlin', and haven't I searched for you ever since. And now I've found you, me darlin' wife—me little Eileen.'

'Hold it right there, buster! I'm not your wife, I happen to be married to the man whose body you are using. And my name isn't Eileen, it's Dawn!'

Unperturbed, the spirit favoured me with an ecstatic grin.

'Aye, me little one. Sure and your name is different now, but you're still me little Eileen, me lovely wife.'

'Will you get it through your head,' I insisted, in near-desperation, 'I am *not* your wife!'

'But of course you are, me darlin'. And now that I've found you again, I'll not be lettin' you go.'

'Listen, sport, *you're* the one who is going. Now I refuse to talk to you any more, so you may as well chooff off!'

I turned my back and resorted to the Twenty-Third Psalm.

The real David arrived a few minutes later and I indignantly demanded to know how the interloper had managed to penetrate Roland's trance.

'It was one who sought to speak with you,' was the placid response.

'Well, tell him to seek somewhere else! His little Eileen, indeed!'

Roland was highly amused when I told him.

'A lovesick spook!' he chortled. 'Now I've heard everything.'

'It's not so funny!' I snapped, feeling quite disgusted. 'The entity was obviously deluded and it just happened to be controlling your body. What if it had demanded to re-establish its conjugal rights?'

'I hardly think that's likely,' chuckled Roland. 'I'm sorry honey, but the vision of you fending off an ardent demon lover is irresistible.'

'Some defender of my honour you turned out to be!' I grumbled, but I was beginning to see the funny side of the situation.

Things like that could only happen to me, I thought. Other people lead sane, ordinary lives while I spend my time talking to people who aren't there and sparring with amorous ghostly suitors! Life might have its ups and downs but mine promised never to be dull!

CHAPTER TEN

Cause and effect: the Law of Karma

Happy as we were at Lavender Bay, we knew that our time there was limited. The house was up for sale and the price was far beyond our slender means. Although we loved the old house, we looked around for a home that was within our price range. After several months of frustration we found a small bungalow in Yagoona, one of Sydney's western suburbs. Only just in time too, for we had no sooner negotiated the purchase than we were told that the Lavender Bay house had been sold and we would be expected to vacate it at the end of a month.

It wasn't easy to leave the house in which we had begun our life together. It was like leaving a part of ourselves behind. When the time came for us to leave, I was reluctant to take the final steps. I walked through every room, footsteps echoing strangely on the bare floors as I whispered goodbye. I thought the house felt sad and wistful too, but perhaps I was only projecting my own feelings onto it. When we closed the door behind us for the last time, I felt a huge lump rising in my throat. I swallowed hard, blinked away the mist from my eyes and tried to smile encouragingly at Roland.

I found it difficult to settle into the house at Yagoona. It had belonged to an elderly invalid and it felt cold and uninviting after the mellow warmth of our former home. I felt as though it was rejecting us. Roland didn't laugh at my fancies, he understood how I felt and he had some encouraging advice to offer.

'This house had become lazy and tired. Wake it up.

Give its face a wash and let the sunshine in. Fill it with love and gaiety and make it feel good, then it will start to enjoy having us here.'

Out came the pails of hot water. We mopped and scrubbed, cleaned the walls and polished the windows. Furniture was arranged and re-arranged, new curtains went up and painted cupboards were given a scrub. We fell into bed each night and slept the dreamless sleep of the exhausted, then rose each morning to start anew. The house grouched and grumbled like a sleepy old man surrounded by a horde of exuberant teenagers. But it woke up, took a fresh look at itself and decided that life wasn't so gloomy after all. And it was ours. As long as we kept up the payments to the bank, nobody could come along and tell us to move. Darryl found himself some playmates and at Christmas time his dreams came true when we presented him with a shiny new bicycle. Taffy, our corgi dog, romped happily in his very own yard and we bought a Persian kitten to purr on the hearth.

There was just one thing left for us to do. To all intents and purposes we were already a family; it remained only for us to make it official. Roland and I were married at the Hurstville Spiritualist Church and my best friend Helen Iddon was my attendant. True to his promise, Keith walked me to the altar. There was no formal reception. When the ceremony was over, our friends came back to our home to celebrate with a noisy, happy-go-lucky party. Our official wedding anniversary falls on 5 March, but the date that is really significant to Roland and I is 2 February, the anniversary of the day we set up home together at Lavender Bay.

We were now just like any other normal suburban couple, paying off a mortgage, raising a child and occasionally battling to make ends meet. The essential difference, of course, is that very few average suburban couples devote their spare time to a pursuit of psychic enlightenment. We suspected that our neighbours might think us quite peculiar if they knew about this facet of our lives but since we were not on intimate terms with them, this did not constitute a problem. Our friends enjoyed discussing the subject with us but none of them felt inclined to get actively involved at that stage, nor would we have made any attempt to persuade them to do so.

However, we were beginning to feel rather isolated and we wondered whether it might be possible for us to form an association with other people who shared our interest in psychic development. I scouted around among my few contacts and discovered that classes for psychic development were being held each week at a place not far away from our home. I telephoned the man who was running these classes and told him about our interest. He seemed very impressed when he heard about David and he said that it would be a pleasure to have us attend.

On our first visit we joined a general class in the main hall. The evening commenced with a few meditation exercises, after which I was stunned to hear the instructor announcing to the class that Roland and I, as practising psychics, would proceed to give a demonstration of trance mediumship! Although taken off guard, Roland did manage to achieve a trance state, but the results were probably nothing like what the instructor had hoped for; his breathing became agitated and he began to moan as though in great distress. Then he flung back his head and cried out in an agonized voice:

'No! Stop it, it's wrong!'

With a jerk he awoke and stumbled out of the hall. I murmured our apologies and followed him. He was visibly upset and all he wanted to do was get home as quickly as possible.

During the following week, we were telephoned by the man who organised the classes. He was sorry that our experience with his class had been uncomfortable, but he still felt that our talents could be exploited in some way. There was a separate class for trance mediums that took place in a side room. Would we be prepared to give that a try? We agreed.

The trance class was conducted by a large taciturn lady who eyed us balefully as we were introduced. I felt instantly uncomfortable and ill at ease, for it was plain that she regarded us as intruders. She carefully informed us that her class was making excellent progress; they had been meeting each week for twelve months and were now beginning to experience the first stages of trance. The *first* stages, I thought, after twelve whole months?

Roland's progress had been infinitely more rapid than that. I was frankly puzzled but I maintained a discreet silence as we allowed ourselves to be bustled into our seats. Our hostess had decided that we should sit on the sidelines and observe her class in action.

The lights were put out and the room fell silent. I waited for something to happen and before long, Roland's breathing took on the now-familiar pattern of approaching trance. I heard the teacher move sharply in her chair.

'Is he trancing?' she hissed at me.

'Yes,' I replied, with some bewilderment.

'Turn the lights on!' she bellowed, and pandemonium began. The room was suddenly ablaze with light and before I had time to collect my wits, the woman had leapt from her seat and seized Roland by the shoulders. Shaking him vigorously, she commanded that he be released from his trance. He awoke with a sudden jolt, lurched to his feet and staggered from the room.

I followed him outside and held his shoulders while he was shaken by spasm after spasm of violent retching. When it was all over and he was seated, white-faced and trembling, on a chair in the hallway, our hostess emerged from the trance room.

'He shouldn't have tranced,' she said in a righteous tone of voice, 'I didn't give permission for it, so it must have been a low entity. I had to get rid of it before it did any harm.'

I stared at her, speechless with astonishment. I was as yet too shocked and concerned to feel anger—that would come later. For the present I could only think of getting Roland safely home before anything else happened. I muttered something noncommittal and guided my shaking husband out to our car.

Although I did not classify myself as an expert in the field of trance mediumship, I knew enough to be aware that this woman was not only sadly unqualified as a teacher, she was downright dangerous! It was patently obvious that she had no idea of how to go about protecting the trance room against invasion by earth-bound entities, since she had been prepared to accept that such a being might have been responsible for

Roland's trance. It also had not occurred to her that in a situation where trances are expected to occur, an experienced medium might enter a trance as a matter of course.

I was shocked by her utter ignorance about the danger of touching an entranced medium. In trance, a medium's body is surging with an intensive buildup of energy. To touch him, except under special circumstances when the spirit guide has made preparations for contact, is like suddenly earthing an electric wire. The built up energy in his body literally explodes outwards and at the very least, the shock can cause a medium to become violently ill. At worst, it could be lethal.

Roland was sick for several days after that incident and it was some time before he was settled enough to trance again. When he did, David told me that it had been he who initiated Roland's trance in that class. His intention had been to offer some helpful advice to the class members. They will never know what they missed, for Roland and I did not return.

Even if I had been willing to give the classes another chance, there is no way that I could have persuaded Roland to do the same. All they had done for him was to cause a great deal of sickness and discomfort. He had also been thoroughly frightened and his confidence in me was undermined because it had been my suggestion that we visit the class in the first place. This meant that my work with him had suffered a severe setback and it was now necessary for me to repair the damage.

Psychic perception is not a special talent that arises only in the wise or those particularly chosen by the Almighty, nor does it necessarily go hand in hand with spiritual enlightenment. Although they may be dormant in many people, psychic senses are perfectly natural abilities that are inherent in all of us. Anyone can learn to use their psychic senses; it is what we *do* with them that makes the difference. Your psychic abilities may function with crystal clarity but they will be of small benefit to you if you are psychologically incapable of seeing beyond the tip of your nose.

Spiritual enlightenment, on the other hand, does not arise naturally and with no effort on the part of the recipient. Like any other form of understanding, it is gained through study and experience. Nor is it something that can be mastered overnight. It is absorbed gradually, stage by stage, in a developmental process that can span a number of lifetimes.

No person currently living in this world can justifiably claim to be an expert on the subject of psychic or spiritual phenomena. The real experts are those who progressed beyond the physical world thousands of years ago. To understand the reason why I make such a claim, it is necessary to know my understanding of psychic development.

The word 'psychic' comes from the Greek *psyche* meaning soul or spirit. In my terms therefore, psychic development is the growth or evolution of a spirit, from its inception to its ultimate fulfilment. Part of this development takes place in the physical world and the appropriate application of psychic ability can assist immensely, but I do not by any means confine the term to the simple manifestation of psychic perception.

David has taught me that *knowledge* is the key to psychic development and that the spiritual worlds are so structured that advancement to higher levels of existence can only be gained through the acquisition of wisdom. Extrasensory perception alone simply will not suffice. He has told me that our progress is judged on the degree to which we are capable of understanding the nature of psychic existence within the framework of our current environment. In other words, if we cannot understand life at our present level, we have no chance of coping with a more advanced sphere of existence.

In a sense, the stages of spiritual development might be likened to classes in a school, except that your rate of progress is regulated by your level of understanding and not governed by the length of time that you have spent in any one grade. All too often, in our physical education system, a student is passed upwards in grade simply becaused of his chronological age. For instance, at twelve years of age, when six years of primary school have been completed, the child commences high school. Scant attention is given to the possibility that the educational process may have broken down for a particular child when he was still in third grade and at the end of his sixth year he is floundering helplessly, with no chance of understanding his studies at high school level. The system says that he must move on, so he is moved on. If he is left crying on the wayside because he simply cannot cope, nobody cares very much, apart from himself and his bewildered parents.

In the spiritual spheres, no soul is left to cry on the wayside. If he has difficulty in grasping an understanding of the particular level on which he is functioning he simply remains at that level until he does understand. There is no time limit, for progress is not subject to an arbitrary system; it is controlled by the spirit's own ability to understand.

It is useless to explain the Second Law of Thermodynamics to a person who has trouble trying to understand the difference between an atom and a molecule. It would be equally pointless to elaborate on an advanced level of spiritual philosophy with someone who could not cope with life at the physical level. Unfortunately, people are not always content to live within their limitations and many students of psychic phenomena insist on over-reaching themselves and then wonder why the supernatural has failed to provide them with the wonderful secrets they were seeking.

In addition to coming face to face with the occasional would-be adversary, Roland and I also discovered that there are people who seem to think of David as being some sort of modern day equivalent to the genie in the bottle. These same people also tend to favour the opinion that, since Roland and I are the channels by which David reaches the physical, we are duty bound to place ourselves—and David—at their disposal whenever they so require. We are amazed by the lengths to which some people will go in the effort to secure David's 'services'.

Quite obviously we are only human and it is physically impractical, if not impossible, for us to place ourselves at the convenience of all comers. It is essential that we draw the line at some point, or else we would have no life of our own. Thus, whilst we do not jealously guard the privacy of our sittings, we have learned where to set the boundaries in order to maintain the level of our own progress. From the beginning, David made it quite clear that he visits us for one purpose, and that is to teach. Wherever there is a case of genuine need, he never fails to render assistance but he always maintains his integrity and refuses to become involved in any activity that would infringe the principles he has come to teach.

Where there is illness, pain or distress, David is always ready to offer comfort and relief. However, he has been requested—often quite forcefully—to 'use his powers' in order to satisfy purely selfish desires which completely disregard the rights and wishes of other people. He has, for instance, been asked to force an errant lover to return to the eager arms of his abandoned lady! Although David gently explained that to do so would be to trespass on the gentleman's right of free will, the lady in question was most persistent and felt herself very hard done by when she was firmly and repeatedly refused. It was quite impossible to make her understand that we simply will not disobey the laws by which we live.

We have also been asked to launch psychic vendettas on behalf of people who feel that they have been offended in some way by another person.

'Couldn't you just make her have a little accident in her car?' I have been asked. 'Not enough to do any *big* damage of course . . . just enough to teach her a lesson?'

For all of David's reminders about being understanding and patient, I often find it difficult to hold my temper with people such as this. If we could achieve such a thing (and we have no intention of trying to find out) we would not even consider it. An act of that nature would be a total contradiction of everything that we believe. There is no way that we would lend our assistance to an attempt to harm someone else. In our view that is witchcraft of the blackest kind.

We cannot be too harshly critical of the people who approach us with such outlandish requests, because they cannot be expected to realise that our activities are governed by precise codes of conduct. We have to bear in mind that we are operating in a field which is not widely understood and is frequently both misrepresented and misused. In addition, the examples that are set by today's society are not exactly conducive to the development of a regard for the rights and privileges of other living beings. In physical life, virtually anthing is condoned as long as one can 'get away with it'. Spiritual understanding, however, adds several dimensions to our outlook on life.

One of the operative principles which we have been taught is one that is usually expressed as the Law of Karma, however it could as easily be categorised as a law of cause and effect. Karma is more than just a mystical principle, it is a natural law which functions automatically and affects everyone regardless of race, creed, social standing or political affiliation. The laws which are created by man may be all too subject to manipulation but karma is autonomous, a power unto itself.

In simplest terms, the Law of Karma ensures that all living souls experience the effects of every one of their thoughts and actions. Note, it is the *effect* of an action that is applicable, not necessarily the action itself. Whatever influence you exert upon others will ultimately be brought to bear on you somehow, irrespective of whether that influence is good or bad.

How does this principle affect you in real life? Let us say that for some reason you aim an irritated kick at a cat, but the animal dodges and you strike your toe against something hard. The full force of your original action has been instantly returned to you in like form, i.e. violence and pain. However, an incident like that is localised—it affects nobody other than yourself and the cat.

Karma operates on a sliding scale, so that the degree of reaction is in direct proportion to the effects of the action that you took. Let us examine a situation which has more far-reaching effects than kicking the cat, and analyse the possible consequences. A man gets drunk, climbs behind the wheel of his car and speeds down the road, weaving in all directions. In his reckless progress, he hits and kills a child. He is immediately responsible for the child's death, but karma does not end there. The result of this man's action will also affect the parents, relatives and friends of the child, in addition to the various personnel who will be required to carry out the demoralising task of dealing with the aftermath. There will be, among other things, shock, grief, rage, loss, disgust, and possibly hatred, all aroused as a direct result of that man's heedlessness. All of these things will inevitably be returned to him. The guilt he feels when he sobers up and realises what he has done will only be the beginning of his karma: the ongoing effects can continue for years and need not stop when the man reaches his grave.

Your identity in a particular life is little more than a facade, for the actions carried out by your body are motivated by the thoughts your spirit chooses to generate. Thus it is the spirit and not the body which bears the responsibility. Karma will follow the spirit wherever it goes, even into subsequent incarnations. Imagine the karmic responsibility of a person such as Adolf Hitler, bearing in mind that it relates not only to those who bore the immediate suffering, but also those who experienced subsidiary effects, such as the innocent people of German extraction living in other countries who suffered persecution because of the hatred that Hitler aroused. Hitler's body may be dead, but his spirit must continue to bear retribution until the last iota of debt is expunged. I would not care to experience any of that soul's future incarnations.

On the other hand, consider the kind of karma that is set in process by a dedicated surgeon who saves the life of a child. In addition to sustaining life, he removes a great burden of care and suffering from the parents and relatives. As a result he will experience ongoing love and gratitude from them, in addition to his own personal sense of fulfilment.

Since karma is the direct result of our own actions, it can be influenced to the extent that we are capable of controlling those actions. Thus if we consider our deeds carefully and weigh up the possible consequences in advance, we can substantially reduce the chances of laying up a store of bad karma for ourselves. Remember also, karma does not stop at the grave, nor does it wait for some preordained day of divine judgement. It can come into effect instantly and continue through any number of incarnations.

If Roland and I were to accede to another person's demands and carry out an act that we knew to be harmful, the responsibility would be ours. It would be pointless for us to protest that the other person was to blame for telling us to do it: we are capable of judging the consequences for ourselves and making independent decisions. Karma is not concerned with intentions but with results.

As I have mentioned, the effects of karma can be immediate or delayed, brief or long-lasting, depending on the nature of the relevant actions. As far as possible, karma operates within the span of the lifetime in which the particular deeds were carried out. It would be frustrating if we always had to wait for another lifetime before we could reap the rewards for our positive efforts and it would be rather unfair if we were always being repaid for misdeeds that we could not even remember. Karma which carries forward into a fresh incarnation does so because there may not have been sufficient time for it to take effect during the previous life or because it required a set of circumstances which were not in existence at that time.

Karma is a system of just rewards. It will neither grant blessings that have not been earned, nor will it administer undeserved punishment. True to the old saying, you reap what you sow. There is no point in moaning about the raw deal life is handing you if you are continually doing things that activate a negative karmic response. For instance, I know a few people who are not prepared to make any positive efforts for themselves because they want everyone else to pander to their whims, shoulder their responsibilities and generally wait on them hand and foot. They usually want the best of everything and may ruthlessly manipulate other people in order to get it. They are often experts at what I call the 'poor little me' technique: Life has been cruel to them; Mummy and Daddy always favoured the other children; their spouses never understood them; their children are ungrateful and their friends are unreliable. They lose jobs because their workmates are jealous of their obviously superior qualities, never because they happen to be lazy or inefficient. Their marriages break up, friends and children desert them and it is invariably somebody else's fault, never theirs.

Such people may continually place unreasonable demands on their associates, ride roughshod over the rights and needs of other people and totally ignore the tremendous strain and distress that they spread wherever they go. Inevitably their lives are characterised by misery and failure but instead of learning the obvious lesson from this, they merely add it to their list of grievances and see it as all the more reason why other people should rush to heap favours on them by way of compensation.

In principle, nothing is impossible but in practice trying to help such people comes pretty darn close. They come to us with an endless recital of woes and misfortunes, then say 'Fix it'. We can neither remove their karma nor alter the world to suit their specifications, but that is precisely what they expect from us. When we do try to help, by pointing out how they can reverse the negative trend in their lives, we are treated to a disdainful stare and a comment like, 'I might have known you were no better than the rest. The trouble with this world is that everyone is too selfish to help someone in need. Well, don't worry about me, I'll just find a dark corner somewhere and lick my wounds'.

When people like this become involved in the supernatural, we have a real problem on our hands. Since they are seldom willing to exert the time and effort in learning how the supernatural functions, they invariably wind up in a worse mess than ever, only now of course they have someone else to blame. The powers of darkness are out to get them, or they have fallen victim to the machinations of some diabolical cosmic conspiracy. This brings them to the edge of paranoia and it becomes even more difficult for anyone to make them see reason.

I do not claim to be an authority on the supernatural or an expert on life itself, but simple logic tells me that if my actions continually result in disaster, there must be something wrong with the way I am doing things. To me it seems foolish to assign my misfortunes to a mythical gremlin when it would be more productive to reassess my own attitudes and try to discover where I am going wrong.

David has reinforced this line of reasoning by telling me that the process of self-analysis and adjustment is one of the ways in which we develop. The problems we encounter in life are opportunities for us to exercise and increase our powers of perception and reasoning.

Getting angry, blaming others, or throwing tantrums are merely signs that we have not developed enough to cope with physical situations, in which case we can hardly consider ourselves ready to face existence at a higher and more complex level. We do not progress by trying to evade our problems but by learning how to overcome them.

There can be no benefit in consulting an expert if he bases his answers on principles that we do not understand. Psychic development involves certain basic principles, as does any other area of learning. If I were having difficulty with third-grade principles, it would be unreasonable to put me in a class with high school students and expect me to understand what the teacher was saying. It would also be unfair to expect the teacher to neglect his other students and personally tutor me when there were other teachers trained and available to teach at my level of understanding. To reach the high school teacher's class, it would be necessary for me to apply myself to the lesser grades until I had developed the ability to comprehend the lessons in the higher class. In David's words, 'I cannot come to you. You must first come to me'.

To work safely within the field of psychic phenomena, it is necessary to understand its causes. To understand the relationship between cause and effect, it is necessary to understand its *reason*. After witnessing the disasters that resulted when people with little understanding proceeded to meddle with psychic phenomena, I felt especially fortunate to have David as a guiding influence. Not only did he make certain that I understood the reasons and principles behind the phenomena that we have experienced, but he was also on hand to ensure that we were not placed in the predicament of having to cope with things that we did not understand. Should such a situation develop, he would always step in and handle it for us. I felt very strongly then that if it were not for David's presence, Roland and I would never have achieved any significant development. My opinion is still unchanged.

CHAPTER ELEVEN
Roland, the psychic

Whenever Roland is asked to pass an opinion relating to David or the spiritual principles that he teaches, his usual response is a diffident shrug.

'What's to tell?' he smiles. 'I sit in a chair and go to sleep. The rest is up to Dawn and her spirit friends.'

This seemingly passive stance has led quite a few people into the mistaken assumption that Roland is little more than a submissive pawn in a complicated ritual that he can neither comprehend nor control. Nothing could be further from the truth!

The fact is that Roland and I function as a team and for that partnership to be effective, we must each understand not only our own roles, but also the part played by the other. Roland is by no means ignorant of the nature and purpose of the forces which work through us, there is simply a facet of his own personality which makes him prefer to hold his own counsel unless it is necessary for him to speak.

Roland is a reasonable, rational and highly intelligent man and as such he thinks very deeply before committing himself to any particular course of action. Nor will he take a step before he has ascertained that the ground ahead is firm and sure. It was this aspect of his nature which caused him to test both David and I very thoroughly before he would accept the philosophy that we were proposing to him.

The healing of his crippled arm was only the beginning for him. It proved to him that there was, as I had claimed, a force that is capable of transcending the bounds of physical limitations, but it did not clearly define the nature of that power, so he then set about assiduously studying it in intense detail. Why, out of all the people in the world, had we been selected as its channels? What was its purpose and what would it require of us? What would it require of him? Was it as benevolent and altruistic as it purported to be? These and many other questions had to be answered to his satisfaction before he would commit himself completely.

It is significant that it took something of the magnitude of the healing of his arm to convince him that psychic energy even existed, even though he had been trancing for some time prior to that event. To his mind, an event must be indisputably proven to have a particular origin and he was quite prepared to accept that his trances might as well be attributable to some mental aberration of his own as to some unseen super-being from another dimension. He knew the facts about his arm: he had been told by experts, i.e. neurosurgeons at one of Sydney's top hospitals, that whilst it may be possible for some restoration of use to be made, it would not be fulfilled without considerable effort and risk. Even if some improvement could be made, the prognosis was non-committal as to what degree, as there had been nerve cell damage in the area of the fracture. Surgical restoration was not attempted and Roland resigned himself to the prospect of living with a useless forearm. Therefore, when the arm *did* improve after I had specifically pinpointed it as an object lesson, he accepted the obvious.

Having accepted, he then set about making himself thoroughly familiar with the encompassing dimensions that had been opened to him. Roland is not the kind of person who is content to sit back and allow things to happen to him. If he cannot maintain some degree of control, he will not allow himself to be used. He would have been perfectly capable of blocking his trances (and indeed, David would not have continued to initiate them) if he had not been satisfied as to the reliability of their origin.

He placed the onus squarely upon David and his requirement can be expressed in two words: 'Prove yourself'. David set about doing so from the beginning and his attitude has always been clearly full of respect and concern for Roland's welfare and rights as an individual. The first few trances may have been unexpected and spontaneous from Roland's point of view, but they were at that time David's only means of letting us know that he was around. He would not have continued to cause them if Roland had refused his consent and when Roland placed conditions upon his performance as a medium, David assiduously adhered to them.

David has made it clear that both Roland and I underwent extensive training before we entered our present incarnations, with the specific intent that we would meet and form a psychic team. Just how far that training went is something I do not know and if Roland is aware, he has chosen not to say so. It must be understood that the first stages of our training as psychics were designed to remind us of the things that we had forgotten in our journey through the physical. Just like everyone else, we had to endure the trauma of birth and the confusion of childhood, which had the effect of overshadowing the intrinsic spiritual knowledge that it was David's first task to re-activate within us.

As I will explain in the chapters that follow, this awareness is latent within all of us and bringing it to the surface is simply a matter of learning to recognise and direct it. This is what Roland and I set out to do, but whilst our abilities are similar and to some extent interchangeable (for example, I have been known to trance occasionally) they are applied in alternate directions.

For my part, I have very little interest in the physical aspects of life. That does not mean to imply that I do not enjoy it; I love trees and flowers, birds and furry animals, sunny skies and listening to the rain on the roof. All of these and hundreds of other things are the work of the Creator and I rejoice in them. Where people are concerned, however, I become a little more reticent, for although I know them all to be spirits like myself, they do not appear to feel any such kinship. David has explained that this is because they have lost touch with their spiritual origins and are not aware of the divine spark within themselves. That it something that I can understand intellectually, but emotionally I find it difficult to cope when I see people doing terrible things to each other and observe little children with the eyes of savage tigers, attacking each other with a ferocity that terrifies me. I recoil from it: to me it is a personal pain from which I seek to escape. I cannot bear to see needless suffering and harassment.

As a result I am happiest when working in the ethereal realms. I am more at home there and I frequently leave my body to perform work of a healing or comforting nature on the Astral plane. When I do work in the physical, it is usually with earth-bound spirits or teaching other people the gentle truths that David has taught to me. Thus my energies are always directed into the spiritual.

Roland, on the other hand, takes spiritual energy and directs it into the physical. He knows and understands the world we live in; he is in control and the physical holds no fears for him. He may not like everything he sees, but he does not allow it to deflect him from his determined course. He is the one who performs the physical acts of psychic healing, for instance. He is also the one who has taken an interest in Quantum Physics, to see how closely their theories resemble the knowledge he possesses. Such activities I happily leave in his capable hands because I know that they are more his forte than mine. No doubt I could understand his choice of subjects if it were necessary but there is no need and there are other areas of activity more suited to my particular nature and outlook.

The very fact that we do have different interests and talents is what gives us value as a team. If each of us covered the same territory, there would be no need for there to be two of us, for one could perform equally well. There is a tremendous amount of ground to be covered in the spiritual, more than enough for two, or even two thousand people to concentrate on various aspects, each adding another dimension to what has been produced by the others.

This is one reason why Roland and I find religious exclusivism so silly. As though any one person or sect could be capable of knowing entirely the mind of the Creator! Each group presents a portion of the truth, certainly, but the world would be a whole lot better off if everybody admitted that no one person can know everything. As Kahlil Gibran once said, rather than to say 'I have found *the* Truth' it is better to say 'I have found *a* truth'. Even Christ admitted that there were things he did not know! There, perhaps, lies a lesson in true humility.

110

It is a humility of this kind, along with an innate caution and reserve, which causes Roland to prefer a background position. If he is asked a direct question he will give a specific answer but in general he prefers to leave the talking to me. This sometimes suits me, because I am a natural chatterbox. At other times, however, I wish that Roland would reveal more of himself, for he possesses a degree of knowledge and ability that would startle most of the people who think they know him well.

On several occasions, when I have been merrily chattering to my friends, discussing some spiritual principle or other, Roland has quietly interrupted to correct me on a point that I have misinterpreted, or drawn my attention to an aspect of David's teaching that I had forgotten or overlooked. He is never pedantic, nor does he lecture, but he has never been mistaken, either!

He claims that he himself is not sure where his knowledge comes from, and tends to believe that it is transmitted direct from David whenever the need arises. However, to me it seems to be intrinsic in him. In many ways he is a bit of a mystery man, maybe even to himself. Perhaps even he would be surprised if all the power within him were suddenly unleashed and he saw what it could do. Perhaps not: I often imagine that there is very little that is capable of surprising Roland or catching him off guard. He is nothing if not completely controlled, and by his own will. Perhaps some day he will surprise us all!

PART TWO
Psychic Principles and Understanding

CHAPTER TWELVE
The basics: energy

Once Roland and I had made the decision to work with David, our training began in earnest and it was not long before I realised that I had hitherto been nibbling around the edges. The psychic world had been shown to me but I was as yet little more than an enthusiastic spectator.

I had been standing on the perimeter of the supernatural, watching the performance of those who had come to teach me. For me to learn the same skills would take many years and even now I am only beginning to comprehend the awesome scope of the world I have entered. At the beginning I did not know what to expect; I had committed myself to working with David, yet I had scant idea of what was entailed. I only knew that, having glimpsed it, I could not turn aside.

It was not simply a case of learning new skills to add to the abilities I had developed during my life so far, but of altering my whole perspective on life. I had been living in a world which moved at great speed, or so it seemed to me, and in which I could hope for little more than the chance to earn enough to keep body and soul together. If there was any meaning or purpose in the machinations of the society in which I found myself, it escaped my comprehension.

There was order and reason in the supernatural, but I could find little of the same in physical life. It seemed to me a raging flood of struggling humanity with no particular purpose. Life's theme seemed to be a frantic scrabble to keep one's head above water with more and more people giving up the effort.

Within the supernatural all seemed calm and well ordered. If there was disruption at any level, it occurred for an obvious reason and only in the lower regions, close to the physical. It could be dealt with by skilled beings who devoted their time to such pursuits, but there seemed no such salvation for those of us who live in the physical. In the supernatural there was no horrific, throat-cutting struggle for supremacy, just order and control, along with the calm acceptance that there is meaning in all that is.

For the life of me, I could not see how that order and meaning could possibly penetrate the physical, but David assured me that it did, however it would take a trained eye to see just how and why. That was to be my lot. I could not hope to understand the levels above if it was impossible for me to comprehend the level upon which I exist at present.

'You wish to know the answers to three questions,' said David. 'Those questions are: "Where do I come from?" "Why am I here?" and, "Where am I going?" To answer you, I say this: you come from the Creator and to the Creator you will ultimately return. You are here as a part of your development. When you have learned enough you will grow beyond this level and enter one higher and so it will go until you have learned all there is to know.'

'What happens then?' I asked eagerly.

'You become as one with the Creator.'

'Yes,' I moved impatiently in my chair, 'but what do I *do*?'

'Do? You simply . . . be.'

'Be what?'

'Just be.'

I tilted my head to one side and surveyed the guide critically. Surely he wasn't having fun at my expense, but there had to be a more specific answer than the one he had given. Suddenly my face lit up—I thought I had the answer.

'Like it says in the Bible—I am that I am—is that what you are saying?'

114

'What I am saying,' smiled the guide, 'is that you just *am*.'

'But what is it like? What do you do? How does it feel? Describe it to me.'

'My daughter, I can describe only that which I know. I am a teacher, my purpose is to teach. I am not yet "just amming".'

'Well why tell me about it if you don't know?' I demanded, somewhat petulantly.

'My daughter, you asked,' was the patient reply. 'Were I able to answer the question as you asked it, you would not understand because your mind does not contain sufficient experience. You are like a man who decides to build a house and begins with the roof, then wonders why it will not stay up. First you must build your foundations, and your walls, then afterwards the roof. Even then, there remains more for you to do, for your house is still merely a shell. Begin with the foundations my daughter.'

As always, I was somewhat shamefaced at David's reply. With a few gentle words, he was able to show me to myself and I saw that my ardent desire for learning far outstripped my comprehensive ability. There was so much that I wanted to know, and although I could see that I must begin at the beginning and proceed with thoroughness and attention to detail, I wanted everything at once. It was not easy to take things slowly and proceed step by step when there was a whole panorama of exciting prospects laid out for me to survey.

Before I could fully understand the spiritual, I had to pay a little more attention to the physical. After all, if we are going to understand what the supernatural is, then we should be fully aware of what it *isn't*, otherwise we may see spectres and wraiths in every shadow and hear ghostly voices on the wind. How does one define psychic phenomena? David made that my first project. It was for me to come up with a definition that gave a very clear description of the phenomena, without leaving any loopholes which could create confusion.

Roland and I put our heads together on that one and we discarded a great many lengthy and erudite descriptions in favour of the simplest possible interpretation: 'Psychic phenomena is an act or occurrence that has *no physical origins whatsoever'*. That is not to say that it has no physical effects either; it can of course produce any number of startling physical effects, but its source cannot be found in the physical world.

In order to see how we arrived at that particular definition, let us have a clear understanding of what is and is not physical. Take a close look at the physical, or material world. Think of something that is physical—the chair in which you are sitting, for instance—how do you *know* it is physical? You have five physical senses which tell you that it is: not only that, but they also help you to determine what *kind* of substance you are looking at. You can, for instance, easily tell the difference between a chair that is made of wood and one which is made of metal. To you, that chair is real and solid. You can feel its texture, it supports your weight, you can probably even smell it. Yet, while your senses tell you that it is solid and substantial, your mind tells you otherwise. You know that it is really constructed from millions and millions of atoms, each one a separate entity. It is not one solid thing at all, but a composite of tiny specks of energy which are comprised largely of space. Atoms have a number of things in common: each has a nucleus which contains positively charged protons, orbited by negatively charged electrons. Physicists have commented that an atom is really nothing more than a concentrated speck of energy. When it comes right down to tin tacks, an atom is not matter at all, but energy. However, when grouped together, atoms perform in accordance to known laws of physics to produce effects and objects that we recognize as physical.

Atomic structure varies. A chair looks different from a piece of carpet or from a human body because the atoms within those forms have clumped together in different ways. They interact differently together, but at the root of all matter, all is energy—energy that can form into material things, visible and tangible to our five senses.

But what of the energy forms that are intangible to our senses? Let us go back to the opening statement—the paranormal, or psychic, has no physical origins. In other words, it cannot be constructed from atoms, and it need not look or act like something which does have a physical atomic structure. Yet it can produce physical effects. If a poltergeist starts pelting your best china around the room, you will certainly see physical crockery smashing into physical pieces. That is a physical effect. The force which is producing the effect, however, is not a physical one. You cannot see it or touch it, you can only see its results. It is some kind of alternative, non-physical energy force. How do we define that?

'I want you to think for a moment,' said David one evening. 'Think, and see if you can tell me something which cannot be defined as physical energy, yet produces a physical effect.'

I stared at him in blank dismay. Think, he said! My mind seemed to be functioning in reverse gear. I could think of several energy forms, but each one could be traced directly to the physical. I could find no form of energy that could remotely pass as non-physical.

'What about thought?' prompted David.

At first my mind rebelled. That was not a fair answer. Besides, the act of thinking was purely physical, it could be charted on an electroencephalograph and any junior nurse knows that the brain functions by electrical discharge. Of course it was a physical process. Then I noticed a quirk of amusement around David's mouth, and I stopped.

He had not said that the *act* of thinking was non-physical. The word he had used was *thought*. That was something else again. From whence comes the original idea that sets the brain in motion? Where did all of our celebrated masters get their inspiration—what elevated energy pattern carried Da Vinci's inventions, years before the world at large was ready for them? Did they already exist somewhere? Had he found a way to plug into them? What is thought? You can chart and photograph the physical act of thinking, but you cannot capture a thought by using any physical means.

Kirlian photography is a process which has produced some fascinating pictures. These show that living tissue is surrounded by a glowing aura, which has a number of odd characteristics. A photograph of a leaf which has been cut in half will show the aura intact. If a moving picture process is used the aura can be seen at first

117

following the contours of the cut leaf, but within a short space of time it begins to open out until it accommodates the space and shape that would have been filled by the complete leaf.

This process also shows that human beings have auras. I seriously doubt that we could cut a human being in half in order to observe the effect on his aura, but we can be reasonably certain that the human aura would be just as impervious to physical effects. It would also offer an interesting explanation for the 'phantom itches' felt by amputees, in which they feel that there is an itchy spot on the missing limb. Perhaps auric photography would show a complete limb even though the physical one had been surgically removed.

Psychics throughout history have stated that human beings have auras, now our scientists have proved it for themselves (with little credit given to the mystics who have known about it for years). What is this aura? David says that the human body is surrounded by an egg-shaped aura, which is where the soul lives.

He further explains that the human body is merely a device that is needed if you are to function in the physical dimension. You need a physical vehicle, so you have one. But it is a vehicle, it is not *you*. This body is ideally suited to life in our environment. It is not suited to life on Mars or Venus; it has been specifically designed for the conditions it will encounter on Earth.

I had been accustomed to thinking of myself as a physical being: a body that walks and talks and does all the things that other bodies do. I know, of course, that I am a soul, but in the beginning it was hard to think of myself as such when I was very obviously confined to the limitations of my body. I could not take off and fly through the air, nor could I levitate an article on the other side of the room. I knew that it was possible, of course; I had even seen it done. Once, while I was sitting at my typewriter, a small egg-timer lifted from the shelf behind me and floated gently across the room to nestle in my lap. Some force had moved it, but it had not been me. It only served to make me more frustrated with the limitations of my unwieldy body. How I wanted to be able to do things like that, but I couldn't. I was merely a lump of clay.

118

This was the first notion that needed to be dispelled. David gently informed me that I, as a spirit, am not limited by anything except my own mental outlook. If I truly believed in my ability to levitate objects and understood the energy processes by which it could be made to happen, I could do it. One does not have to depart the physical world in order to develop such skills. He told me that we inhabit our bodies, and we do it in a rather intriguing way. We surround them. We are souls with physical bodies, not the other way around. And our thoughts? David tells me that they originate within the soul—inside the aura. So, when we are thinking, we are carrying out a physical process. When we originate a thought, however, we are being psychic.

I had of course heard about the aura before I became acquainted with David, but I had not thought about it in quite the way he described it. If anything, I had thought of it as something that radiated outwards from my body. As for thought being a psychic energy form, that was completely new to me. I hadn't thought about it in that way at all. To me, it was an automatic process and I paid no more attention to it than I did to the daily actions I carry out in the physical, such as operating a typewriter or driving a car, yet all of these things had to be learned at first. They are not automatic. Thought, it seems, has a definite starting point and who knows what process of learning and development it was necessary for me to undergo as a spirit before I mastered it?

David told me that those who can see the aura are able to perceive a number of things about another person, ranging from his state of health to whether or not he is telling a lie. If one of the organs in your body is diseased, the malady can be detected in the aura long before a physical diagnosis can be made.

We are capable of original thought and our bodies are surrounded by an aura which is unaffected by physical phenomena. This means that there is something about us that is psychic. Why? What is the *purpose* of being psychic? If you are psychic—and we all are—you are not doing anything abnormal, you are merely being a soul. In other words, you are being yourself, or so David says.

After setting our parameters and defining what is and

is not psychic, for the sake of consistency it became necessary to refer to 'psychic energy' as distinct from the energy forms that are normally recognizable within the physical. David himself is loath to give labels to anything, but he allowed me to do it, in the understanding that I could not follow his comprehensive and rather abstract patterns of thought. For me, there had to be a distinction somewhere between what is physical and what is not, although as time went on I became increasingly aware that the boundaries are very diffuse and the physical merges with the psychic to such an extent that it is often difficult to distinguish between the two. However, my understanding was made easier when I reminded myself that the word 'psychic' originated from the Greek *psyche*, which means soul—a fact which I find myself repeating constantly to people who question me about my involvement in psychic activities.

What is the *purpose* of being psychic? I have been questioned on this matter by a number of people, many of whom seem to believe that my involvement with the 'occult' is an unhealthy thing. Once again, I am faced with a word whose original meaning is quite innocent, but which has become tarnished through its use in current vernacular. Anything that is occult is simply unseen or hidden; therefore, what is understood and known to me cannot be occult in my terms. It is only a mystery if you do not understand it.

As for the purpose of being psychic, it derives from our own purpose. Why are we here? There must be a reason, otherwise we would be somewhere else. If, as David says, we are non-physical entities, or souls, then we do not belong permanently in a physical world. To come here, we had to enter a vehicle through which we could operate in the physical world. That vehicle is constructed from physical material, and it will return to its basic components when we have finished with it. But what of ourselves? Why did we come here?

You don't get onto a bus just for the sake of being on a bus, unless you happen to be kinky about buses. You get onto a bus because you want to go somewhere and do something. You entered your physical vehicle, your body, because you wanted to walk around in the physical dimension for a while and then leave. Why? The only thing that we can be certain about in this life is that we will leave it at some time in the future. Whatever our purpose is, it does not lie in the physical. If so, what is the reason for coming here in the first place? There has to be a reason, and that reason was one of the things I sought.

David gave me a mental exercise to perform. He asked me to see if I could recall something that had happened when I was seven years old. It was quite easy to do, and I was confused as to why he felt that it was important. I was even more confused when he asked me to relate something that happened when I six, five, four and so on. When we got to the earliest stages of my life, I became confused. I could remember lying in a cot and being unable to communicate my thoughts to the people around me, but I could not have given that experience a time zone. I could have been anything from one week to eighteen months old. Then David asked if I could remember the moment of my birth. I looked at him and wondered if he were playing mind games with me, since everyone knows that it is impossible to remember such a thing.

But, as always, David had a purpose. Whatever my reason for coming here, he told me, I knew what it was before I came. But the birth process is traumatic and it is a known fact that pain and trauma set up mental blocks.

There is an added disadvantage, in that for the first decade or so of life, we are subjected to conditioning by people who have their own ideas about why we came into this world. Those ideas usually bear little relation to the facts, but the conditioning process is such that by the time we grow up, we have accepted it as the only available explanation, whether we realise it or not.

In childhood, we can even have been punished or ridiculed for showing tendencies which could not be slotted neatly into somebody else's pigeon-holes. This, too, can produce a condition of 'psychic amnesia'. Every person is a soul, therefore every person has psychic ability, yet the majority of us are firmly convinced that no such thing exists because the psychic potential has been driven so deeply underground that it becomes totally forgotten. Even a person who is fully aware of his psychic ability may have trouble in putting it into practice because of some mishap which has caused it to submerge.

Until quite recently, I found it almost impossible to see anything clairvoyantly. I understood what clairvoyance was and I knew what I could expect to see, yet I could see nothing other than the physical. I could not understand why this should be so until I remembered an incident which took place when I was very small—perhaps two or three years old.

I went away for a holiday with an aunt who was a member of a particularly strict religious sect which regards anything to do with psychic phenomena as evil. We were staying with a friend of my aunt's, and I became quite fascinated with one of the rooms in her house. It was a funny, old-fashioned room, panelled with dark brown wood and in it was a nice old man with whom I used to hold endless conversations.

Inevitably my aunt and her friend began to wonder what it was about the room which interested me so deeply and I was caught in the act of conversing with my friend. My aunt wanted to know what I was doing, a question I found puzzling since I thought my actions were self-explanatory; however, with all the candour of extreme youth, I told her.

What followed this shocking revelation was the most severe thrashing I have ever had. I was slapped repeatedly whilst my aunt kept saying, 'There is no old man. You cannot see an old man. You are telling lies; you are a very wicked little girl. There is no old man. You cannot see—you cannot see—you cannot see. . .'

Not surprisingly, I stopped seeing the little old man. No doubt my aunt thought she was saving my immortal soul, but what in fact resulted was that I became clairvoyantly blinded. I forgot how to register clairvoyant impressions and for almost thirty years after that, the situation remained unchanged.

Many children have invisible playmates. If they are lucky, their parents merely smile knowingly and allow them to retain their precious 'fantasy'. Others are punished for telling lies or they are told not to be silly. As children, we are constantly told to come back to 'reality': 'Stop daydreaming. . .Get your head out of the clouds. . .Wake up to yourself.' Is it any wonder that we forget? I wonder what kind of society we would have if we encouraged our children to tell us about their associations with the people we cannot see?

The whole point is that by the time we have reached physical adulthood, all memories of our psychic origins have been thoroughly submerged and therein lies a problem. If you cannot remember why you are here or what bus you should be travelling on, how on earth are you to get where you want to go? Some people never remember; they just wander around lost and in the end they hop onto the first bus they can find. True, they eventually leave the physical, but to go where and do what? Chances are, they will find that the bus does a round trip and they end up exactly where they started—in the physical once more.

Far better to know why you are here and make sure that you are on the right bus when it is time to go home. You can only do that if you understand what it is you are trying to do and if you do it the right way. But if you cannot remember, you need someone to come along and say to you: 'Hey, these are the rules of the game'. In our case, this is what happened when we met David. It is also the driving reason behind this book, because David's information applies to more people than just Roland and me. We are all searching for a reason. David has given one to us and we want to share it with anyone who wishes to accept it for themselves.

Life can be utterly confusing, even for the best of us. Most of us find it a struggle and there seems to be very little rhyme or reason in it. I do not wish to strike up a battle with orthodox religion but I personally found no satisfaction in it. To me, it simply did not make sense and in fact I found that it only made life more complicated. I was faced with the instruction that I must play a certain game without understanding the rules or even knowing what the object of the game was supposed to be.

Think of a game that you see on television, one that you do not like. It may be football, or golf, or motor racing. Whatever it is, you cannot see any sense in it at all. Chances are you don't understand the rules of the game. A man may sit glued to the television set for five hours with a pile of beer cans steadily growing on the floor beside him while he is engrossed in a televised golf tournament. His wife can see no sense in it at all and cannot understand why he doesn't do something useful, like mowing the lawn or playing football with the kids.

To the wife, golf is a meaningless activity in which a lot of grown men who should know better go to a great deal of trouble to hit a silly little white ball with a stick, then walk five miles up a paddock just to hit the silly thing again. She does not understand the rules of the game but her husband does. He knows what the players are trying to achieve and he understands the difficulties that they encounter. He can feel the distress of a player whose shot does not go the way it ought, and the triumph of a player who scores a hole in one. To him, it means something, because he understands the rules of the game.

If we do not understand the rules of the game in life, it too, will seem meaningless. We must know what we are trying to achieve. We must know the reasons which brought us here. Those reasons lie in our psychic existence—they relate to you as a soul, not to your physical body. Unless you do understand the rules of the game, you might be taken for a ride by someone who claims to know all the answers—at twenty-five dollars a visit—and by doing so you can be trapped into accepting someone else's theories in place of the facts.

Everyone, somewhere deep down inside themselves, is searching for a purpose in life and all of us are frequently assailed by the perplexing question: what *really* happens when we die? Certain religious philosophies tell us that we have approximately seventy-five years in which to progress from original sin to perfection. If we fail, we will be forever consigned to the flames of Hell, where we will presumably shovel coal for the rest of eternity. If we succeed, we will be rewarded with a halo and a pair of wings and will spend the rest of eternity sitting on a cloud trying to learn how to play a golden harp. That may be someone else's idea of Heaven, but personally it would bore me to tears.

The traditional ideas concerning Heaven and Hell simply do not make sense, even to the limited under-standing of a human being. There is something lacking.

If we are to believe in a God who was clever enough to create the Universe (and there is no reason why we should not), then we must assume that He has enough intelligence to provide an after-life which contains some sense of meaning. So, what are the alternatives?

In order to find out about a non-physical world, we need to use non-physical methods. Psychic understanding is needed but if we do not even know that the psyche exists, our search for enlightenment might bear a very close resemblance to a dog's pursuit of its tail.

Before David could begin to teach me in earnest, I had to be brought to this stage of understanding: that I accepted the reality of the psychic worlds and the beings who inhabit them. All of the experiences that are related in the earlier part of this book were merely the preparation for the study I was about to begin. Now that I had seen for myself the operation of psychic energy and had spent a reasonable amount of time in conversation with a being from the psychic world, I was ready to understand the principles that operate within that world and also in our own. Without that preparation, I might not have been so ready to accept David as he presented himself. Experience always gives the best basis for understanding.

In having David as an instructor, I was very lucky. There are many psychics who admit quite openly that they do not understand the origin of their unusual abilities. Peter Hurkos, the famed psychic detective, has confessed that he has no idea of how or why his mind functions as it does. His gift frightens him and he wishes that it would go away so that he could go back to painting houses. Had I gone on experiencing the kind of psychic flashes that I had in the beginning, without ever finding an explanation for them, I might easily have found myself in complete sympathy with him, for the only thing that is truly frightening is the inexplicable.

There are many people who have never experienced any conscious manifestations of psychic phenomena, yet they believe in it all the same. You may not be able to bend spoons, solve crimes or predict the future with any degree of accuracy, but something happens when you see somebody else doing it. You are forced to admit to yourself that there is *some* force, some alternative source of energy, which does not conform to the natural laws of the physical world as we know it. In short, your attention is directed away from the physical, back to the soul, or psychic plane. Your memory is triggered.

The purpose behind demonstrations of psychic phenomena, whether or not the mediums are aware of it, is simply to show that the psychic world exists. When some psychic phenomenon occurs and its occurrence directly involves you in some way, your attention is directed to the non-physical, or soul plane. If it stays there for long enough, you begin to experience it for yourself.

Our attention is focused so intently on the physical world in which we are operating at the present, that we fail to notice the more subtle currents of the psychic world, even though they surround us all the time. There are any number of spiritual beings close to you at any given time, but unless they can find a way to penetrate the physical, you could remain unaware of them throughout your whole lifetime.

A number of years ago, psychologists carried out an experiment in which a cat was used as the subject. They connected a wire to the nerve which led from the animal's ear to its brain. The other end of the wire was attached to a dial which registered electrical impulses. A loud noise was produced close to the cat's ear and the needle on the dial swung sharply in response.

A cage of mice was then put in front of the cat, who concentrated intently on them. When the loud noise was produced this time, the needle on the dial failed to move at all. As far as the cat was concerned, the sound did not exist; just as the psychic world does not exist for thousands of people. It is there, but they are concentrating so intently on the events of the physical world that they remain unaware of anything else.

If a person denies the existence of a psychic world, he is denying his own existence as a soul. He is one of those who suspect that we are only physical beings who may or may not possess a soul. The only thing that has any reality to him is the material world. He is really only half alive and the tragedy is that he doesn't even know it.

We are thinking creatures, and a lot of our thoughts, along with the actions that follow them, relate to purely physical things. If I punched somebody on the nose and they retaliated by stamping on my foot, a lot of mental and physical activity would be taking place. The brain would be registering a pain response, along with anger.

If my opponent were wired to an electroencephalograph, this activity would register on the machine. It would be possible for you to see my opponent thinking about stamping on my foot before the action took place. You would not see the thought, but you would see the mental activity.

Not all our thoughts are related to the physical. Many of them are concerned with our existence as spiritual beings. If we do not *know* that we are spiritual, then those thoughts are bound to be misinterpreted. Our prime motivation comes from the spiritual, or psychic part of ourselves. We are powered from a non-physical source, the soul. We *are* souls. Not only does the Bible tell us so, but most religions teach the same thing.

The Bible also tells us that we have an existence outside the body. 'I knew a man in Christ above fourteen years ago (whether in the body, I cannot tell: or whether out of the body, I cannot tell) . . .'. 2 Corinthians 12:2, King James Edition. Exponents of traditional religion may have their own interpretation of that passage, but to me it seems that the meaning is quite specific.

Psychic energy works for us when we learn how to motivate ourselves from our spiritual source. The spiritual part of you is not confined within physical limitations, because it is not of physical origin. You are a soul: your physical body is a vehicle in which you travel through this environment. If you like, it is a highly complex robot. That is not an easy concept to absorb, when one has spent a lifetime thinking in terms of the physical and very little else. It took months and months before I began to have a sensation of freedom that I was able to trace back to this piece of information.

David compares the physical body to a small boat in which you are travelling along a river. If you are sitting in the boat and are confined to the limitations which affect it, you will be unable to plan very far ahead, because you can't see beyond the next bend in the river. If someone is travelling in a helicopter above you, he will be able to see you and also the river ahead of you. From his vantage point, he may notice that another boat is travelling in the opposite direction, towards you. He may call to you through a loud-hailer, telling you that you are on a collision course, and you might be quite startled to hear his voice. If you know nothing about helicopters, you might even think that he is a messenger from the Gods.

We have already likened the little boat to the human body in which you are travelling. Now, let us say that the man in the helicopter is a soul. Since you, too, are a soul, you have a helicopter of your own. The moment that you realise you can operate your boat more effectively if you put it on remote control and direct it from your helicopter, you begin to make life a great deal easier for yourself.

What makes people psychic? The very fact that they exist. While you walk, talk, think, or do anything at all, you are being motivated by your higher self. Psychic development is not a matter of *becoming* psychic, but of realising that you have always been that way. Once you begin to understand this, you can run your little ship more effectively, because you will know *what* you are doing, *how* you are doing it and, more importantly, *why*.

You are already psychic. Psychics are not specially gifted people who have been singled out by some great power from beyond, they are ordinary people, like you and me. There is nothing special about me and there never has been. I have the same problems and aspirations that anyone else has—the only difference is that David managed to make himself known to me and teach me that there is a far greater world that lies both within and without the one that I perceive with my senses.

I always place a strong differentiation between psychics and mystics. In my terminology, a psychic is someone who has operational psychic abilities, but who may or may not understand the principles which underlie those abilities. A mystic is someone who understands the forces that are at work in psychic phenomena and that person may not even demonstrate any of the abilities that we have come to regard as psychic, simply because he has

128

advanced beyond the physical level and is operating on a grade that is unseen by most of us. However, the only thing that makes them any different from other people is the fact that they understand the rules of the game. They know that there are certain natural laws which affect all life and they have an understanding of the ways in which these laws operate. Some have more understanding than others, but they all have some degree of awareness.

What are the uses of psychic awareness? What can it do for you? What do you want it to do? Can it make you rich? For those of you who are thinking in terms of learning how to predict the Soccer Pools for the next few weeks running, I have sad news. It would be wonderful if it could be done, but I have not managed to achieve it so far and David is never very sympathetic when I broach the subject to him. His only reply is a smile and the remark: 'My daughter, if winning would do you any good on the level at which I exist, I would give you the numbers. But it is a physical thing and I am a spiritual teacher'.

Money is the currency of the physical world. We do physical work and get paid in physical currency, which we use to purchase things which answer our physical needs. If you wish to gain an abundance of physical possessions, it would seem logical to spend your time studying the rules by which the financial world operates. If you want to get rich, you would be better occupied studying finance and economics than psychic development.

If a person truly understands the meaning of the word 'psychic', he pursues a course of psychic development because he recognises the fact that he has needs which cannot be answered in the physical. He needs something more—something that is not available here. He is aware that he has an existence quite apart from his physical body and he wants to know more about it.

You are also aware that there is something outside the physical and whatever it is, it is exercising a call for you. If it were not, you would not be reading this book. Since it *is* outside the physical and has no physical origin, common sense tells us that it must lie in the realm of the psychic.

We all experience reality shifts—the common term for them is day-dreams. Whatever you wish to call them, their effect is to take you away from the physical world for a time. Whether you are sitting at a desk in an office or standing by a machine in a workshop, you begin to day-dream and suddenly you forget about the physical reality that surrounds you.

You may hear birds singing, smell a delicately scented breeze and even feel the sunlight on your shoulders. Then *thwack,* the office boy drops a pile of papers onto your desk, or someone slaps your back in passing and you are jerked back to this reality. For that brief space of time however, you were somewhere else. Where were you?

Close your eyes and think of a room that you know very well. It can be any room, other than the one you are in at the moment. Perhaps it could be your bathroom. Just picture it as though you were standing at the door looking in. Take a good long look at it and then open your eyes. Now, where were you?

The physical part of you did not move, nor did your thinking process. These things both remained where you are sitting, but what of the non-physical part of you—where was that? Was it not looking in through your bathroom door? Call it memory if you like, but how do you define memory? In a physical sense, your memories cannot be seen or experienced by anyone but yourself. They do not originate from a physical source, but from within you; and you are a soul. Some part of you was standing at your bathroom door and that part was the non-physical you, the soul.

All right, you can't imagine anyone wanting to stand around in the ethereal, looking at bathrooms for the rest of eternity. Neither can I, but this ability to be somewhere else in a fully conscious state while your body remains in a fixed environment can be developed so that you can travel a great deal further than your bathroom door. You can use this ability in order to go places and do things, in comfort and completely free of charge. You can use it to explore the realms that exist outside the physical, and if you do you will learn a great deal.

I have had a number of out-of-body experiences, some indescribably beautiful ones as well as a few that I would rather not relate at this stage, for they required me to visit the shadowy realms inhabited by lost souls—a horrific and heartrending experience. Each journey is memorable but one of my favourites is the very first time I consciously achieved soul travel.

I had been trying for months and getting nowhere fast, because every time I felt the slight lifting sensation that heralds escape from the body, I would feel a surge of excitement and promptly bounce back to full conscious awareness of the physical. This time, however, I was not trying, which is probably why it was so successful.

I was in bed, drifting in that twilight consciousness that is the forerunner of sleep and I was blissfully unaware of my surroundings. There was a moment of blankness, then I realised that I was swaying slightly, to and fro, as though my bed were a cradle and some unseen hand were rocking it. I opened my eyes and found myself floating near the ceiling. This time I managed to stay calm. I remembered reading somewhere that this is the moment when you should look down upon your recumbent body, so that you can be fully aware that you really have left the physical. Just as I turned my head to look, I distinctly heard David's voice:

'My daughter, do not look down. You are not experienced enough to resist the pull of your body. Stay as you are.'

I closed my eyes for a moment, to regain stability and when I opened them I found myself drifting through a peaceful void. It is almost impossible to describe the experience, for the atmosphere that surrounded me was both blank and full of vibrant colour; it was nothing yet it was everything; empty yet full of life. I had a sensation something similar to swimming underwater only without holding my breath or feeling a drag against my body.

'I'm doing it, I'm really doing it!' I thought in delight. In answer, David's voice floated towards me:

'Keep quiet and keep coming!'

I drifted downwards through a warm, rainbow-hued mist and as it cleared I saw that I had set down on the outskirts of a great parkland, facing a roadway. I looked around in amazement for I seemed to be in the midst of a busy township. The roadway seemed to be made of white earth; there were no cars, only people, drifting along, quite intent upon their own business but not unaware of me. Some of them smiled at me in passing. On the other side of the road were buildings, both ancient and space-age in design—sweeping white structures arranged in tiers, set into a hill, with the façade of each layer resting on columns upon the layer below, rather like a wedding cake.

Then, across the street, I saw him. At first I didn't know what to think, for he seemed to be wearing a priest's cassock but as he walked towards me I saw that in fact it was a simple brown garment over what looked like a white skivvy collar. He was the most beautiful man I had ever seen, with wavy golden hair, sparkling blue eyes and a dimpled smile that revealed even white teeth. No one had to tell me that this was David.

As he walked towards me, I looked again at my surroundings. What in the name of Glory was a city doing in the spirit world? David reached my side and threw an affectionate arm around my shoulders. Gazing laughingly into my eyes with those blue pools of mirth, he chuckled:

'Well, what did you expect—a vacuum?'

I cannot say how long it was that I stayed there, because time simply did not exist, but I walked and talked with this wonderful man, and truth to tell, I fell more than a little in love with him. If I had thought myself lucky before, I felt a hundred times blessed now. For that experience alone, all of my studies would have been well worthwhile but it was not to be a mere pleasure trip. There were things for me to learn but I soon discovered that in that delightful realm, learning is only another one of the pleasures that are there to be experienced.

The sphere to which I was transported should not be confused with the idea of Heaven, as propounded by the churches, although it certainly seems heavenly in comparison with the physical world. It is one of the many spheres within the spiritual world where spirits may meet together, exchange knowledge and generally take pleasure in each other's company. For a student such as I, it is a wonderful place to visit, for not only does it fill my soul with pleasant contentment, it affords me a great opportunity to learn more of the things I wish to know.

Of what particular value is all this learning? All people have a basic drive to know and understand, but there is more to it than just accumulating information. You must be able to put that knowledge to some use.

I have already mentioned that physical wealth is related directly to your existence in the physical world. You can accumulate as much as you like and no doubt you will enjoy it, but the day will inevitably come when you must get back onto the bus and go home, and you cannot take it with you.

If you wish, you can give it all to a priest, in order to buy your way into Heaven. You will leave behind you one very happy priest, but when you arrive at the steps of the Golden Throne, you are in for a slight shock. Your credit rating does not travel with you.

Physical wealth and social standing are not a passport to Heaven, which is why Jesus said that it is easier for a camel to pass through the eye of a needle than for a rich man to enter the Kingdom of Heaven. You can be wealthy and still earn your way into the higher realms, but you do not do it on the basis of wealth alone. The rich man who plonks himself down on the right hand of the Creator and says: 'Right, God, I've arrived. Now, bring on the Pharisees and I'll whip a few for you,' is bound to be surprised by his reception. His *spiritual* credit rating only entitles him to ride as far as the first bus stop.

Knowledge and understanding, the things that you store in your memory bank, are the operative currency in the next world. If you have spent your days looting and pillaging in order to build up a stockpile of wealth, that is your own choice and you are free to make it. But it is unlikely that you could also devote much time to the accumulation of spiritual currency. If that is the case (and if you were cheating, it almost certainly is), you will only be able to stay in the cheapest hotels because that will be all that you can afford. If you don't like rubbing shoulders with the unsavoury characters who share your abode, you may comfort yourself with the knowledge that all the nice people are staying in high-class resorts and you can eventually get there if you decide to *learn*.

Should you devote all of your time to the accumulation of spiritual wealth to such an extent that you deprive yourself physically? Quite the reverse. At one stage during my development, I became so enthusiastic about making spiritual progress that I began to reject everything that originated within the physical. David corrected me with six words: 'My daughter, don't forget to live'.

The keynote in this philosophy seems to be centred around moderation in all things. For instance, there is nothing wrong with having a drink or two, so long as it is not taken to excess and causes no problems for you or the people with whom you come into contact. The same applies to smoking. Many people prefer not to smoke, on the premise that it is better for their health. I will not argue with that, but in a spiritual sense, David has only requested that we do not smoke during our sittings. What we do at other times is entirely our own affair.

Understand that life is a part of your learning process and the experiences, pleasant or otherwise, that you undergo during your lifetime are a form of feedback, designed to teach you. Can you really understand the beauty and harmony of Nature and see the Creator's hand at work in the world if you don't get out into the fields and smell the buttercups?

Understanding your spiritual origins and the reasons which prompted you to come here will help you to understand the rules of the game. A person who does not understand the rules plays very badly. If he is forced to continue playing the game, he becomes frustrated and apathetic and wants nothing more than to give up and go home. He is failing, and more than that, he is probably also proving to be a handicap to those who do understand and want the freedom to play their own roles in the game.

The object of any game is to set up obstacles for yourself, or have them set up for you, so that you can exercise your knowledge and skill by figuring out how to overcome them. If you are a real enthusiast, you may continue to set progressively more difficult goals until you become a champion. Whichever way the game is played, if it is being done with understanding it has purpose.

Is life nothing more than a game? That depends largely upon your attitude towards it. But no matter which field of human endeavour you choose, you will always find ways in which to test yourself so that you can develop. To succeed in anything, you need a working knowledge of the rules or you are not going to get very far. Your knowledge must be sufficient for you to operate by yourself. You want to know how to do it; you do not want it to be done for you.

Psychic development will teach you the rules; it will not play your game for you. It will help you to develop as a soul and build into your memory bank some usable currency, which will be extremely useful in the spiritual world, which is where you are inexorably headed. You came into this world with one—and only one—expectation which is absolutely certain of being fulfilled: that you will eventually die.

Is there really a life after death? Does this spiritual world of which I speak really exist, or is it a figment of the imagination? Every major religion tells us that life after death is a reality and so do the psychics. If that were the only evidence on which an argument for a spirit world could be based, perhaps we would be justified in saying that it has not been proven.

But what of the people who have died and returned to tell of their experience? Three things are missing from a cadaver—heat, energy, and intellect. There is no brain activity, nothing to be charted on an EEG. To all intents and purposes, that person is incapable of consciously registering anything at all. Despite this, a great number of people have been clinically dead for a time and have been revived. These people have had interesting tales to tell. During the period in which their brains were inactive, they underwent experiences on a *conscious* level and they brought their memories back with them. Many of them have told of watching the surgical team frantically trying to resuscitate their physical bodies. The descriptions given by them tally in detail with the actual events as related by the medical staff concerned. This, in minds which are incapable of thought?

They have related other things also. They have mentioned feeling as though they were travelling along a dark tunnel towards a bright light. They have walked and talked with loved ones who have already died. These experiences are shared by hundreds of people all over the world, not merely one or two. By the simple act of *remembering* their experiences, they have proved that memory is unaffected by physical phenomena such as death. To deny the existence of another world in the face of such evidence is really hiding one's head in the sand. There is a world of spiritual existence, to which you will return after your physical body has died. But what of the here and now? Can spiritual development be employed to answer some physical needs or must we all wait for a misty hereafter before we can see the benefits of our endeavours? It can certainly be used for physical purposes and one of its most startling applications is in the field of healing. Believe it or not, it is possible to heal the majority of physical ills without drugs or surgery, by employing psychic energy. I have personally witnessed a number of such cases.

I have seen psychic energy being used to dissipate a virulent kidney infection, a process which took no more than ten minutes and was carried out in the presence of a qualified medical practitioner. Another time, a spinal complaint of some twenty-eight years' duration was also healed by our guides, using this psychic energy. These and other examples of healing are dealt with in greater detail in a later chapter of this book.

Many psychics choose to seek the art of healing by psychic energy, others find that it comes upon them unasked. My own choice was to teach, a role for which I believed I was ideally suited, if only because whenever I discover something new and interesting I have a compulsive urge to tell everyone else about it.

Your choice may be something completely different and it is entirely your own to choose. You are an individual with free will to make your own decisions. Psychic energy can be used for any number of purposes. Like electricity, it is mindless in itself. Electricity can be used to heat your home, provide lighting, and cook your food. It can also operate life support mechanisms in hospitals. Do not forget, however, that it also powers the electric chair. Whether power is used to sustain life or curtail it is the decision of the person who wields that power—and that same person bears the responsibility for his decisions.

This brings us to the key issue—your very reason for reading this book—*how to develop*. You are already doing that because you are sharing the knowledge that was given to me by David himself. In the following chapters I hope to give you more information, which may help you to develop even further. Any item of information is useful, for knowledge and understanding are the keys to development at every stage in your life.

There is an exercise that David gave me to do at the beginning of my training, which you may practise for yourself. It is simple enough, although you may have some difficulty with it at first. I want you to set aside five minutes each day for meditation. It can be any part of the day, so long as it is the same time each day and you can be sure of being undisturbed for the full five minutes.

When you sit down to meditate—*relax*. Do not try to meditate *on* anything in particular, just allow your thoughts to rove freely in whichever direction they care to take. It does not matter if you go over the events of your day, if your mind insists on reminding you of all the other things you could be doing. Nothing matters except that you do not consciously exert any direction onto your thoughts. Learn to allow your mind to go. It is not as easy as it sounds. I will be developing this technique further throughout the book, but I would like you to give each stage a full week's practice before moving on to the next level. Remember, if you don't keep to the routine you cannot expect it to work for you.

The *only* way to develop properly and in safety is to gain a good working knowledge of the natural laws which apply to psychic activity. In other words, learn the rules. Psychic awareness can be stimulated suddenly, it is true. Peter Hurkos started to display his abilities after he had fallen from a ladder and fractured his skull. But it is not a very bright idea to spend your time leaping from ladders in the hope that you might land on the precise spot that will stimulate your psychic awareness. For most of us, psychic development is achieved through a process of learning and practice.

Our book will not make you psychic. We would be liars and cheats if we claimed that it could. You already have the full range of psychic abilities, all you have to do is learn to recognise them in yourself. If the book helps you to do that, then we have fulfilled our purpose.

137

CHAPTER THIRTEEN ·
Meditation: the levels, protection

The groundwork having been laid, David began to move me into more specific areas of study. His aim was to build my understanding from the ground up, helping me to relate to the worlds that I could not see, yet which would henceforth form a very real part of my life. I was already beginning to understand that the psychic worlds are no less real than the physical, for my visits to those other regions had shown me that they were every bit as real and valid, and in many cases, much more vibrant and full of energy. I fell into the habit of referring to those worlds as Alternate Realities, illustrating that I had come to accept them as such, rather than thinking of them as far-off, mysterious regions that bore no relation to reality as I understood it.

I also began to understand that it is not physical distance which separates these spheres; it is only the level of our comprehension which keeps us apart from the beings who inhabit other realities.

From the beginning, David instilled in me a basic safety factor and in this lay a technique which was to prove useful in other respects also. It was that I should never accept anything as true just because I had been told that it was. I must always endeavour to prove things for myself.

What he was trying to do was help me to open my channels of communication, so that I would not always need to use Roland as a means of communication. He told me that when the final channels of communication were opened, I would need no message through Roland to tell me so, for I would know for myself.

My meditation exercise was enlarged upon. He asked me to continue with it, but he also explained more about what we were trying to achieve.

As I mentioned, it is important that this exercise is done at the same time each day and that it lasts for approximately five minutes. I also suggested that it is not necessary to concentrate on anything in particular but to allow the mind to rove wherever it wishes. The aim is to get to a point in meditation where the mind becomes blank, however it is no use trying to *force* it to go blank, for that would defeat the whole purpose of the exercise. The idea is to relax.

There is no trick to the technique, unless simple perseverance could be called a trick. If the exercise is carried out often enough and the routine is maintained, eventually the mind does slow down and become quiescent. Experience is a very valuable teacher and it is for this reason that I asked you to carry out this exercise for yourself. It is all very well for me to tell you what I achieved, but no doubt you would like to achieve the same things for yourself, if you have not already reached that stage of development. The whole aim of writing this book is to share the knowledge and experience given to us.

The meditation exercise is one of the small building blocks that can be used as a foundation for future development and we will be enlarging upon it as this book progresses. If you try to *force* your mind to go blank and think of nothing, you are actually doing the opposite of what is required. Relax, and *allow* it to go blank in its own good time.

When the mind is allowed to wander, it eventually tires of meandering aimlessly through scattered thoughts and it begins to seek a direction. If you are not providing that direction by focusing into the physical, the mind will focus elsewhere—in the psychic. This is the first stage in learning how to switch yourself off from the physical so that you can pass through a reality shift and experience the psychic.

It is all very well to meditate, go blank, think of nothing, but if you don't understand why, it won't mean very much to you. It may seem like a lot of hocus-pocus and you won't make a serious effort to succeed. From my point of view, I have always wanted to know why I am being asked to do something, and David explained that what I was aiming for was to open the channels of communication between myself and him. The effort was by no means one-sided, for he was trying equally hard to reach me.

To help me see things from his perspective, he asked

me to imagine that I was located in some high spot, looking down on a crowd of people, all rushing around busily, bumping into each other, disappearing into buildings and scurrying out again. In short, a scene of confusion. Imagining that I had a spotlight, I was to try to focus it on a particular person for long enough to catch her attention so that she became aware of my presence and that person was to look like me.

As David said, wouldn't it make the job a whole lot easier if that person would just sit still for five minutes? She would not have to do anything herself except sit still and allow the spotlight operator to reach her with the beam of light.

The gap that we are trying to bridge is not a physical one, it is one of comprehension, or thought. As I pointed out in the previous chapter, thought is a form of psychic energy. The more we understand, the easier it becomes to bridge the gap.

It is not easy to explain a multi-dimensional concept when the words at our disposal are only three-dimensional, and David was often forced to resort to exercises in imagination in order to help me understand what he was trying to explain.

To help me visualise the relationship between the physical world and the realms that surround it, he made up a rather interesting exercise: let us say that the Earth, that is the planet itself, represents the physical world. The next layer of existence could then be represented by the atmosphere which surrounds this world. In spiritual terms, we are now speaking of the Astral plane, which is the first level of non-physical existence. The first bus stop, if you like.

If you were travelling away from the earth, you would first pass through the atmosphere. After penetrating that, you would emerge into space, which is a vacuum, a void. In the spiritual progression also, there is a void which lies at the limits of the Astral.

The meditation routine requires a mention here, for I experienced a very distinct sensation which related directly to the description David was giving me. It was so interesting that I held a discussion with him about it, and by chance I had the tape recorder running at the time.

The following excerpt is a verbatim transcription of the conversation.

It began with a question from me: 'When I go into meditation I pass into a silent period. I'd like to discuss it with you and find out exactly what level it is, and what can be achieved there. When I get to that level, I think—well, I'm here, and there's nothing here yet. Do I put something here, do I pass through it, or do I use it as a springboard to something else?—in other words, what the heck am I supposed to do with it now that I've got it? Could you discuss that with me and explain more about it? Tell me how to develop it for a useful purpose'.

'My daughter, tell me of your observations.'

'Well, I relax in meditation. I "change channels", if you like; alter the shift of my focus from the immediate physical to the mental level. Then I get a "noisy period" where there are scattered thoughts, scattered voices which don't make conscious sense to me, so I just accept them and let them go. I don't try to hold them. Then there is a distinct *snap!*—and I am suddenly in silence. Not emptiness, but there is auditory silence and something I can only describe as visual silence. There seem to be currents. Flowing shades of light and dark move around me. I experimented with this level today. I had a pain in my back and while on that level I tried creating a point of light which I focused on the aching point in my back. The point of pain became hot—the pain is now gone. Obviously there are valuable things which can be achieved on that level, and that can even be surpassed. I'd like to know more about it.'

'I am where I am, you are where you are, yet we are together. I am here, yet I am there: you are there, yet you are here. Neither of us has moved, but we have traversed. That which you see, that which you hear and that which you experience is now yours to know. We have, since we have *been*, traversing to attune ourselves so that we may *be*. Do you understand so far?'

After several minutes' rapid thought, I nodded and David continued: 'That which you experienced as your "noisy period" is as you accelerate your vibrations and you pass through that layer of understanding which is immediate above your own, upon which you exist.'

'Is that what we term the Astral?' I interjected.

'That which is immediately above you in vibrations. As your vibration increases or accelerates it becomes more garbled, flows past you more quickly, and when you reach the extremity of it, there is a barrier through which you are propelled to the next level of awareness and understanding. It is, in the term that has been used by your fellow men, that which is called "Limbo". For it is a space between the level below—which is immediately above yours, and the next. It is silent, for it is a space.

'Immediately above your reality is your next level— through which you *all* shall traverse. It is noisy, it is violent, but not so much as in your reality. For you to traverse from that level to mine requires a safeguard. It is the nature of things. There is this zone—as you traverse it, in its silence, you are observed as you approach us.

'If we *wish* it, you traverse and you appear on levels near to us—for I am not at that level, I am higher. But there are those at that level who see those who traverse the Void—the Veil, if you wish. And they see and they tell, for it is for them to do so. I see you through eyes of those who are *known* to you as David. I am told and I see, and I see you come. It is my wish that I converse with you, and so you traverse it. If I did not wish it, then you would be returned—first to your "noisy level" above your reality, down through it into your world.'

'Then this relates back to what you told me some time ago,' I said, 'that I could develop to a point where I would be able to speak with you on your level, because some things are too intense to be brought through to mine. There are things that I must see and learn on your level and this is then part of that development. Is that so?'

'That is so. It will not be rapid. It shall take time for you to learn, but you have time, and so do I. Do not wish it impatiently, for you have time, and far better you do it safely and steadily and surely and *know*, as you do.'

'So what I do when I reach that silent area, or "limbo", is simply accept it?'

'It is there. You must traverse it. It shall not change.'

'But I don't have to make any effort, or try to force anything?'

'You are floating free. You are seen, you are observed.

142

If it is to be that you are to come to this side, then you shall be drawn.'

'Is it valid that I use my time on this level to ease pain in the physical body?'

'It is there. It is the area upon which you draw that which heals. Far better—if for yourself and not for another—whilst you are there, that your technique alter slightly. As you see your light and you draw it into you to ease what ails you, far better whilst there, that you place the light in the area that is ailed and radiate the light from it outward. The light is within you, it is not external. It works if you wish it—for you live in a world where you draw help unto you. There, it is *within* you and you radiate it out—in opposition to the movement where you are.'

The 'noisy period' to which we were referring occurs in what we know as the Astral level. This is the spiritual level immediately above the physical and although many psychics aim to penetrate this level in meditation, it is not a good idea to remain there. The Astral is inhabited by souls who are awaiting reincarnation and whilst some of them may be able to pass on some interesting information, the *real* spiritual wisdom lies in the levels above the Void. It is for this level that we should aim.

When, in meditation, you experience those noisy thoughts and rapid, blurry pictures in your mind, do not attempt to retain them or decipher them because they are only the first stage in your progress. Let them go and pass on upwards, trying to reach the Void.

What follows this noisy period is a sudden silence. It is so sudden that people often hear a snapping or popping sound at the moment of breakthrough. The silence that you experience is warm, calm and almost euphoric. This is the Void.

At this point we need to spend a little thought on the subject of reincarnation. It is a subject which has been the centre of a certain amount of controversy, because there is a division between those who believe in it and those who do not. I will establish my opinion by stating now that I do believe in it, and in fact I can see little sense in life if reincarnation is not a fact.

When you have learned all that can be learned in the

143

physical, you pass through the Void for the last time and enter the realms of true spiritual existence. In the meantime however, there must be a spiritual sphere where you can spend your time between incarnations, for you do not pass out of one body and immediately enter another. This transitional realm is the one we know as the Astral and it is immediately above our physical reality on a vibrational level. It is graded from levels on which the most primitive souls exist to levels where there are spirits who are almost ready to make the transition into the spiritual spheres. Many of these higher spirits can be of assistance in your development if you happen to become acquainted with them; some function in the role of spirit guides for people here in the physical who are not quite advanced enough to reach the higher guides. But if you are making a deliberate effort to reach the higher spiritual levels through meditation, it is not the Astral for which you should aim.

You now need to think in spiritual terms rather than relating things to the physical, because you are no longer operating as a physical person. You are developing as a soul and you must learn to think like one. It is a totally new concept of thinking and do not expect it to be easy at first. You have had a lifetime to develop your present thought patterns and I am now asking you to relate your thoughts to things that you cannot even see yet. However, you will find that it becomes easier with practice.

The Void is actually patrolled by beings who are known to us as Guardians, which is as good a name as any. Their task is to see that nothing which carries contamination of any kind is permitted to pass through the Void. They have the ability to deflect such things back to the place from whence they came, and they do this by exerting a force which pushes everything away from themselves. It cannot be used by a determined intruder as a means of access because it draws nothing to itself.

Everyone has the ability to launch themselves up from the physical and into the Void and it is this ability that your meditation is designed to develop. If you do it properly it will have the desired effect, but if you attempt to capture and hold the rapid 'astral' thoughts, you will have difficulty. By focusing your attention on those thoughts, your tendency will be to take off in a sideways direction instead of upwards.

The guardians actively seek those people whose actions indicate their readiness to pass across the Void. This does not happen only at death, it is a condition of thought which can be achieved in a fully conscious state of mind. I know, because I have done it countless times.

Perhaps we could imagine each guardian with a spotlight, searching for people who are sitting still. If the light is focused on you, you can use it as a direction-finder to guide you towards your objective. Remember though, it is a psychic energy force and unlikely to physically appear as a light. It is more likely that you will feel the illumination inwardly.

Once you are touched by this light and you reach into the spiritual, you can attach your own line of communication and you will have a two-way passage between the spiritual and your existence in the physical. In other words, you will be able to fly your own helicopter.

It is in this way that you form the link that joins you with your guide. This is a being who is more highly developed and who exists permanently in the spiritual spheres, as David does. While you are following the round of physical incarnations, you come under the care and direction of this being and you will continue to do so when you graduate to the spiritual, for this is a tie that is never broken. The guide is what some people may prefer to call a guardian angel, but whatever name you care to use, his function remains the same. He is there to take care of you in a spiritual sense.

The aura which surrounds your physical body is where you have your existence as a soul. Your body is simply a vehicle that gets you around in the physical world. It is, if you like, a robot. A highly complicated and sensitive one, but a robot nonetheless. The body itself is mindless. Certainly it has a brain, and the brain has an important and complex function. It carries out the physical thinking process by which the thoughts originated by the soul are converted into physical action.

You—the soul—may have a desire to carry out some action in the physical and experience the feedback that results from it. This is how you learn, by experimentation. You form a thought, a mental image, which is imprinted onto the brain. The brain then converts this psychic energy into electromagnetic impulses which are fed along the nerves, to activate the required response in the body. The body does not reason, it simply reacts. It will carry out whatever function is directed through it by the brain. This is all very well as long as the thoughts imprinted on the brain arise from one soul, but what would happen if there were *two* sources of thought?

Let us consider what happens in a radio set. If it is tuned to a certain wavelength, it will reproduce the sound that is being broadcast on that wavelength. If two radio stations are operating on wave lengths that are very close to each other, your radio will reproduce both. The result will be a horrible cacophony. The way to avoid this is to have your radio so finely tuned that it can distinguish a slight variation in frequency. It also helps if the radio stations are prevented from using wavelengths that are too close together.

Like a radio, your brain will faithfully reproduce any thought that is imprinted onto it. As long as the resident soul is the only one who can reach the brain with thought imprints, there is nothing to worry about. If thoughts from more than one source reach the brain, it will do its best to reproduce them all.

In the case of a trance medium, something similar to this process is taking place, but if it is done under the supervision of a guide, there is no cause for alarm. What is alarming is when some soul other than a beneficial one finds a way of penetrating your aura and influencing the patterns of thought which operate within your brain.

If this happens, what will be seen physically is a very confused person who is prone to extreme and sudden changes of mood and who often does things which seem totally out of character. The sufferer may even complain of hearing voices in his head or seeing strange lights around himself. If the confusion is severe enough, we have another name for it—insanity. I am not, of course, inferring that every person who has ever been classified insane is really suffering from auric invasion. What I am pointing out is that insanity can be a consequence of that kind of invasion.

146

This confusion is not only mental, it is physical also. There is a continual flow of energy between the body and the soul, through the aura. We call it vital energy, the eastern mystics call it *prana,* but the name is not really important. What *is* important is that this energy continues to flow in a steady, uninterrupted stream. If it comes in irregular jerks over a prolonged period, the body mechanism will begin to break down, just as your car would, if you had an intermittent blockage in the fuel line.

As I mentioned in the last chapter, psychics who can see the aura can often spot a developing illness before a physical diagnosis is possible. This is due to the fact that trouble often originates in the aura. Since the soul expresses everything about itself through the physical body, anything wrong in the aura will be reproduced in a physical sense and illness will be the result.

When the aura is invaded by an alien life-force, the effect on the body can be very similar to physical invasion of the body by a virus. Illness that arises from such a source will persist despite the efforts made by physicians to locate and eliminate the cause, for as long as the alien force remains within the aura. Often a doctor will assume that the cause of such an illness is psychosomatic. Once again, I am not suggesting that all psychosomatic illness is really the result of auric invasion but in a great many cases it is, and only a trained psychic could tell the difference.

When your aura is invaded by another entity, the common term for the condition is 'possession'. This is not strictly correct however, because what really takes place is a struggle for possession or control of the physical body.

Inhabiting the Astral are souls who have not managed to make the transition into the spiritual world after death. They will have to be born again physically and complete the round of existence again and again until they learn everything they need to know. They are not necessarily *bad*; as I pointed out earlier, the Astral itself is subdivided into several levels and the highest of these are inhabited by souls who are developing quite well and simply need a little more training and experience. Those souls, however, are not interested in invading the auras of other folk, for they know better.

147

The lower levels of the Astral are the closest to our level of physical existence. In these levels can be found souls who are in a highly disturbed state, often because of some trauma associated with their deaths. Try for a moment to put yourself into a position similar to that which one of these souls may have experienced.

Let us say that you are driving a car—quite a bit too fast—and you hit a patch of grease on the road, causing your car to run out of control. It collides with a telegraph pole at some speed and you lose consciousness instantly. A few moments later, your physical body is dead.

By the time you regain your senses, the ambulance has removed your lifeless body and all that remains on the scene is the wreckage of your car and the inevitable group of spectators. Without being aware of it, you have wandered some distance away from the car and you now believe that some fortunate chance has thrown you clear. You approach the people who surround the vehicle and you hear one of them commenting that the driver must have died instantly.

Anxious to reassure everyone that you are unhurt, you press forward and speak to the man who made the comment. He ignores you, so you speak again, a little louder. When he continues to take no notice, you reach out to touch him—and your hand passes through him.

After the shock of seeing your very first 'ghost' has subsided, you try to touch another person, then another. The result is always the same, your hand passes through everyone you try to touch. You are now living in a nightmare from which you are unable to escape. How long do you think it would take for you to dissolve into hysteria?

A soul who has undergone this kind of ordeal may lapse into a state of total confusion, not knowing where he is or what he is doing. Without realising it and certainly through no deliberate act of his own, he can be drawn into the aura of a living person. Regardless of whether or not he is aware of what is happening, the result will be the same. His confused and erratic thoughts will begin to imprint themselves onto the brain of his host.

In a later chapter, I will go into the subject in greater detail, for it is an area that every mystic should be conversant with if he is to avoid trouble, both for himself and for those with whom he will come into contact. For the present however, we are dealing only with the basics as they were first taught to me by David.

Possession is not the only danger to a careless psychic. Your aura, if not properly sealed, can be penetrated by thought impulses from entities who never enter the aura itself and not all of these souls are drifting around in the Astral. Some of them live right here in the physical and are deliberately manipulating the energies at their disposal. This is not always done for a sinister purpose. Many talented psychics use this method to perform acts of healing upon people who are some distance away. Others, not so altruistic, manipulate others for reasons of their own, usually selfish and never beneficial for the person being used. When psychic energy is being used in order to penetrate the aura of another being with malicious intent, we call it psychic attack.

I fell victim to an attack of this type a few years ago and it reached the point where I became physically ill before I was made aware of what was going on.

Through an acquaintance in a psychic research group, I became friendly with a lady who affected a very deep friendship for me and took a great interest in our activities as psychics. She was almost constantly on my doorstep and seemed most eager to sit for hours in deep conversation with me. At first I was quite happy to have her company but as time wore on I became listless and weary almost constantly. I did not associate this feeling with my lady visitor. I simply thought that I had contracted some virus which would no doubt clear up in time.

The malaise did not ease. In fact it became worse and when it reached the point where I started to suffer frequent giddy spells and found great difficulty in dragging myself out of bed in the mornings, I decided that I needed to see a doctor. His opinion was that I was suffering from anaemia and he took a number of blood tests, which revealed that there was nothing at all wrong with my blood, nor could any infection be isolated.

At this point, I decided to consult the guides, for I reasoned that if the cause of my malady was not physical, then it must be originating from the psyche. I was told that this lady was coolly and deliberately draining my energy from me for her own use and I was told how to close down my defences so that my energy was no longer available to her.

Whenever I was in her company, I was to imagine that I was enclosed in a glass bubble, through which no energy could escape. I was also to keep my mind firmly set on the idea that she would not be able to reach through that protective sheath. I did this, and although I said nothing to her about it, it was not very long before she lost interest in my friendship and her visits ceased.

How does a person become exposed to these hazards? The most common way is presumed to be a lighthearted involvement in occult activities, unaccompanied by any real understanding of the principles involved. This is certainly an open invitation to psychic abuse, but it is not the only means by which unpleasantness can be encountered.

If you intend to carry out any form of psychic activity, it is highly advisable that you be aware of the dangers and that you learn how to avoid them. However, avoidance of psychic activity itself is no guarantee of safety, particularly if you possess any noticeable level of psychic ability.

Some people believe that if they never have anything to do with psychics or psychic phenomena, they will automatically be protected against danger. This is a dangerous misconception because what is in operation here is a natural law which affects everyone, regardless of whether or not they acknowledge its existence. I have seen small children who do not know the meaning of the word 'psychic' infested by as many as seven entities at once.

The natural law which affects this area is one of attraction and repulsion or, in simpler terms, 'like attracts like'. This does not necessarily mean that if you attract an unpleasant entity, you must be unpleasant yourself, it is more a matter of vibrations. I do not particularly like using that word, because 'vibrations' is a term which has been greatly over-used and not always in the correct way, however it does apply to this field of activity and so it must be understood in the proper context.

During psychic development you are working to

increase the quality of your psychic energy. Note, I said quality, not strength. Some of the lowest forms of psychic energy are immensely powerful. Energy has a resonance, or vibrationary pattern, that is capable of affecting other forms of energy. In physical terms, Caruso was reputed to have shattered glass with the vibrations of some of his top notes. He was using a certain vibrationary frequency in order to achieve a desired effect. As you develop your understanding, you refine your energy and we say that you progress upwards, or that you raise your vibrations.

You are continually broadcasting on your own vibrationary frequency and as a result you announce yourself to other beings who are attuned to that frequency and they can draw close to you. High vibrations attract highly developed beings and vice versa. It is quite impossible for a vibrationary link to be formed between two people on totally different wavelengths; there is simply no point at which the two can merge.

People on a low wavelength would remain unaware of the presence of higher beings from the spiritual spheres even if those beings did approach them, for the same reason that human beings are unable to detect the high-pitched sound of a dog whistle. The vibrations are outside of the range of perception.

To reach a communication with your guide, you work at raising your own vibrations. Many things can assist you in this: knowledge and understanding, contentment, happiness, fulfilment, tranquillity, positive emotions such as love and compassion. Any and all of these and many others can be of great assistance.

Other influences can have the reverse effect and actually bring your vibrations down. Harsh emotions such as anger and hatred, alcohol and certain drugs; these things not only lower your vibrations but they also weaken your aura's resistance to penetration. Perhaps the most insidious trap of all is simple illness. When your vitality and vibrations are lowered, you must be on guard against the entities who operate permanently on a similar wavelength.

I am by no means insisting that you should never allow alcohol to pass your lips and it is obvious that I cannot instruct you never to fall ill. What is advisable is that you do not attempt any form of psychic activity while such influences are in force in your body.

When you are feeling tired, off-colour, irritable, or sick, read a book, watch television, or indulge in some favourite hobby or other pastime. Do anything except attempt psychic activity of any kind. It is not only the beginner who can be adversely affected if this warning is ignored; no matter how highly developed you are, you can still fall victim to psychic infestation if you do not take proper care. It has happened to me on occasions when I have not been as careful as I should. At those times, help was immediately available to me but the fact remains that I should have taken more care.

I once walked into a situation which was potentially lethal when I should have known better. I had been working with a woman who was having trouble with earthbound entities in her house. The place was full of them and they were causing all kinds of problems for her. She made several visits to our home, and on each occasion it was necessary for us to clear her aura of one or two entities which had clung to her.

She was due to go into hospital for a major operation and she was highly apprehensive about it, so to dispel her nerves, she decided to throw a party on the eve of her admittance. She wanted all of her friends to be present and she begged Roland and me to go also. At the time I was suffering from a heavy dose of influenza and could hardly stand up but she was so importunate that I did not want to disappoint her. Roland strongly advised me to stay home and so did my friend Helen Iddon, who was also going to the party. However, after taking a few 'flu capsules, I pronounced myself ready for anything.

I had been at the party for about fifteen minutes when I suddenly felt as though all of my energy had drained away from me. I sagged and almost fell from my chair. Roland and Helen rushed to my side and my hostess took charge and led me into her bedroom, telling me to lie down for a while and see how I felt after a rest.

As I lay on the bed, she bent over to take my shoes off for me, just as Helen and Roland walked through the door. Helen looked grim and when she spoke, I was startled by the ferocity of her words.

'That's no physical illness, get her the hell out of here—*now*!'

I could not find the energy or the will to move and had it been left to me, I would have lain where I was, but Helen would not hear of it. She and Roland manhandled me into a sitting position and between the two of them, they virtually carried me out to our car. I'm sure Roland broke a few speed rules getting me home, and once we were inside our own house, I felt fine and I couldn't imagine what had come over me at the party.

The following day, Helen called to see us and while she was there, Roland tranced and David arrived. Helen asked about the previous night. She said that when she had seen me lying on the bed, she had felt the distinct impression that she was looking at a dead body. I might add that Helen is a qualified nursing sister with a very practical, no-nonsense attitude to life, who does not panic even in the most pressurised situations.

David told us that my grip on the physical had become extremely tenuous, weakened by the severity of the influenza and the drugs I had taken. Under attack by the entities present in the house, I had been defenceless. In his words 'The soul was withdrawing and what lay on the bed was an emptying shell'.

'Phew!' I breathed, 'I didn't know it was that close.'

'My daughter,' said the guide in a gently grave tone, 'you must never forget the rules that you have been taught. You are not immune to danger.'

The best protection that you can have is the constant presence of your own guide, and I am sure it was David who galvanised Helen into action when I needed immediate help. A guide is continually on guard to defend you against attack. However, even with such communication established, the link becomes tenuous if you yourself do not take care.

In addition to avoiding psychic activity when your vibrations have been lowered, it is also highly inadvisable to attempt to carry out any activity that you do not fully understand. You would not attempt to operate a complicated piece of machinery if you did not know how it worked, and the psychic machinery is equally dangerous to those who do not know the laws of its operation.

Remember also that protection is available to you from the spiritual spheres themselves. No matter which particular religious affiliation you may have or by what name you call the Creator, a prayer for protection before proceeding with psychic activity is always beneficial. It will draw to you those spirits whose task it is to provide protection. A prayer will also bring help to you if you should encounter problems while operating in the psychic spheres.

If you have any reason to believe that you have run into trouble or that someone close to you has collected an astral entity, don't attempt to deal with the situation yourself, unless you have had the necessary training and experience. Dealing with this kind of infestation takes a great amount of training; it is not a beginner's pastime. If you suspect that something has gone wrong, seek out someone reputable and qualified, who knows how to deal with the problem. If you do not know anyone with these qualifications, perhaps a call to the local Psychic Research Association or Spiritualist Church could bring you the name of someone who can help.

You would not attempt to drive a car if you had never been taught how to drive and if you had no knowledge of the road rules. You would also be rather obtuse if you were unaware that some of the drivers you are likely to encounter may present a danger to you. While driving, you take care to avoid the wild thrill-seekers and the weaving drunks, because these people present a hazard to you. Common sense tells you to be fully prepared for sudden threats from other drivers.

It is the same with psychic activity. Stay within the sphere of action to which your knowledge and experience is attuned. Don't try to operate in areas where you are unsure of the terrain and where unknown hazards may abruptly confront you. As your vibrations become more highly attuned, you will automatically progress into higher areas of development, but it will in that case be done in safety. Don't try to attempt anything before you are ready. Like road safety, psychic protection is largely a matter of knowing the conditions under which you operate and abiding by the rules.

CHAPTER FOURTEEN
Guide structure and the links

After teaching me about the basic structure of the spiritual worlds (and it *is* a very basic understanding, since the actuality is one that the human mind would find difficult, if not impossible to encompass) David turned my attention to the actual guide structure and the links that make it work. It is one thing to accept something simply because it happens, but if you are going to have any control over your own role in the proceedings, it is also necessary to understand what makes it work. As always, David's lessons were simple and began with the most basic concepts, closest to the things that I already understood. As a teacher, he is gifted in a way that I could never hope to emulate, for my knowledge is nowhere near as expansive as his. The best that I can do is paraphrase his lessons and put them into a terminology that we humans can best relate to and therefore understand.

I was surprised and gratified to find that in doing this, I was fulfilling one of the purposes that David had in mind for me, for he told me that he wished me to work as a translator for him. His last incarnation in this world was over two thousand years ago and he is unfamiliar with the English language and with the way life is viewed by people of our time. I must say that this does not seem to affect his keen insight, for he often shows a far greater understanding of me than I have of myself.

David had been training me to work as a teacher, so that I could pass on his teachings to those who wish to know them. In doing this work, I became a link in the chain of information. I formed a part of David's work. That gave me a real feeling of belonging. But it was not enough for me to know that I functioned in this way; I had to understand how the chain of communication works, both so that I could make the best possible use of it and also so that I could explain it to others. So, let us discuss the beings who function as spirit guides, in particular, their relationship with us, how the guide structure operates and why we need such a system in the first place.

Roland and I are not in the business of putting people in touch with deceased relatives. In fact, as far as psychic work is concerned, we are not in business at all, because we feel the information we have to give to those who seek us out is too valuable to bear a price tag. But for the sake of the exercise and to give us a starting point, let us assume that you know virtually nothing about the spiritual spheres, but you have a desire to contact a person who dwells within them. How would you go about it?

If the person you sought were living in the physical, the method would be simple. You would merely pick up your telephone and dial his number. Let's say that your friend lives in another state or a district some distance away from your area. To telephone him, you would first dial the area code for his district. This would connect you through a series of exchanges to the main receiving exchange in his city. When you dialled the local prefix, your call would travel through other links until it reached the local exchange in your friend's district. The last digits would connect you with your friend.

All of this happens very quickly and you are not really aware of the complicated switching that is taking place while you dial the number. You play your part by dialling the numbers and you trust that the telecommunications system will do the rest.

If your friend is no longer living in the physical, you need another means of communication. If you are developed enough to have lines of communication established with your own guide, the procedure is simple. If not, you would need to find someone who could make the connection for you.

There have always been and always will be people who claim to be mediums. Some of them are, some are not, but those who are genuine have a guide structure set up and this enables them to communicate with the 'other side'. You can visit one of those mediums and ask them to make the connection for you. They then become your first link—or exchange—in your line of communication.

Perhaps you wish to contact Uncle Fred who died five years ago. How do these mediums go about making the connection? They cannot locate Uncle Fred themselves because they know nothing about him. They have no idea of what his personality is like, or where in the spiritual spheres he is to be found.

The medium forms a connection through the recognized guide structure. The medium will contact the next link: this could be a higher astral entity or one of the guardians and this person carries the connection through to the medium's guide. The guide contacts Uncle Fred's guide, who locates Uncle Fred and the connection is made. You and Uncle Fred may then speak to each other through this line of communication.

You can see that there are similarities between this procedure and the one that takes place when you make a telephone call. The difference, of course, is that it takes place on a non-physical or psychic level.

A psychic medium is just what the name implies—a medium, or channel through which the psychic worlds can reach us. A medium is a bridge, connecting this level of existence with another. Messages between the levels are relayed through them and all the links in the chain of communication function in the same way as the medium. Roland refers to his trancing as 'playing switchboards', which is not so far removed from the truth. The medium himself is not an oracle, he is just the channel through which information can be relayed. Occasionally we have met people who expect us to be able to predict world events or the results of a horse race simply because we claim to be psychic. We find that most annoying, because we are simply not in that line of activity, and anyone who thinks of our work in that way has patently misunderstood what we are trying to do.

Although the connections are established with great rapidity, it seems rather a complicated way of making a connection with a person who is living in the psychic spheres. Is it really necessary to arrange things in this way?

Let's go back to the radio set I mentioned in the last chapter. It operates on a set frequency and it will pick up broadcasts within the range of that frequency and none other. The police radio is a different system and operates

157

on a frequency beyond the range of the average domestic radio. No matter how energetically you twiddled the dial, you could not receive a police broadcast on your mantel radio.

As a physical being, you operate within a set range of vibrationary frequencies. You must, in order to stay here. You have physical senses which receive frequencies within the range of the physical. The average range of human hearing is between 80 cycles and 16,500 cycles. There are sound frequencies which lie outside that range, but we cannot hear them. Yet we do not insist that they are not there, just because they are inaudible to us.

The human hearing listens to what is known as a window across the sound spectrum. Our visual range operates within limits too: the ranges of light frequency are measured in angstroms. This is a window through which we view the light spectrum frequency.

The infra-red frequency is above our audio range but below our range of vision. An infra-red camera detects heat in frequencies but we can neither see it nor hear it. We cannot see or hear x-rays either, but if you were to stand in front of an x-ray machine for long enough you would certainly be able to observe the results. These rays are very high frequency and are capable of penetrating body tissue. Prolonged exposure to them would do untold damage to your body.

Some of our sittings with David can last up to two hours and we have been holding sittings on a regular basis for several years. Could you imagine the results if David were operating on an x-ray frequency and we had been directly exposed to him for that length of time? The damage to our bodies would by now be irreparable. David's vibrations are undoubtedly much higher than x-ray frequency and we could not stand such power in close proximity to us. Yet for us to progress in knowledge it is necessary for us to have extended access to that frequency.

In the physical we operate within a window of frequencies. Immediately above us, the Astral also operates in a window which steps down into the physical and ranges on up, to the Void. For the sake of our exercise, we will say that the physical range is from A to B

158

and the Astral ranges from B to C. The next level is the Void, to which we will allocate a frequency range between C and D, and D will represent the lower range in the first level of spiritual existence. Our guide may be operating on H frequency, which is way above the limits of our physical perception. How does he get his frequency—his transmission—onto our receiver here in the physical?

He steps it down. He transmits at his lower range, which is the higher range of the level below him. Someone on that level receives his signal and converts it down to his own lower frequency, feeding it out at that level to the next and so on, until it reaches physical range.

When it reaches physical frequency we can detect it. If it is spoken through a medium we hear it; if your ashtray lifts off and does a rapid aerial circuit of your living room you will certainly observe it visually. Should this energy come close and touch you, you will feel it, probably as gooseflesh or a prickling sensation on the back of your neck.

Since all of this is possible, why should you bother spending so much time and energy in an effort to raise your own vibrations?

As the energy is swept down from its origin, it is progressively filtered so that it reaches us at a level we can comprehend. It has gone through a number of links and the signal has been weakened to our tolerance level. Now what happens when you put a high-fidelity record onto your stereo and play it with the volume turned as low as it will go? You lose most of the bass and mid-range tones; in other words, you miss out on a great deal of the transmission.

If we raise our vibrations high enough, we can eliminate one of the links in our chain of communication and receive the signal at a higher level of comprehension. We could take our message direct from the Void instead of receiving it through the Astral.

Scientists know that if they place photographic equipment into a rocket and fire it off into space, they can photograph the stars with more clarity than would be possible if they set up their cameras at ground level. Although the atmosphere is less dense than the earth, it is quite thick in comparison with the space that surrounds it and because of this comparative density, it bends light rays as they pass through it. It also contains a great deal of pollution and like a misted glass it will obscure certain details of the images that are viewed through it.

A similar principle affects the impulses which travel through the Astral. Although they are still coherent, they lose a certain amount of clarity. If you raise your vibrations so that you can launch yourself into the Void, you will be able to receive the signals with a greater strength and clarity and you will be able to direct your energy with greater effect.

When you raise your vibrations to this extent, you achieve something more than clear reception. You eliminate the necessity for further reincarnations because you no longer need the shelter of the physical world. It is only necessary for you to remain here for as long as you are unable to tolerate the higher frequency levels which operate in the spiritual spheres.

When you are capable of operating in the Void, there is no longer any need for you to have psychic energy filtered down to you at a physical tolerance level. Some psychic mediums are able to communicate with spiritual entities at a higher level than others; the first link for some may be an astral entity and then a guardian, whilst others can link directly with a guardian. They are connected through further links to their guides. There are, for instance, five links between Roland and David, and each one is capable of speaking through Roland himself.

What lies beyond the guide? When you reach his level, have you progressed as far as it is possible to go or is there something more? David has told us that there is. While he guides us, he is in turn guided by beings higher than himself. No doubt these beings are also guided by others, but there must be some point at which all things culminate. Somewhere in the heavens, there has to be someone who sits at a big desk and says: 'The buck stops here'. There is, and this supreme being is the Creator. Ultimately, all of the teachings come from him.

Every religion in the world recognizes a God of some kind. Whether that being is known as Krishna, Allah, Jehovah, or Mr Smith, what is being acknowledged is that somewhere there exists a supreme being who created everything that exists.

There is a school of thought which subscribes to the 'Big Bang' theory, suggesting that the heavens were formed as the result of a tremendous cosmic explosion. Go out of doors some fine evening and contemplate the stars—hundreds of millions of them. In size, most of them would make our planet look like a speck of dust. That is an awful lot of rock, floating around out there.

Imagine it all joined together in one lump—one incomprehensibly large rock— and then suddenly going *bang*! Then try to work out how the rock got there in the first place and what kind of energy source it would take to cause something that huge to explode into smithereens.

One of Roland's favourite jokes concerns a little boy who held a grasshopper in his hand and said:

'Hey, Grasshopper, did you know that all the flowers and all the birds, everything in the whole world, was made by God? Would you like to see God, little grasshopper?' So saying, the child squashes the creature with his fist. Put yourself in the grasshopper's place for a moment; imagine its view of the little boy and the impression of awesome power a small child would produce in a creature so tiny. Then multiply the sensation of power to an almost incomprehensible degree and we will say that degree of power represents the Creator.

How would you feel if that degree of power walked into your living room and said: 'I would like a cup of coffee. *Now!*' I'll bet you'd find some biscuits to go with it! Now, if that degree of power looked at you over the rim of its cup and said: 'Four seconds from now, I am going to annihilate you', apart from thinking that it is a strange way to say thanks for the cup of coffee, what would you do? The sheer inevitability of it would be overwhelming.

Of course I am not suggesting that the Creator would do any such thing; I am just asking you to imagine that amount of power being unleashed upon you. Even if it was unleashed in all sincerity and kindness, it could still be totally, sincerely, kindly, *wrong* and be the means of your total destruction. The mere act of opening your front door to that amount of energy would be enough to

161

blow your whole neighbourhood to kingdom come!

As the Bible says: No man can look upon the face of God and live. We simply cannot withstand that amount of energy. Yet this God created you and knows how your development needs to be directed. Somehow he must get his message through to you, and he must do it without causing you any harm. So he filters it through the guide structure, cutting down the power until it reaches our tolerance level.

We tend to think of the human body as an incredible device and so it is. We can do marvellous things with it. But it will neither fly through the air nor breathe under water. A dog can hear a wider range of sound than we do and the tiniest microbe can make us so ill that we die. When we think about it in those terms, the human body is really frail and its range of abilities is severely limited.

The resonance frequency used by the guides cannot be detected with our physical senses, so it is broken down in stages. There may be as many as fifteen or twenty links between you and your guide and yet there is no time lag when you speak with him. You do not have to wait while your words travel along a network of links because outside the physical there is no time; there is only one continuous *now*.

Psychic development is spiritual growth and all growth arises out of understanding. If we understand what happens when we are working with the guides and know that these links exist, if we understand how the system works, then it becomes easier to operate within it.

Since I have mentioned the Void a number of times, you could presume that the function of the Void is quite important, and this is true. It forms a buffer zone between the Astral plane and the spiritual spheres. I have mentioned that the guardians act to deflect any intruders who are not sufficiently developed to enter the spiritual planes: you could assume from this that the guardians do this work so that the spiritual planes cannot be contaminated by the presence of low entities and this is true. But it also works in the interests of the entities themselves, whether they realise it or not.

Think of being locked in a sound chamber while high frequency sound is fed continuously through a speaker at maximum volume. It would not take very long to drive you mad. The effect of being surrounded by powerful, high-frequency vibrations such as those which operate in the spiritual spheres would be much the same if you were not ready to be exposed to them. You can understand from this the importance of preventing the undeveloped souls from reaching through the Void.

Every person who works with a highly advanced guide has the responsibility of functioning as a guardian and this is something that Roland and I must bear in mind when we hold sittings with David. We have found, through trial and error, that even when David's energy is filtered down to the higher ranges of our tolerance, there are people who cannot withstand it, because even within our own sphere, the individual levels of tolerance can differ a great deal.

We once had a visitor who was a competent psychic in his own right and is quite an authority on the subject of Astral travel. We had been corresponding for some time and he expressed a profound desire to have an opportunity of speaking with David. When he finally came to Sydney for a holiday, a sitting was arranged. David had been speaking for a few minutes when things started to go wrong. Our visitor first showed signs of stertorous breathing and gasped for air quite alarmingly. Then his arms and legs stiffened and began to jerk as though he were having a fit.

David urgently warned me that this man was simply unable to tolerate the high energy level and that he (David) would have to leave. With that, he departed and Roland awoke from the trance. Our visitor was semi-conscious and jerking convulsively and it was several minutes before we could restore him to normality. Since that time, we have been very reluctant to hold sittings for people who request an audience with David unless we have first established by degrees that they are able to withstand the high energy levels generated by the guide's presence. In that respect, Roland and I are functioning as guardians.

That explains the purpose of the guardians, but have you thought of the possibility that the Void itself may carry out certain functions? It does and we can

163

understand them quite easily if we begin with a game of imagination.

You are a mad scientist and you have hatched a diabolical plot to poison the entire city's water supply. You have collected some virulent bacteria and cultured them on a glass plate which you have hidden in your drain, where the bugs have a nice, moist, smelly environment in which to flourish. Unfortunately for you, Superman or Wonder Woman (or some other Caped Crusader) gets wind of your scheme and destroys all of your carefully concocted plans by swiping your precious plate and hurling it into outer space, where the sterile environment kills off all your lovely, lethal bugs. All that remains is a clean glass plate orbiting a distant asteroid. And one badly bruised mad scientist.

As personalities, we are also cultured within the physical environment. From infancy we are taught what is and is not acceptable behaviour within our society and we build for ourselves a façade which fulfills those requirements. It is like a mask, which conceals the true personality and shows others only that which we wish them to see. Jung called it the persona. We become so accustomed to wearing this mask that we sometimes believe it to be our true personality. When we do something that is out of character with the qualities we expect from the persona, we are bewildered with ourselves.

How often have you said to yourself: 'Now, why did I do that? That isn't me at all'. I have news for you—if you did it, it's you all right!

When you enter the Void you must leave the persona behind, because it has no place in the spiritual spheres. It belongs to the physical and that is where it must remain. As the sterile environment in outer space stripped away the microbes from our hypothetical glass plate, so the Void strips away the persona, revealing you just as you are—warts and all. It is because of this that the guardians can instantly tell whether or not you have any business being in the Void and whether you should be firmly sent back to your place of origin.

Remember, it is not 'sin' which renders you unacceptable. It is a simple matter of development. It would make

164

no sense to enrol a child at university if he were still struggling with the kindergarten curriculum, and there would be as little point in allowing an undeveloped soul to enter the higher spheres. For the time being, your aim is to reach the Void. When you do, however, it is not the end of the story, but the beginning. From that point onwards you can *really* do some developing and it will be all the more enjoyable because you will fully understand what it is you are trying to do.

CHAPTER FIFTEEN
Clairvoyance, clairaudience, trance principles

I have occasionally encountered some odd looks when I have mentioned to an acquaintance that I am psychic. Strangely enough, if I say that I am interested in parapsychology, the same reaction does not occur anywhere near as often. It is almost as though there is something odd or abnormal about being psychic. Of course there is not; we are all endowed with psychic faculties, whether we recognise them or not. It is through these abilities that we are linked to the spiritual. Spiritual messages reach us via our psychic senses, so it is desirable to have a good understanding of how this communication takes place on a physical level.

In a discussion of this nature, we can only generalise because it would be unfair to assume that there is a copybook standard to which all psychics must conform. However, certain elements are common to all communications that reach the physical through spiritual senses and we can become familiar with these. It gives us some idea of what to expect.

Communication is a broad subject, so for the sake of convenience, I will break it down into categories:

· Clairvoyance and visions
· Clairaudience

- Automatic writing
- Conscious communication
- Trance mediumship

CLAIRVOYANCE

This is just what its name implies—clear vision. I have already mentioned that physical vision is restricted within a certain span of light frequencies. Radiations on a frequency outside that range would be invisible to ordinary eyesight.

If you are clairvoyant, you have the ability to see on a wider scale of frequencies; you can see things that are invisible to other people and you do it quite naturally. You may not even realise that other people cannot do it. I know of a few people who think it is quite normal to see a play of colours around the heads of other people, and they have been very surprised to be told that what they are seeing is the human aura, which is invisible to almost everybody else.

The normal range of human perception has widened progressively over the centuries, so that the average person today is capable of seeing a wider spectrum than our ancestors knew. Several scholars have pointed out that Xenophanes knew of only three colours in the rainbow: purple, red and yellow, and even Aristotle referred to 'the tri-coloured rainbow'. Today we class people as being colour-blind if they are unable to see colours of a certain light frequency. However, it would seem more realistic to say that their eyesight has not developed according to current standards of vision. There may actually be nothing wrong with their eyes, it could be that their ability to interpret what they are seeing is limited.

On the other hand, a clairvoyant sees *beyond* the accepted 'normal' range of eyesight, so perhaps we could say that in comparison to a clairvoyant, *all* people are colour-blind! A clairvoyant impression can register in one of two ways. I explained the function of thought in an earlier chapter and I told you that the brain itself will translate into a physical frequency anything that is imprinted onto it. Whatever you see on levels outside the physical will become a conscious impression for you in some way.

Just as you can close your eyes and picture a remembered scene in your mind's eye, an impression reaching you from the spiritual may be seen in the same way. You see something in your mind as though you are imagining it, but it is really reaching you from another dimension of existence.

Alternatively, you may see it as though you are physically looking at it, although it will be totally invisible to someone standing beside you. That is why one or two people in a group may clearly see an apparition while their companions remain unaware of it.

Clairvoyance can be literal or symbolic. If you are exploring an old house at midnight and you suddenly came face to face with a ghost, you would be seeing literally. Under less eerie circumstances, you may see spirit forms during a psychic circle, or seance. Either way, you are seeing what is actually there and your impressions are therefore literal.

You are seeing symbolically if your vision must be interpreted before it can be understood in a physical sense. For instance, you might see a blazing sword embed itself in a stone—it makes no sense until the symbolism behind it is unravelled. A good example of this kind of clairvoyance can be found in the Bible, with the dream of King Nebuchadnezzar. In the dream, the monarch saw an image which had a head of gold, chest and arms of silver, lower body and thighs of brass, and legs of iron. The feet were of mixed iron and clay.

He watched a large stone, 'cut out without hands', as it struck the feet of the image, shattering it into tiny pieces. Daniel interpreted the dream by saying that the head of gold symbolised the kingdom of Nebuchadnezzar, whilst the lower portions were lesser kingdoms that would follow. The stone that shattered the image, however, represented the kingdom of God, which will ultimately overcome all worldly empires.

Since time only exists within the physical dimension it stands to reason that when you are seeing clairvoyantly you will not be restricted to any time period. You operate in the psychic, timeless zone. You can watch a scene that is currently taking place in another part of the world; you can see an event take place before it actually happens or

167

you can observe an historical scene that occurred hundreds of years before you were born.

Clairvoyance sometimes opens the way to some amusing incidents. I remember one occasion when a young lady named Sue visited our house for the first time. She was with her boyfriend, who was very interested in our psychic activities and had told her about them. Sue was inclined to be sceptical, but she was curious to know a little about what being a psychic entailed. She asked me what kind of things I was able to know about other people. Immediately I had a mental image of an illuminated sign which read 'Dentist'. I gave Sue a gleeful smile.

'Are you planning to go to the dentist, or have you already been?' I asked. Her face was a study in awestruck amazement. She gasped 'I went yesterday! How did you know that?'

I grinned. 'I would never be able to explain,' I answered.

As this chapter is concerned with the various terms with which you will come into contact when speaking with other psychics and as the purpose of the exercise is to give you an understanding of those terms, we will not go deeply into the techniques of application at this point. I prefer that you undertake more meditation and then go into the actual techniques in the next chapter.

However, there is an exercise that I would like you to begin, in order to facilitate the opening of your psychic channels a little further. You must have a little understanding of the techniques before you can fully understand the following items of information. I want you to think of yourself as a detached observer. Relax yourself as you have done in the past, let your physical self go and *observe what is happening to you*.

Don't try to influence your thoughts, emotions or senses but take note of the thoughts or sensations you experience. This is not going to be easy at first but persevere. You can practise it if you like but don't neglect your regular meditation period; that is of utmost importance.

CLAIRAUDIENCE

The principle behind clairaudience is much the same as

in clairvoyance except of course that instead of seeing things, you hear them. As with clairvoyance, the impression can reach you in either of two ways: you may actually hear voices speaking to you or you might carry on a silent conversation in your head. It is easy in the latter case to assume that both sides of the conversation arise in your own consciousness and sometimes this is so, but often when we think we are talking to ourselves we are actually conversing with another spirit.

It takes some practice to learn the difference, but eventually you begin to recognize a certain feeling that accompanies the words, a slight air of authority, that tells you this communication is coming from elsewhere. Often this 'still, small voice' will tell you things about which you had no prior knowledge, yet which prove correct in every detail. In such a case, you could be almost positive that this is an instance of clairaudience.

I usually experience clairaudience in the 'silent conversation' form, but there have been occasions when I have actually heard voices. Once I was standing in a shop, waiting to be served, when I heard a lilting female voice, just over my right shoulder, calling my name. I spun around at once, but there was no one standing anywhere near me. Nor was there anyone in the shop who was known to me. At a later sitting I asked the guides if this had indeed been clairaudience or if it had been my imagination. I was told that it had been a spirit voice that I had heard. When I asked what had been the purpose of the call, I received the reply: 'Just testing'.

No other person can teach you how to tell the difference between this kind of communication and simple wishful thinking. This is where your own discrimination needs to be applied to the full.

During my nursing days, I fell ill and had to take several days off work during a course of lectures and I missed a number of important lessons. I borrowed notebooks from the other students and studied my heart out each night, but as the course drew to a close and the end of term examination approached, I became quite nervous about my chances in the subjects in which I had missed several lectures. On the day of the exams, I sent out a mental SOS to the guides.

'I'm not asking you to give me the answers to questions that I would not normally know,' I told them, 'I am just asking you to help me remember clearly everything I have studied, so that my marks will not be too low.'

I was quite relieved to discover that I had adequate knowledge to cope with most of the questions, but there were two in particular in which I simply had to take a guess. They were multiple choice questions, in which I had to select the right answer from a group of four. With each question, I instinctively made to answer in a certain way, which my reason told me could not be correct, so I went along with my head instead of my instincts, arguing furiously with myself the whole time.

When the examination results came back, I found that my 'instinctive' answer would have been the correct one. Later on, in another sitting, I was told that I had been given the assistance of a spirit doctor and he was not at all impressed with my argumentative attitude when he tried to help me with those answers!

Joan of Arc was clairaudient; she heard voices which told her what to do and it was by following the guidance of her unseen friends that she carried out a number of successful campaigns for the King of France. Because of her ability and the prevailing religious fancies, she was burned as a witch, but five hundred years later the church relented and made her a saint. I'm not sure whether Joan was impressed, but it was a nice gesture!

Another saint provides an example of a psychic who used clairvoyance and clairaudience together. This is Bernadette, who as a young girl saw a vision of a beautiful woman, whom she believed to be the Virgin Mary. The vision conversed with her on several occasions although people who accompanied her were unable either to see or hear the lovely lady. Bernadette heard the ethereal visitor ask to have a shrine erected on the site of the visitation and this is now the healing sanctuary of Lourdes.

AUTOMATIC WRITING

In automatic writing your own psychic ability is functioning, but instead of retaining the information as it reaches you, you allow it to flow through you, causing your hand to form the appropriate words with a pen. You

170

may be aware of the words before they are written or you might have no awareness of them until you read the script. Either way is valid.

There is no reason why you should not be able to perceive a message clairvoyantly and clairaudiently as it is being written, is is simply dependent upon how active your psychic senses happen to be at the time. I often get mental pictures accompanied by words or phrases, and by putting them together I can work out what the message is meant to be.

Some time ago, my ex-husband rang me to ask if he could take Darryl away for the weekend. Immediately I had an overwhelming negative reaction and it was all I could do to stop myself from shouting 'No!'. I managed to keep my cool and instead I suggested that Dennis call in on his way out of the city and we would discuss it. My excuse was that I needed a little time to consider.

After finishing the telephone conversation I sat down to think. I decided to meditate and try to get some specific information from the guides.

'It's no good just telling me to say no,' I explained in my mind, 'you have to give me a logical reason.' The picture that flashed into my mind was reason enough. I saw a cream-coloured sedan with the rear passenger-side caved in from a collision. Knowing that Darryl normally goes to sleep on the back seat during a long journey, it did not take long for me to deduce what this meant.

There was still a problem, however, because of Dennis's attitude to psychic phenomena. He would simply not accept an intuitive flash as reason enough to deprive Darryl of a trip to the country.

'Help me,' I begged the guides. 'Give me a good reason for refusing.'

Ten minutes before Dennis arrived, Darryl began to wheeze. By the time his father walked in the door, a full-blown asthma attack was in progress. I tried to hide my relief as I pointed out that the child was obviously not well enough to go anywhere. At the time, Dennis did not own a car and he had hired one for the journey. When I saw that it was a cream sedan, I decided to try to warn him against taking the trip. Naturally he dismissed my warning with a smile.

'Still into all that psychic nonsense?' he grinned. 'I'll be all right, you'll see.'

No sooner had Dennis departed than Darryl's asthma attack stopped as suddenly as it had begun. We did not see Dennis for several weeks after that, and when he next visited he had a story to tell us. On his way back to the city, he had been coming down a mountain road when a semi-trailer behind him lost its brakes and careered into the rear passenger side of the car that Dennis was driving. Dennis had spent the next few days in hospital, but Darryl, who would no doubt have been asleep on the back seat, might easily have been killed.

Some people operate exclusively on a clairvoyant level, others only use clairaudience. Some use both in conjunction with still other senses. There is no arbitrary pattern. Most people have a predominant sense which they tend to favour and it is certainly easy to slip into the habit of relying only on the dominant sense. There is nothing wrong with this, but I personally think it is better for you if you give the other senses a chance to develop also.

Your level of consciousness need not affect the quality of psychic behaviour. Psychic faculties can operate efficiently whether the psychic is conscious or not and for the sake of convenience we can divide mediums into two categories: those who operate on a conscious level and those who function as trance (or unconscious) mediums. Conscious communication can take any or all of the preceding forms. Whilst you remain wide awake you may describe visions or pass on spirit messages. You can simply relax and place yourself in a receptive state of mind, or you may work out some method of concentration best suited to your own personality.

One interesting message that I received in this way was delivered to a Maori lady in her own language. I speak no other language than English, and I was more surprised than she when the message for her came through in her own tongue. I received it syllable by syllable, phonetically.

If the idea appeals to you, you might decide to use a crystal ball, but remember that when you gaze into it and see pictures beginning to form, they are coming through your own consciousness. There is nothing magical about a crystal ball and in fact you could achieve the same results at considerably less expense by using a saucer full of black ink. If you do want to use a crystal ball, there are several things to remember. Firstly, the glass should have no flaws in it, otherwise there may be distracting light refractions which disturb your concentration. When not in use, it should be wrapped in a dark cloth and kept safely away from the light. It should not be exposed to bright light during the sitting because the light reflections could be unsettling for you. Like any inanimate object, it will absorb vibrations from anyone who handles it, so if you want it to remain a pure focus for your own subconscious, you should not allow anyone else to handle it.

You could use a ouija board as a very basic (and clumsy) method of automatic writing, but I strongly advise against this method because of the technique involved. When you use a ouija board, you issue an open invitation for spirit beings to take control and guide the planchette, spelling out the messages they wish to deliver. This is all very well if you are in direct communication with your own spirit guide, but if you are you will already have much more efficient methods of communication. Ouija boards are usually used by beginners with very little real knowledge, therefore they are likely to attract only lower astral entities and that can spell trouble.

The motion picture 'The Exorcist' is based on a factual case in which a young boy became possessed after playing with a ouija board. How much of the events dramatised in the movie actually happened I do not know but doubtless the child attracted an entity of the lowest kind and great suffering resulted, both for the child and his family. It is always wise to remember that there are evil beings in the next world, just as there are in this one, and to make sure that you do not carelessly expose yourself to them, for they are not easy to get rid of once they have taken a foothold.

CONSCIOUS VOICE COMMUNICATION AND TRANCING

These are similar in many ways, except for the obvious fact that in the former, the medium remains awake. He may hear a message clairaudiently and deliver it verbatim or he may be able to still his thoughts to such an extent that the guide can imprint a message directly onto the medium's brain, so that the body responds to a direct signal from the guide. This method is the one that I use. I suspect the reason lies in the fact that I am an inveterate stickybeak. I like to know what is going on and it would not thrill me at all to hear second-hand accounts of the scintillating conversations that took place during my nap.

Whether conscious or not, a medium is not a marvellous oracle. The messages which come through cannot be attributed to the medium as a person. A medium simply acts as a switchboard, providing a channel for communication between the spheres.

When spirit communication comes through me, I experience a curious sensation of detachment. I can feel my body moving and speaking yet the thought process which activates it is not my own. I have noticed distinctive changes in the tone and timbre of my voice, sometimes to a remarkable degree. On one occasion, I startled both myself and Roland by speaking in a very definitely masculine voice. I could even feel the difference. My voice vibrates in my throat but that time I could feel it rumbling somewhere in the region of my chest. It was a most intriguing sensation, but it has only ever happened once.

During communication, I am at once a participant and an observer, which is an odd sensation until one becomes accustomed to it. There is a dreamy quality about the experience yet I remain fully aware of everything that takes place.

Roland, on the other hand, can use either method. He is usually quite content to sleep while someone else does all the talking, and on those occasions he is functioning as a trance medium. He switches off his own consciousness and allows the guide to take control of his body. He begins each trance sitting by allowing himself to drift into unconsciousness, and depending on the prevailing circumstances, this can happen slowly or with some rapidity. Once he reaches the desired level of uncon-sciousness, there is a change in his breathing pattern. His breath comes in deep, rapid gasps for a few moments, which is the transition stage in which the guide is actually

174

taking over. After this, the breathing settles down to a regular rhythm.

Shortly after this, communication begins. His eyes may or may not open and his body may remain in one position or become quite animated—once again, there is no arbitrary pattern. What is significant is that the being now speaking is not Roland, but a completely independent personality. As with conscious mediumship, the personality shift can be mirrored in altered mannerisms and vocal characteristics (although I have to admit that I have never heard him speak with a female voice).

When a trance sitting ends, the procedure is reversed. The body goes to sleep and enters another phase of altered breathing, after which the medium awakens. Roland usually remembers nothing of the events that took place during his trance, but I have heard of mediums who can remember in vivid detail all of the trance proceedings, even though they were unconscious at the time.

While a medium is trancing it is advisable to have another person present, who is capable of acting as a control. This person sees to it that the medium comes to no physical harm. If an emergency should arise, it is the control's responsibility to ensure that the medium is safely awakened. The control also needs to be aware of the particular hazards which can threaten a trance medium, so that full protection can be assured.

It is *not* safe to awaken a trance medium by shaking or touching him in any way. An entranced medium should never be touched unless the spirit guide has first guaranteed that it can be done in safety (and obviously, you need to be very sure of your guide's ability). When a medium is entranced, his vibrations are raised to the highest physical level so that they can merge with those of the guide. Other people in the room will still operate on their accustomed levels, and for one of them to touch the medium would have an effect roughly equivalent to thrusting a knife into an electric toaster while it is switched on. A short-circuit of this kind can make a medium very ill and can even cause serious injury.

A trained control who works regularly with one medium and co-operates with the guide can learn to judge when it is safe to touch the medium, but wisely checks with the guide in any case. A control's first responsibility is to the medium. There is no place here for grandstanding or theatrical posing.

In our sittings I act as control for Roland and at these times I ask everyone to remain seated and to preserve a clear radius of three feet around Roland's chair. This is treated as 'off-limits' for the duration of the trance and it is done to ensure that he is not accidentally touched. Even after the trance has concluded, the sitters are warned not to touch Roland until several minutes have elapsed. This came about after an accident in which Roland received a painful injury.

We had concluded a sitting and I had left the room to make coffee for our guests. While I was in the kitchen, a conversation started and Roland began to argue with one of our guests, a girl named Jeanette, about a particular passage in the Bible. Jeanette took hold of a Bible and opened it at the appropriate section, offering it to Roland to read for himself. As she passed it to him, her fingertips lightly brushed his knee. The touch was so light that she hardly noticed it, but the effect on Roland was violently explosive. He cried out sharply in pain and doubled over, clutching at his knee. He later told us that the feeling had been as though someone had grabbed all the nerves in his knee and suddenly ripped them upwards. When we examined his knee, we found an angry raised welt, which took three weeks to subside. Poor Jeanette was full of abject apology, but it was an honest accident and if anyone was at fault, it was me, for not staying in the room until the danger period had passed. I have never made that mistake again. David later explained to me that the touch had actually 'earthed' Roland, and the built up psychic energy in his body had literally exploded outwards through his knee. I shudder to think what would happen if he were ever touched suddenly whilst in full trance.

I also greet the spirits when they begin to speak and establish their identities before allowing the sitting to continue. I will not pursue a conversation with a spirit which refuses to give its name any more than I would with an anonymous telephone caller. I must know to whom I

176

am speaking and that being's purpose for coming before I will proceed. Our guides always preface their conversation by giving their names or providing a key phrase which has previously been agreed upon. If they fail to do this, I remind them and even the most advanced of them will comply with good humour, for they know that I am only carrying out the instructions that have been given to me by David. It is a simple precaution against deception and one that I strongly recommend. A genuinely advanced guide has no reason to object and you have every reason to be suspicious of any character who is reluctant to identify himself.

A trance medium and control, functioning as a team, can become involved in some interesting procedures. Such a team can actively assist the spirits who work in the field of psychic rescue. The aim in this work is the formation of a link between the higher spirits and those who are earthbound, or trapped in the lower Astral.

Earthbound spirits vibrate on a low level and it may not be possible for higher beings to lower their own vibrations to the necessary degree. Although they might be able to do it, the chances are that their appearance would serve to alarm the spirit they are trying to assist. A physical person is a more familiar sight to an earthbound spirit and therefore more reassuring. Being at once in the physical and the spiritual, a medium can bridge the gap so that the rescuer can be linked with the earthbound personality. The lower spirits are actually drawn through the medium's aura as they are raised to a higher level of existence.

From a physical viewpoint, this procedure is quite interesting. The earthbound souls sometimes carry on a conversation, through the medium, during the process. This is one way in which the control can help to raise the earthbound soul: by explaining the situation and calming any fears the spirit may have, the control helps to increase that being's level of understanding and thus raise its vibrations. In a later chapter, I will be dealing with this subject in greater detail.

The importance of the control's ability to cope is stressed here, because what takes place during a rescue is very similar to possession, although of course it is done deliberately and under carefully controlled conditions. If the wrong move is made, however, the earthbound entity may become enmeshed in the medium's aura which can produce a difficult and potentially dangerous situation for all concerned. I have seen this happen only once, when a person panicked and made a sudden dive behind me as I was dealing with a particularly nasty entity. I would prefer not to see it again.

No matter what type of psychic ability you use, your energies are neutral in themselves. You choose whether you will use them for altruistic motives or purely selfish ones. The choice you make is entirely your own. You have free will and no advanced soul would ever attempt to force an influence upon you, even though it might seem to be in your own best interests. Higher souls carefully respect your freedom, but freedom also means that you are responsible for your own actions. It is wise to think carefully before you become involved in psychic activity and make very sure that you fully understand your own motives.

CHAPTER SIXTEEN
Development exercises

In this chapter I would like to share some development exercises that were given to us by David. They are quite simple in concept, but do not expect them to work magical or instantaneous results. They are designed to stimulate your psychic abilities and assist in the opening of your channels, but like anything else, these things take time. Perseverance and patience are needed, but if you keep at it, you will gradually achieve results. The degree of your success will depend on how sincerely you wish to develop properly and safely. Psychic development is not an area in which you should aim for rapid or startling results; it is in this respect a little like driving a car. It is much better to take your time and abide by some simple safety rules than to seek to astound your friends with your cleverness. Don't be tempted by people who ask you to show off, for they are only demonstrating their own lack of understanding You should develop these things for your own benefit and pay no attention to people who urge you to show off or take a quicker route to success. Cover the ground slowly and thoroughly and make sure that your foundations are firm.

Our advice is that you perform these exercises in conjunction with your meditation. How often you do them is a matter for your own discretion, but I would recommend that you limit yourself to what you can comfortably achieve. It is not advisable to force the pace and place undue stress on your energy levels.

Throughout the various segments of this book we have placed a certain amount of emphasis on your meditation periods. We have told you that meditation is the springboard from which you can reach the spiritual. By the time you have read this segment, you will have seen just how valuable your meditation periods can be.

If you follow the meditation routine regularly, you will eventually be able to experience what we call a 'reality shift'. When the mind is not absorbing stimuli from the physical, it turns to the non-physical, or spiritual plane, for its stimulation.

Have you ever noticed, when you have been deeply engrossed in a daydream, that it takes a few moments to collect your thoughts before you can readjust to the world around you? It is particularly noticeable if you are abruptly disturbed by a touch or a sudden noise. You might give a little start and blink in confusion for a moment or two. If you have company, you may say something like: 'Oh, I was miles away, off in a world of my own'. That is a reality shift. Your physical body, of course, has been in the same place all the time, but your attention has wandered. Your thoughts—your conscious awareness—had shifted from your immediate surroundings. Remember the cat I told you about in an earlier segment? While its mind was totally focused on the mice, it was oblivious to anything else and even failed to notice a loud noise.

At these times, there is an awareness in a corner of your mind that you are comfortably settled in the physical, but that awareness has dimmed to a semi-conscious level.

179

Your vitality is centred around your non-physical self. In a sense, you have withdrawn into yourself.

We asked you to meditate regularly, at the same time each day, in order to facilitate the connection between you and your higher self. At the time we likened it to sitting still and allowing time for a spotlight operator to get you into focus.

We asked you to imagine yourself as the spotlight operator, looking down onto the hustle and bustle of everyday life, trying to locate and focus on one person—that person being yourself. That was not an idle request. We asked you to do it for an important reason: we wanted you to divide your consciousness, to get your awareness onto a higher level.

It is common for people to assume that if they are consciously operating on a psychic level, concentrating on the spiritual environment which surrounds them, they must automatically be totally oblivious to the physical. This is not entirely so. You can watch events taking place in another part of the world on your television set: you do not have to actually leave your home and visit those other places to see and hear what is going on there. Except for certain types of high-level psychic activity, which usually involve trancing, most people are able to operate efficiently as psychics withoug losing touch with physical reality.

Exercise 1

This is a continuation of the imagery relating to the 'spotlight operator'. Understanding that the spotlight operator represents your higher self, relax and imagine yourself in that situation. Begin by relaxing for a few minutes as you do in your meditation period. Once your mind is quiescent and your body relaxed, imagine that you are sitting somewhere high, looking down upon someone who looks exactly like you. At the same time, imagine that you are focusing a beam of golden light which surrounds the person you are surveying.

If you like, you can vary this exercise by imagining that you are viewing yourself through a tunnel rather than from a high location. In fact, it is a good idea to do this, because it will help you to maintain flexibility of mind, which is always an asset in psychic development. It is only necessary to spend a couple of minutes on this exercise. The principle behind development lies in reinforcement by repeated practice rather than in bursts of extended activity.

The purpose of this exercise is to help you loosen the bonds that tie your attention to the physical and reinforce the sensation of awareness on a higher level of thought. Once you have mastered the technique of stepping away from the physical and lifting yourself above your accustomed level of thought, you will find that it becomes much simpler to deal with the problems that you encounter in everyday life. At 'ground level', it is often difficult to surmount your problems simply because you are unable to see beyond them. The development of psychic awareness and the ability to move onto a higher level of thought make it much easier for you, because it enables you to analyse your situation in the light of your overall understanding.

In a previous chapter, I spoke about operating a boat by remote control from a vantage point in a helicopter. That is the facility I would like you to develop. It is amazing how problems diminish when you are able to take a few paces backwards and analyse them in the light of higher understanding. A problem is only a test that you set for yourself in order to grow.

Whilst it may seem that you are merely playing games of imagination, the underlying theme is a practical one. The obvious barrier to psychic development is the fact that throughout your life, your mind has been trained only to accept those things which arise in physical reality. It may be possible to make a sudden switch from operating exclusively on a physical level to function as a psychic in every sense of the word, but it is not advisable because in such cases the risk of psychic and emotional shock is very high. It is much more comfortable to move gradually through a transition phase which contains a little of both worlds, and this can be accomplished by the use of imagination.

Once you are conditioned to recognize psychic stimuli, you are certain to find that things occur during your exercises which were unplanned and unthought of. For instance, I have previously mentioned the Void in this context.

Once you have grasped the technique of allowing your thoughts to wander, you may find that there is a point at which they become garbled and seem to dash through your mind at great speed. Let them go. Do not try to retain them for long enough to decipher them because they are only the first stage of your progress. These thoughts occur at the Astral level.

As I mentioned earlier, what follows is a sudden silence. It is so sudden that people often hear a snapping or popping sound at the moment of breakthrough. The silence that you experience is warm, calm and almost euphoric. This is the Void.

Once you reach the Void, you feel complete calm and pleasant detachment from the cares of physical existence. When you have reached that stage a few times, try an experiment. Float gently for a few minutes, then try to suddenly carry out a physical action such as lighting a cigarette or standing up. You will find that there are a few moments of disorientation and that it takes a little while for you to get yourself together in the physical. It does not take long, but the sensation is quite distinct and it happens because you are switching from one reality to another.

When you have practised enough, you will find that it becomes second nature to switch yourself into the sensations which accompany the Void. It no longer requires a concentrated effort of will and you can flick into it after only a few moments of relaxation.

As this facility develops, you will begin to notice that your awareness is expanding and your sensitivity increases. You become more perceptive and intuitive in every aspect of life. Roland has often noticed this principle in operation when he is at work. It is quite common for him to suddenly start thinking about a particular person fifteen seconds before that person enters the room or calls him on the telephone.

Bear in mind that he is not making these things happen. He does not influence the person to walk into his office just by thinking about it. It is simply that his aura has become highly sensitive to the vibrational changes in

182

the atmosphere around him and he has learned how to interpret the impressions that reach him.

As this facility developed in Roland and me, we found that we began to develop instantaneous telepathy between us. Not only would one begin to speak about something as soon as the other thought of it, but there were a number of other incidents which in themselves were quite startling examples of telepathy.

I once saw an attractive wig on display in a local shop. It had been marked down in price and on impulse I thought it would suit me rather well. My own hair is long and blonde, whereas the wig was short, wavy, and auburn. I thought it would be rather fun to have it, but I never make a purchase out of the ordinary without first checking to see if it is all right with Roland. I wanted his consent to buy it, but at the same time, I did not want to tell him what it was; I wanted him to come home and find a redhead waiting for him at the door.

I rang him at work. 'Can I spend fifteen dollars?' I asked.

'Well, that all depends,' he replied. 'What do you want to spend it on?'

'I don't want to tell you. I want it to be a fun surprise.'

'Okay, I'll tell you what. You spend the money and I'll try to guess what you have spent it on. I'll write my guess down on a piece of paper and give it to you when I come home. We'll see how close I am.'

When he got home that evening, I greeted him at the door just as I had planned, wearing my new wig. His face split into a grin of delight and he handed me a piece of paper. On it he had written 'hair, hairpiece, wig.'

Some time ago, I began a correspondence course in creative writing. Every time an envelope arrived from the school, I experienced a moment of tension because I knew that it contained a marked assignment and it was important to me that I made good grades. I averaged good marks throughout the course, mostly B plus and the occasional A, which pleased me no end.

One morning, while Roland was at work, the familiar brown envelope arrived in the mail. I opened it and to my immediate delight, I discovered that I had been marked with an A plus. I was so thrilled that I headed straight for

183

the phone to ring Roland and tell him the good news. Just then, it rang. I answered it and Roland said 'What are you so excited about?'

He had been working quietly at his desk when he suddenly felt a bolt of electric thrills running through his body. At the same time, he had a mental image of me, so he reasoned that something good must have happened to me. At the time, we were separated by a distance of at least five miles.

Once this stage of development has been reached, it is possible to develop it further, to the point where you can influence the people and events which surround you, however it takes a great deal of practice and it should be remembered that such actions carry a great load of responsibility. It is not permissible to override the free will of another person, nor to use your abilities in any way that could cause harm to someone else.

Even though you may feel that interference may in fact benefit another person, it is not allowable to take such an action without the consent of the other person. It is not for you to change the course of another person's life; there may be very good reasons why that person is taking a course which seems illogical to you.

Your ability can be used for a number of beneficial reasons, however, and one of the most notable of these is healing. As I have told you, the body is powered and motivated by the energy which flows through it from the aura. If there is an interruption or a blockage in this energy flow for any reason, physical illness will be the eventual result. Psychic healers use their own energy to clear the blockage and re-establish the clear flow of energy through the body of the sufferer.

I have mentioned before that a clairvoyant who is able to see the aura clearly can often pinpoint an illness even before it has manifested itself in the physical body. This is because the clairvoyant can see the point at which the energy flow is being blocked. Like anything else, the ability to see auras can be developed with practice. It is simply a matter of knowing what to look for and, more importantly, how to look. This will take time and patience, but with perseverance you will find that it becomes second nature.

Exercise 2

If you can get a friend to co-operate by acting as your subject in this exercise, so much the better. If not, you can use a plant, preferably a pot-plant so that you can relax in the comfort of your living room. Once more, it is important for you to be quite relaxed before you carry out this exercise. As before, relax as you do during your meditation periods and allow yourself plenty of time. Do not try to hurry things.

As you relax, you will probably find that your eyelids begin to droop; don't let them close entirely, but make no attempt to keep them wide open. If you are using another person as the object of your exercise, gaze steadily at that person's eyes.

As relaxation overtakes you, you may find that your gaze begins to drift a little and your vision may begin to go a little blurry. Don't try to clear it, because you are not trying to focus on the physical but into the psychic. After a few minutes, you should be able to see a hazy outline around your subject. With people it is usually most noticeable around the head.

The outline may be quite close to the person's body or it may extend for several inches. You will probably first see it as a misty white colour or you may be able to see other colours in it. It is most common for people to see the aura as misty white at first; the ability to see it in colour develops with practice.

The more deeply you relax, keeping your awareness concentrated through your eyes, the easier this exercise will be.

Although you see the aura through physical vision, you are also using clairvoyance because you are looking at something which does not exist within the physical range of frequencies. If it did, everyone would be able to see it. As I have already explained, clairvoyance is the ability to see things which lie outside the physical range of visual frequencies. It can also be developed with practice.

Exercise 3

Once again, use your meditation technique in order to reach a deeply relaxed level of consciousness. Now, visualise a familiar room in your home. It can be any

185

room you choose. If you recall, this exercise was explained in part in a previous chapter but we are now going to take it a step further.

I want you to close your eyes and get the picture firmly established in your mind. Keep your eyes closed until you have achieved this. Once it is done, open your eyes slowly and see if you can maintain the vision with your eyes open; that is, see it as though you really are in that room. It will most likely be very difficult at first and it may be some time before you are able to achieve it but it will be of great benefit in the development of your clairvoyance if you persevere.

Sometimes we get clairvoyant 'flashes' or moments of intuition which come when we least expect them. These also can be used as keys in your development. Emotion acts as a carrier wave for psychic activity, and if you are alert enough you can note the emotions that you were experiencing at the time just prior to the flash of intuition. Were you feeling relaxed and happy, buoyant, or quietly introspective? Analyse these sensations and learn to re-create them within yourself when you are carrying out your exercises.

When you meditate, always put yourself onto a higher level of thought and feeling. Detach yourself from mental involvement in physical events and aim for a feeling of complete relaxation and well-being. Be aware of yourself as a spiritual entity, immortal and untrammelled by worldly cares.

To reinforce the feeling of detachment from the physical, there is an exercise that you can do while lying in bed. Close your eyes and imagine that your bed has been turned around so that your position is reversed and your feet are located where your head normally rests. Once this is achieved, it is rather a unique sensation, especially if you open your eyes after you have mentally relocated yourself. You find that you feel quite disorientated for a while because the room appears to be completely out of alignment.

After you have practised these techniques for a while, you may be able to come up with some variations of your own. Anything that stimulates your higher consciousness and helps to break the bonds which tie you to the physical is of benefit in the development of psychic awareness. You may also find that unexpected things occur while you are doing your exercises. You may, for instance, think that you have heard someone speaking or you might see sudden flashes of light. Don't put such things down to imagination because they are signs that you are reaching the level of breakthrough for which you are aiming.

Last of all, remember that ultimately, your psychic development is up to you. We can tell you how to recognise the signs of development, but it is for you to seek them out. If you apply yourself to your quest in a steady, confident manner, you will get results. It may take time, but it is important for your own sake that you do not try to rush things. In psychic development you cannot skim lightly over the surface and expect to achieve instant results. Your knowledge and understanding need to be deep and strong; you must also learn to cultivate a state of patient tranquillity. In today's helter skelter world, this is not easy, but it can be done. You can do anything at all—if you really want to.

CHAPTER SEVENTEEN
Sensitivity, psychometry

In the preceding chapters we have dealt piecemeal with what goes into the makeup of the people we call Psychics. If we put all the pieces together into a cohesive unit, the overall concept can best be described as a 'state of mind'.

To be sure, psychics have their share of worldly problems—who doesn't? The distinction lies in the way in which those problems are viewed. It is not enough for us to be told that there is a reason for all things, we need to know what the reasons are, how they apply to us and what we can do about them, otherwise our problems only constitute a burden instead of providing us with the learning experience for which they were intended.

The mere possession of functional psychic faculties is not an answer in itself, but it can be used as a means of *finding* the answers. It is possible, through psychic awareness, to open up whole new dimensions of thought which enable you to examine your situation from a greater perspective. This brings you closer to the achievement of your ultimate goal—a unified self.

The key to all of this is *sensitivity*. If you are sensitive to pollen or a particular type of dust, you don't have to first know it is there for it to affect you. You do not need to use any of your five given senses to go searching for it before you start sneezing or your eyes begin to water. The mere fact that it is there and you are sensitive to it is sufficient for you to experience the effects of it. Once you discover the source of your reaction and the reason why it affects you in a certain way, you can work out the most appropriate course of action in order to deal with it.

It is the same with psychic phenomena. However in this case it must now be assumed that you are actively doing all you can to be affected by it in an effort to draw it to you. In reality you are continually being bombarded with psychic emanations; the trick lies in learning to tune yourself in to them.

Some people have a natural affinity for certain levels of vibration, others acquire it through necessity or desire. In either case, once 'tuned' to this frequency, they become keenly aware of it whenever it is present.

I recently watched a television programme in which a woman was describing her experiences as a victim of child abuse. Both parents were alcoholics and the father was prone to fits of insane violence whenever he had been drinking, to such an extent that he presented a very real threat to life and limb. The woman mentioned that she and the other children somehow acquired a sixth sense about this: when coming home from school, they had only to turn the corner into their street and they would instantly know if their parents had been drinking. In this case, the children's very survival depended on them being aware of when to stay out of harm's way. There were no physical signs that could have warned the children at that distance, they had simply learned to tune in and identify the wavelength on which their parents were broadcasting.

Not very long ago, I had an experience which also

highlights the way in which we can become aware of a situation that is occurring outside the range of our physical senses. On a whimsical impulse, I had bought myself another pet, a tiny mouse, whom I promptly christened Hercules. Roland's reaction to this was somewhat dubious, on the very logical grounds that I already possessed three cats and he was not over-confident as regards Hercules' chances of survival. However, I pointed out that there are ways of eluding the danger. During the day, Hercules' cage is kept in the most frequented room so that we can keep an eye out for his safety. At night the cage is placed on top of a wardrobe, inaccessible to marauding pussycats.

On the night in question I sat up writing until quite late and stumbled wearily off to bed, quite forgetting that I had not moved Hercules to safety. I had been in bed for about half an hour and was just drifting off to sleep when I suddenly came awake and remembered that Hercules was still in the living room—along with all three cats! I went to get him and found him cowering in a corner of his cage, with a very intent puss trying to figure out how to get her paw through the bars.

Coincidence? Perhaps—but the frequency of such apparently coincidental occurrences in our lives is so high that to believe in nothing but the element of chance is really stretching credibility to the limits.

Did your mother seem to have a sixth sense that warned her whenever you were about to get into mischief as a child? Perhaps you are still wondering how she managed to do it. I have news for you: she got the pertinent warning direct from your own guilty little mind. Think back, if you can, and remember how you felt at the time. Maybe you were on the verge of sneaking your hand into the cookie jar and all your senses were concentrated on doing it without getting caught. Were you feeling a sense of nervousness—flutters in the tummy, faster heartbeat, tremulous hands? And wasn't your concentration focused on the fervent hope that your mother would not enter the room at that moment? You couldn't have given her a clearer warning if you had broadcast your intentions over a loudspeaker!

By the very act of concentrating on your mother, you

linked your mind to hers and all of those nervous, guilty sensations that you felt were instantly transmitted to her. She may not have known exactly what they meant but she certainly realised that it was time to come and see what you were up to.

Modern technology has produced instruments which are capable of detecting changes in the electrostatic field which surrounds the human body. Whilst Roland and I cannot claim to be conversant with the details of this area of knowledge, we have noticed that it has produced some interesting findings.

A medical practitioner friend of ours told me some time ago about a thought-provoking incident which occurred during some experiments with an electrostatic field. It had been discovered that the field would produce distinct and measurable changes at the location of some bodily illness or malfunction and research was being carried out in an effort to discover whether such changes could be utilized as an aid in diagnosis. During this procedure it was found that the electrostatic field of one subject, a man, registered the appropriate changes over a section of his lower leg. According to all of the available knowledge, there should have been some physical malfunction in that area, yet nothing could be located. The man's leg was perfectly normal.

Some three days later, the man had a nasty accident and broke his leg—in the precise location that had been pinpointed by the electrostatic changes. That raises some intriguing questions, doesn't it?

Scientists have been aware of this electrostatic field for a number of years. From the USSR comes a well-documented case involving telekinesis, in which this field was measured and its responses plotted. The subject was a woman named Ninel Kulagina, whose fame has travelled worldwide as a result of her startling abilities. As a young woman, at times of considerable mental and emotional stress she would cause crockery to fall from shelves, lights to go on and off and doors to open and close—all with no physical intervention. She developed and harnessed this ability, thus making it possible to reproduce under laboratory conditions. One test, conducted by scientist Edward Naumov, involved Ninel clasping her hands together over matches scattered on a table and concentrating on causing them to move to the table's edge and drop to the floor. Over sixty films were made of this woman performing seemingly impossible feats, which included the separation of a raw egg which had been broken into a tank of saline solution. From a distance of several feet away, Ninel managed to move the white and the yolk completely apart.

It was during this test that the electrostatic field surrounding Ninel's body was measured. The man conducting the experiment, Doctor Gernady Sergeyev, found that at the moment the egg began to separate, the electrostatic field began to pulse at four cycles per second.

The human brain can be 'trained' to operate so that it can emphasize certain waveforms in the alpha, beta, delta and theta wavelengths by means of a biofeedback device. An electronic 'gizmo', (my profuse apologies to all electronics buffs) the biofeedback machine has electrode inputs to its circuitry and usually a light or sound signal on its output, switchable to each of the wavelengths mentioned. The person using the device endeavours to register a response on the indicator through relaxation and concentration on a selected wavelength.

What of this electrostatic field? How is it possible for it to register an injury days before it happens? What is its connection with psychic activity? Is science on the brink of being compelled to openly acknowledge the existence of the aura?

PSYCHOMETRY

Psychometry is the art or ability to detect subtle emanations from inanimate objects. The ability is not difficult to acquire; the art lies in being able to interpret the impressions correctly. It can be a wow at parties but it can also be used for other reasons, not the least being to enhance your growing sensitivity. It is a means by which you can have immediate feedback on your accuracy, therefore it can be used as a ready-reckoner of your developmental progress.

It works this way: take an object that somebody has been wearing close to the skin. It can be a ring, pendant, locket or whatever (*not* a watch—too many moving parts that can confuse the issue), and fondle it lightly through both of your hands. Let your vision go blank and observe your emotions. See how it makes you *feel*. Emotion is a carrier wave for a lot of psychic information—you need to learn to interpret these feelings.

While you are playing with the object, understand what you are doing. The emotions that the wearer has felt have been experienced through both the aura and the physical body. Happy times, sad times, shocks—the full gamut of human emotions are there to be read. How? Just as the electrostatic field registers the emanations from a subject, so the trinket is imbued with the same vibrations. Attune your sensitivity to the currents that have flowed through the metal and you will feel what the wearer has felt—the fondness for an old house, the disappointment of being badly let down by a loved one, the grieving of a loss, the euphoria of a success. Relax. Let the information come *to* you, don't try to wring it out of the object. A word of caution: before you attempt a reading, make sure that the object has never been worn by anyone other than the person who gives it to you, otherwise you are likely to pick up conflicting and confused vibrations.

Speak your mind—don't discount something because you think it might be incorrect or unimportant. How are you to know? It is not your role to judge or decide. You are only the medium through whom the information passes.

I once attended a development group in which the participants were practising psychometry. Because of the danger of losing valuable objects, the exercise was performed on flowers. I was asked in advance to bring a flower from my garden and this I did. The girl who received my flower to read sat frowning in concentration for quite some time, then at length she sighed impatiently.

'It's no use,' she complained, 'I can't get anything. I just keep seeing great billows of smoke!' Her face cleared somewhat when I informed her that she was quite correct. Just a week previously, the fence near the bush from which I had plucked the blossom caught fire and was blazing away quite merrily before it was noticed and extinguished. No wonder the lass was confused: it was not my impressions she was reading but those of the flower itself. That says something to anyone who has ever wondered whether plants have a consciousness!

On another occasion, a friend who had been given one of my bracelets to read expressed a great deal of confusion because the strongest impression he could feel was of a pile of broken glass and he failed to see how it could possibly have any significance for me. Nevertheless, it was quite appropriate. At the age of five, I was playing with some other children on a fire escape. When I reached the top, an older child impatiently pushed me out of his way and I fell—straight onto a pile of broken beer bottles that had somehow accumulated on the ground below. I still bear a large scar on my left elbow as a memento of the adventure.

Don't fall into the trap of censoring your impressions. Telephone wires do not judge the veracity of the conversations they carry, only the participants can do that. Let the person for whom you are doing the reading attest your accuracy and sensitivity for you.

Don't decide to tell someone what you think they want to hear. There are two reasons for this, the first and most obvious being that you would only be handing them a load of bunkum and experience will tell them so. In addition, you would not be keying yourself open to the encompassing level of existence that is there for your sensitivity to detect. In other words you would be kidding yourself and wasting your time because the exercise would be utterly useless in terms of psychic development. When you are at one with yourself, you have no need to pretend. No one person can know everything: if you don't know or your sensitivity is off, say so. It releases you from the burden of having to maintain a pretence.

SENSITIVITY

This word—sensitivity—has been stressed from the outset in this passage because it is a key factor in your development. The currents that flow from the spiritual dimensions are subtle, especially when compared to the raucous vibrations which abound in the physical. Through *awareness* or acuteness of your honed sensitivity you are able to detect the subtlety of changes around you and your perceptivity grows; you develop your clear-sightedness. All of this is done at a non-physical level, using non-physical energy. It is done using non-physical means, but understand that you are in a physical environment and for you to perceive it, for you to be able to react or instigate, you must be able to physically detect it. Therefore this non-physical energy must produce a physical effect.

It does this in the most natural of ways: you feel it. It is expressed to you via *emotion*. Emotion is the carrier wave over which psychic information is modulated. Ever been fired from a job? Do you recall the panicky feeling that went with the news? How do you think that emotion would look on an electroencephalographic readout? What effect do you think would be registered if a Kirlian photograph were taken of your aura at that time?

Ever had the feeling: 'I can't explain it, but I just know something is going to happen. . .'? How *did* you know?

Perhaps you have been somewhere for the first time and have been overcome by a feeling of deja-vu that physically touches, saying that you have been in that situation before. If you have, then try to re-create the emotion now.

All of these examples have one common denominator: recognition of an emotion. They are, however, subtly different in the way that they have expressed themselves to you. Each portends a different event and each carries a different meaning, yet they have all been expressed to you via the same medium. Now try an experiment that you have tried before: close your eyes and visualise standing at your front gate. How do you feel? What physical sensations are you impressed to feel as you 'stand' there?

Try it again and this time not only ponder the emotions you feel, but analyse where they are located in your physical being. They are tangible, physical impressions of a psychic, non-physical energy source which is being manipulated by you. You are experiencing them by drawing them to you. They exist in the timeless zone; they are *always* there, they will always be there when you call on them. What you are doing is *thinking* yourself into that location. As we said in an earlier chapter: thought is an energy source as distinct from physical energy.

You should now be able to see the point I am making: when you experience something, look for its origin. Differentiate between the psychic and the physical. Operating this way, you are constantly reinforcing into your consciousness the awareness of this other reality or higher state of being. You are drawing into your awareness a level of vibration that you have not encompassed before. You are entering a transitional phase in your evolution as a spirit.

Where does this take you? As was noted in a previous chapter when we were discussing the levels or spheres: immediately above the physical layer of existence is found the Astral, or Astral plane—a higher state of being. Above that are the spheres themselves. Only the Void separates the two. Entry to the spiritual spheres is not possible without the guidance of your higher self. It follows, *ergo*, that progression through the spheres is denied until you are at one with that higher self.

It is taught that there are many progressions or spheres, each adding its own dimensional reality to our experience, each one originating within the experiences of the higher self. Only when the higher self and the consciousness of your reality are in coincidence can there be an exchange of information between the two.

NIRVANA

Nirvana is a term used in Buddhist theology to signify the extinction of physical existence, or the extinction of all desires and passions and attainment of perfect beatitude. Western scholars roughly equate it with the Christian heaven and it is generally accepted as being the ultimate plane of existence. When a soul has achieved or attained Nirvana, it is free from the necessity to reincarnate.

Hands up, all those who thought Nirvana was the end of the story! So what did you imagine would become of you, once you reached that plane? Did you really think that you would thenceforth float around in eternal nothingness and, if so, didn't you find the idea just a wee bit appalling? All that effort just to get nowhere and be nothing!

Nirvana is only the end of the *physical* story. From that

point onwards, the scene changes to the spiritual spheres. During the round of physical incarnations, a soul is little more than a chrysalis. Nirvana is the point at which it is transformed into a butterfly. As a matter of interest, the ancient Greeks knew a lot more than they let on. It is no accident that their word *psyche* not only means a spirit, but also a butterfly.

There is an ultimate plane of existence, but it is certainly not Nirvana. It is known as the plane of *Minerva*, which means union with the Godhead. Traditional religious philosophies do not cater to this possibility. Always in their doctrines the two must stand apart; the creation can never be part of the Creator. The creation is viewed as the *work* of the Creator and there stands the distinction. Everything we learn, however, points us inexorably toward the view that we are part of the Creator. We must be; we are part of the Creation itself. The energy that motivates the body you live in; where does that come from? You are the result of that energy, but where does it come from in the first place?

It can be seen that the 'seventy-five year span of life used to progress from original sin to perfection' syndrome means there must be an awful lot of rejects who never make the grade because there simply isn't enough time. However, in the spiritual spheres, time is not only irrelevant, it does not exist. On that subject, David says this: 'Time is a condition of physical existence. Where I am there is no time—only one continuous *now*.'

As this book is primarily concerned with the conditions that apply before we reach the stage of Nirvana (which, of course, is the same as passing through the Void), we will leave this subject for the present and go on to other things. However, I should mention at this point that this, our first book, was never intended to be the ultimate book on spiritual existence. Such a book could never be written, for Infinity could not be confined within the necessary boundaries. Nor do Roland and I know everything there is to know; only those who have reached Minerva can do that. However, there is a lot more that we *do* know and we are learning more all the time. It is our hope that we will be able to share this knowledge with you in future volumes.

CHAPTER EIGHTEEN
Spiritual relationships

Once, when I was discussing our philosophy with some newly-acquainted friends named Steve and Barbara, I noticed a quizzical expression beginning to form on Steve's face.

'You aren't by any chance trying to start a new religion, are you?' he enquired.

That question caused me no end of amusement. It is a well-known fact among my friends that, in my opinion, this world needs another religion about as much as it needs another nuclear bomb. There is enough confusion over religion as things are, and there have been more brutal massacres carried out under the flimsy banner of religion than for any other human cause.

This does not mean that I have no belief in God. In fact, I have a very powerful faith in the Creator and I am quite certain that he is a great deal more understanding and intelligent than orthodox religion would have us believe.

I have often been asked whether I am a Christian and if so, why I do not attend the Christian church. My answer to that is that if being a Christian means believing wholeheartedly in the teachings of Christ *as he taught them*, then I am a Christian. As to attending the Christian church, I will commence doing so when I find one that truly presents the Christian philosophy—and practises what it preaches. For the present, I do not believe that such an institution exists.

Christ said 'Render unto Caesar the things that belong to Caesar, and to God what belongs to God' yet today we find religion and politics going hand in hand. 'Love your enemies and do not kill' say the priests—yet they go out into the battlefields, bless the guns and tell the young soldiers that it is all right to slaughter the enemy because God is on our side. What blasphemous hypocrisy! I would rather have nothing to do with religion than conform to the dictates of an organisation which cannot even maintain peace and honesty within its own ranks.

Roland and I live by the philosophy that David has taught to us because it is honest, consistent, compassionate, and it makes sense. In addition to that, David has proved to us that he has the ability to carry out the deeds which he claims.

What we do *not* do is expect other people to accept our philosophy simply because it suits us. If our teachings make sense to you and you wish to adopt them as your own, we are happy to share them with you. If not, we wish you well on your chosen path.

In the preceding chapters of this book, I have told how I came to be involved with the supernatural and we have related the basic teachings and techniques as taught to us by David, but there is more to come. I would like to explain our philosophy in terms of the evolution of the soul.

There is nothing new in what I have to say. These things have been known for countless ages, but perhaps I may present the picture from a slightly different perspective. Then again, maybe not. However, this book would be incomplete if this segment were not included. Once again, I am relating the things that I have learned from David.

We come from the Creator and to him we will ultimately return. A tiny thought appears in the mind of the Creator; it is imbued with his own energy and it becomes a soul, whereupon it is set free to follow a course of evolution until it becomes a matured spirit— something like an angel if you like. Even then, there is more progress to be made, but we shall come to that later.

I do not know what evolutionary processes take place before we manifest in human form. Perhaps I shall learn before I leave this life, but in the meantime I prefer not to make wild guesses.

I know that our real home lies in the spirit world, beyond the Void, and I know that *every* soul will ultimately make the transition from the round of physical incarnations to the world of the spirit. No matter how base or evil a soul may seem to be in our eyes, it is following the path of progression and will eventually refine itself and cast off the coarse instincts that currently

198

confine it to the lower levels of existence. No soul is irrevocably doomed, for every soul contains that spark of divinity that came from the One who brought it into being.

In physical life we progress through a number of incarnations until we are developed enough to cross the Void. Then we begin our progress upward through the world of spirits. Earthly relationships are transitory, but each of us has a spiritual family and that relationship never diminishes; it can only develop. In the kind of terms that I understand, David is my spiritual father, but of course it must be remembered that spiritual reality varies a great deal from the physical. David has a great many children. I am only one—however, he has occasionally informed me that I am also the cheekiest and the only one who dares to stamp my foot and argue with him. Judging by the tone of his voice when he mentions this, I get the impression that he finds it rather amusing and so far, I have not received an ethereal kick in the pants.

As humans, we are very young spirits. All of us are children, no matter how old our physical bodies may be. Have you ever noticed that there are small children who seem to be gifted with an understanding far in excess of their years, while certain so-called adults carry on like infants? In spiritual reality, the irresponsible adult may be thousands of years younger than the soul which currently inhabits the body of a youngster.

As the soul progresses, material acquisitions and mortal acclaim mean less and less, while spiritual values become more and more important. This is something that happens naturally, over any number of incarnations. It cannot be forced, nor will it be evaded, but it is useless to take the aspirations of the most highly developed souls and attempt to force them upon a young soul who is as yet incapable of understanding them. Far better to explain the purpose of life in terms that the young soul can understand, and allow him to do his best to make progress at his own pace.

This world, the physical, is a classroom and we are all here to learn and develop. It is when we become conscious of ourselves as spirits and begin to understand the nature of the spiritual world that awaits us that we reach the stage of development that is necessary if we are to cross the Void, or pass through the veil. Just as a matter of interest, it is the Void which truly qualifies for the name 'Veil of Isis'.

By using our psychic senses in the way that was intended, we explore the spiritual realms and learn the things we need to know. Certainly you can also use those abilities to tell fortunes or predict the future, but that is not their prime purpose. Roland and I do not do it because we feel that it is a waste of time when what we really want to do is make further spiritual advancement. However, we do not criticise those people who choose to use their gifts in other ways, for it is their right to do with them as they please.

A number of well-known mediums use their gifts in order to deliver messages from across the border of death. They are occasionally criticised for doing this and there are purists who claim that they are wasting their talents, delivering trivial messages which really have no great amount of spiritual import.

Whilst Roland and I do not carry out that kind of activity, we have no criticism to make in regard to the people who do it, for we know that they may be fulfilling a very great need in the people who come to hear their messages. Fear of death is a very real thing to a great many people and for them it is an immeasurable comfort to know that life goes on after the physical body has ceased to function. It is also a comfort to know that departed loved ones have not simply ceased to exist.

I mentioned earlier in this book that Roland's first wife died after they had been married for only eight months. When I met him, he was still grieving for her, for he felt that life had dealt with her very harshly. It was useless for me to try to console him with my own beliefs, for he had no way then of knowing whether or not I was correct.

Some time after we had begun to live together, I received a visit from Diana, his first wife. She told me that she was greatly concerned about Roland in his grief and she wished for him to be comforted. She asked me to help and I told her that I would do my best, but it was difficult, for he would accept nothing that sounded like platitudes.

200

For some time, we discussed the man we both loved, and Diana told me about some of the good times that they had shared, giving me details of events that had taken place in their life together.

She then asked me to assure Roland that she was well and happy and that she wished him to stop grieving and just remember the happy times that they had spent together. When he awoke from his trance, I gave him the message. He looked at me with a blank expression on his face, but I continued to tell him about the talk I had had with Diana. When I mentioned the incidents she had told me about, his face changed and his eyes lit up.

'There is no way you could have known those things,' he told me. 'I am the only person, other than Diana, who knew about them. I did not tell you about them, so you must really have been talking with her. Thank you. Now I can let go of the grief.' With that, my darling husband broke down and allowed himself to cry for the very first time since his beloved Diana had departed this life, but his tears were refreshing for they washed away all of his pain. After seeing this in him, I cannot criticise the people who devote their lives to helping others in the same way.

It is difficult to speak about death without sounding as though I am repeating a lot of platitudes, for most of the things that can be said have already been said countless times by other people. But it is true that death is only a transition. Your real existence lies in the spirit world and life in the physical is only a brief stage in your development.

What really happens when a person dies? How do they feel and where do they go? What happens to them after death? Is there really a Heaven and a Hell?

Unless there is severe trauma associated with a person's death, the process itself is not frightening. When death occurs from natural causes, the process is gradual and the person has entered the world of the spirit almost before they are aware of any change. Have you ever heard the classic tale of the dying person who claims to see departed loved ones gathering around the deathbed? This is something that really happens. Death is not a lonely process, for there is always someone waiting to meet you on the other side and that person will take your hand and

201

guide you to the level of spiritual existence to which you belong.

Sometimes, however, accidents happen and events do not take the desired course. In one of the earlier chapters in this book I wrote about a cheeky Irishman who claimed that I had been his wife and he had come back to claim his own. At the time, it seemed to me like something out of an Edgar Allan Poe horror story. The last thing I wanted was a lovesick ghost hanging around the place and in fact I thought that the character was really a rather sick earthbound spirit. As things turned out, however, he was telling the truth, but I did not find out till several years later.

When he next visited me, he chose a wiser method of approach. He had David introduce him and assure me that what I was about to hear was quite true. David Michael told me of our life together in Ireland. The story is both sad and beautiful. He was a priest, aged twenty-seven, and I was a fifteen-years-old farmer's daughter. In those days a girl of fifteen was considered to be of marriageable age and it was permissible for priests to marry, but there was opposition to our union because he came from a well-to-do family and I was little better than a gypsy. But we were deeply in love and spent fifteen happy years of marriage together. It ended, however, in tragedy.

We lived in a house at the top of a cliff and one morning I came out of the house to find David Michael lying dead on the ground. Apparently he had suffered a heart attack. In the scheme of things, it had been planned by the guides that he would be the one to meet me when I passed over, but things went wrong. Blinded by tears and numb with grief, I stumbled away from my husband's body and wandered toward the cliff. I didn't even see it coming; I just walked to the edge and fell to my death. By the time David Michael came to claim me, I had wandered away into the Astral and become earthbound.

It was necessary for me to incarnate again so that he could locate me. He speaks briefly of a life in France less than a hundred years ago where we did not 'connect' and lived independent lives of no interest to either of us now except for the point that we did not meet. This time, he swears, he will not leave my side and he will be there to meet me when I leave the physical.

Until I really got to know David Michael, I found it a little difficult to understand why he had first introduced himself as 'a teacher and a drunkard to boot', when he had in fact been a priest. I had to learn to understand his personality. For one thing, he is nowhere near as elevated as David in development, although he is by no means undeveloped. He has lost little of his earthiness (of which he seemed to have plenty) but this does not interfere one whit with his spirituality. In spiritual terms, a priest would be regarded as a teacher, for the simple reason that his role is supposed to be that of a teacher of spiritual things. I am not familiar with the Jewish language, but I believe the word 'Rabbi' actually means teacher.

As for his taste for liquor: 'Well, me darlin', 'tis the Irish in me. There's nothin' sweeter than the good auld Irish whiskey. 'Tis the nectar of the Gods—beggin' His pardon'. If I didn't know better, I'd swear that our dear David Michael was in truth a leprechaun—and he would probably cheerfully agree with me.

David Michael is now a regular visitor, for he has vowed to take care of me and never to leave my side. Roland makes no objection to this. Flattering though this may seem, he says that he can understand a man loving me for all eternity once he has had a taste of being married to me. In the interests of humility, I will refrain from comment, except to say that such words are music to my feminine ears.

Last Christmas I decided to buy David Michael a present, and a bottle of Irish whiskey duly appeared under the Christmas tree. We saw no reason why David Michael could not come and have a wee drink per courtesy of Roland, and nor did David Michael for that matter, although he said he would first have to ensure that David was looking the other way, since it was not strictly according to the rules. At least, no one had ever thought to make any rules for such an unlikely eventuality.

I know that I have said it is not wise to indulge in psychic activity when one has been drinking but by this time we had reached the stage where we could trust in the guides and I knew that David Michael would allow no harm to come to Roland. However, what we did not take into account was that David Michael can hold his liquor a great deal better than Roland can. It is normal, when David Michael is present for a lengthy visit, for him to withdraw occasionally and allow the medium to rest, for the continuous flow of high energy would be harmful to Roland if it were not occasionally lowered. The night that David Michael decided to sample my Christmas gift was hilarious!

David Michael enjoyed his whiskey so much that he drank a half bottle in one sitting. The effect on him was undetectable, but it was when he withdrew that the fun began. Roland was so inebriated that he could hardly stand up, and kept muttering things about getting the number of the truck that had hit him. Yet as soon as David Michael returned, he would be as sober and steady as though he had been drinking tonic water. The effect was highly amusing, but at least David Michael had the consideration to make sure that Roland did not suffer a hangover the following day.

Roland's recollection of the evening's events is naturally rather hazy. He can remember coming out of his trance several times, feeling as high as a kite and wondering if his legs would ever again be able to hold him up and he, too, finds the incident amusing.

In the time that David Michael has been visiting us, there has built up a warm camaraderie between he and Roland, even though at first Roland was hardly ever aware of his presence. Recently they have developed the art of both being present at once without upsetting the equilibrium of either Roland's body or his mental attitude. Roland sometimes carries on an open conversation with David Michael, and he has commented with a grin that he hopes no one outside the family ever catches him doing it, or he will find the men in the white coats coming to take him away.

There is a very good reason why this state of affairs can exist, and it lies in the structure of the spiritual personality. When a soul incarnates, it is only a portion of the consciousness which comes into the physical. The higher self is the soul itself, and this personality contains the memories, experiences and accumulated knowledge of every incarnation that has ever been lived by that soul. All of this knowledge is not needed in one incarnation, so the physical personality, whilst it may seem complete from our viewpoint, is really only a fraction of the whole. Roland is in fact a reincarnation of David Michael, for David Michael is Roland's higher self. Roland says that he does not feel this as a conscious thing: to him, David Michael is a separate personality, but he understands intellectually that when he leaves this world, he will virtually 'become' David Michael. If it sounds confusing to you, you should try living with it!

Whilst David Michael has a rollicking sense of humour and a taste for Irish whiskey which make him seem endearingly human, these things do not detract from his spirituality. It is a mistake to think that just because a being has left the physical for the last time, he must lose all traces of personality and become a sort of angelic zombie. When the Creator gave us life he intended us to enjoy it as well as to learn. Certain people may tell us that life was not meant to be easy, but nor was it intended to be a joyless burden. There are joys and wonders in the world that were put here for all of us to share and enjoy, and the spirits appreciate them more than any of us, for they share in the wonder of their creation. This is one of the reasons why David told me not to forget to live. The things in this world that are harsh and unpleasant are the things that have been created by selfish men. The wonder and beauty of nature and the miracle of life is something that exists for us to rejoice in. We should not regard the Creator as an autocratic old man with a big stick. When we find joy in life, we are actually thanking the Creator for putting us here, so rejoice in being alive!

Before I leave the subject of David Michael, there is an interesting footnote that I must add. You will remember reading earlier in the book about the time when I suddenly and inexplicably became afraid of heights. At that time I was about twenty-nine years of age, which is roughly the age at which I fell over the cliff in Ireland. There is no possibility that this fear could have been the result of auto-suggestion, since the fear came years before I heard the story. Make of that whatever you will.

When a spirit completes its last incarnation, it passes through the Void and enters the higher realms of spiritual existence. Prior to that, if the spirit needs further development before becoming advanced enough to make the transition, it will go to the Astral plane. No time is ever wasted, and the time spent in the Astral is taken up with further learning and experience, which become a part of the true soul, or higher self, and function as subconscious knowledge in the incarnated soul.

There is no set number of incarnations through which a soul must pass. Progress is determined by the rate at which the soul develops. Some may be ready to cross the Void after ten lives, others may need fifty. It makes little difference in the end, because ultimately we will all reach the same place.

Of the levels beyond the Void, I can say little, because the very fact that I am living out a physical incarnation indicates that I am not yet ready to make the transition. However, David has told me that this is my last life and that I will cross the Void when I leave here this time.

He has told me that we will continue to learn and develop when we reach those levels and that we in our turn will function as spirit guides for the souls who are behind us in progression. Ultimately, after countless aeons of physical time, we will reach the plane of Minerva, which is union with the Creator. Of that, also, I can say little because it is quite obvious that I have not yet experienced it. Nor has David, for he tells me that he is still working his way towards that level.

It is comforting to know that the traditional ideas of Heaven and Hell are little more than man-made myths and that there is a more pleasant and substantial future awaiting each and every one of us. Whilst Roland and I would not dream of forcing our ideas onto other people, we find them greatly reassuring ourselves and one of the reasons why this book is being written is because we want to share our knowledge with others who may be seeking the same answers that we have found.

CHAPTER NINETEEN
Psychic attack, psychic rescue

Few people would disagree when I say that spiritual rescue is one of the most lively and dramatic fields of psychic activity. It is easy to become hysterical about the subject—I have heard highly respected psychics speaking in shuddering tones about 'demonic possession' and 'satanic influence'. I would be singularly blind if I were to deny the existence of dark forces within the universe; I have been exposed to them on one or two occasions, at which times I have thanked my lucky stars that David was present to deal with the situations. However, we have so far found that they are the exception. The human soul seems to have a unique talent for getting itself into trouble without the assistance of outside agencies.

Strictly speaking, we could say that 'demons' are involved in every case, but only if we fully understand the origin of the word. In the original Greek, the word *daemon* simply meant a spirit and did not ascribe either malevolence or benevolence to the term. Socrates claimed to have been influenced thoughout his life by his own *daemon*, which we would now understand in terms of a spirit guide. However, because of the sinister connotations now placed on the word, I prefer not to use it at all.

Psychic attack and auric infestation are chiefly caused by *human* souls, living either in the physical or on the lower levels of the astral. For the reasons why they carry out such activities, we must look at the human soul itself. Let us consider the manifestations of psychic disturbance: furniture flung around, piles of faeces deposited in the middle of a floor, foul obscenities spat forth in abundance. You would find the same occurrences taking place in an acute mental hospital, yet you would not refer to the inmates as demons. You would understand that they are sick and incapable of acting normally.

Why does the neighbourhood bully delight in terrorising other children? Why do gangs of youths roam the streets, bashing and stealing from anyone who happens to cross their path? What makes a depraved pervert torture and maim little children? What motivated Adolf Hitler to launch one of the most horrifying orgies of terror and destruction in recorded history, and what was lacking in human nature that he was not stopped long before he ever came to power? What depravity did he stir in the souls of other human beings? The answers lie in the weakness and ignorance of the human soul itself.

All the way through this book I have stressed that you are a spirit who manifests into the physical by means of a vehicle that we call the body. You express your personality through that vehicle. Your personality remains the same whether or not you currently possess a physical body; if you are essentially kind and decent now, you will not suddenly become a ravening monster when your body wears out and dies. Equally, if you are a hoodlum in the physical, death will not turn you into a saint.

We cannot prevent psychic attack until every human soul understands the reality of spiritual existence and obeys the natural laws which are designed to keep the universe in harmony. It does not take a highly talented psychic to realise that this is unlikely to happen during my lifetime, or yours. In the meantime, to understand the nature of the phenomenon is to have the means of dealing with it as it occurs.

In every case of attack or infestation of one human being by another soul, we have found that spiritual ignorance is the root cause. In some cases, the spirit is simply unaware that it is no longer alive in a physical sense and is confused and disorientated.

In others, an entity has become vindictive and malevolent because of the harshness of its own treatment during physical life. Many are sad, desperate creatures, miserably pleading for help and relief from their suffering. Working amongst them as I have done for a number of years, I can feel nothing but compassion for their distress, and understanding of the conditions which forced them into their respective dilemmas.

One of the saddest cases I know was first brought to my

208

attention by Coral, a friend who was at the time studying with me. She had a natural aptitude for astral projection and was in the habit of practising it each night after retiring. Just after leaving her body one evening she was startled to see the figure of a fair-haired woman frantically pummelling her prostrate physical body. So great was Coral's surprise that she slipped back into her body and by the time she managed to exteriorize again, the woman had disappeared. Coral felt the presence several times during the days that followed and her impression was that the entity was urgently trying to get help of some kind.

Coral often assisted me in rescue sittings but she wisely refrained from making any attempt at dealing with this situation alone. She asked Roland and I if we would undertake to hold a sitting in an attempt to communicate with the distressed woman. Of course we agreed and arrangements were made for a sitting to be held the following evening.

We waited expectantly as Roland slipped into his trance and I kept searching his face for changes of expression that would give me a clue as to the emotional state of the entity. Although I had by this time performed several rescues I would by no means have classified myself as a seasoned practitioner, but I had learned that body language and facial expressions communicate a great deal of information which can be of help in the rescue procedure.

Roland's body became restless. The movements were agitated and the head was repeatedly moved from side to side in a negative motion. The facial expression was one of agonised suffering and the overall impression was one of a person who was trying futilely to escape from some unbearable emotional pressure. Tears began to flow and the body was wracked with sobs.

None of the movements were particularly feminine and I had a strong impression that the manifesting entity was a male and therefore could not be the same spirit that Coral had seen. However, there was little time for conjecture, as the agitated form in the chair began to moan and mutter. For some time the words were incoherent but eventually they became more distinct.

'I didn't do it!' came the choked cry.

Coral leaned forward in her chair as I spoke softly to the entity.

'What didn't you do?' I asked.

'I didn't do it! I *didn't* do it!'

'Didn't do *what*? Please, try to tell me. I'm here to help you.'

'I didn't. . .didn't do it. I didn't. . .'

I looked uneasily at Coral and she answered with a puzzled shrug. What to do, when we had no way of knowing the source of the spirit's distress? To make a guess and be mistaken could cause insurmountable problems, yet it seemed that the entity would do nothing but repeat the same mystifying sentence over and over again.

All at once there was a change. The restless tossing ceased and the figure in the chair became serene.

'My daughter,' said David, 'the one who has been brought to you was executed for a crime of which he is innocent.'

'What was the crime?' I asked.

'A young woman was murdered.'

'Is it this woman who was seen by Coral?'

'It is. She is trying to reach him.'

'What can we do, David? The entity does not appear to hear me. How can I help?'

'Understand, my daughter, this man protested his innocence to the end but was never believed. He has been lost for a long time and is now confused. He now wonders if he may indeed have committed the act in a moment of madness. Convince him that he did not.'

'How?'

'The young woman is present, but he does not see her. You are the link. Draw his attention to her.'

'I'll try,' I promised. 'Bring him back.'

Roland's body slumped. Then he began to moan softly and make that desperate back and forth shake of the head.

'I didn't do it, I didn't!' he sobbed. I could now sense the overwhelming loneliness and pain of this lost and despairing soul. I wanted to reach out and heal his hurt; the words came unbidden to my lips.

'No, Brother, you did not kill her,' I said.

The figure facing me stopped moving and fell silent. I could almost feel its alert tension.

'You didn't do it,' I said. 'You are innocent.'

The head shook slightly, as though my listener didn't quite dare to believe his ears.

'You did not do it,' I repeated. 'Open your eyes and look. She stands before you. She is alive!'

He shrank back in his chair and his eyelids began to flutter.

'It was all a bad dream,' I crooned. 'It is over. Open your eyes, *wake up!*'

The eyes jerked open and flicked rapidly around the room, then gazed expectantly into mine. I could see the light of hope dawning in them.

'It is true,' I smiled. 'See for yourself. She is here!'

The eyes widened, then looked past me and an expression of enraptured wonder swept over the face. A joyous, tear-filled chuckle surged from his throat, then he sighed.

'I *didn't* do it.' He smiled softly in relief and was gone. Coral and I looked at each other and sniffed. Both of us were blinking back tears.

Spirit entities are people: the fact that they currently do not possess physical bodies is the only thing that makes them different. If an entity is earthbound, it is in that predicament for a reason and that reason is almost always related to trauma of some kind or another, either occurring during life or at the time of death.

An earthbound entity is in a condition of profound shock, usually accompanied by deep depression or confusion. The sudden appearance of a higher being would be as frightening for them as it would for you, if not more so. It would have the opposite effect to the one desired and the higher beings have no desire to alarm or frighten anyone.

The aim in psychic rescue is to draw the earthbound spirit gently upwards at a pace that it can tolerate, until it reaches a level at which it can rest and be healed. A medium already exists in the physical and, if operating in conjunction with a guide from beyond the Void, provides a vibrational bridge that spans all levels of the Astral. The energy can be manipulated by the guides so that an entity can be drawn into it at one level and removed at another. As mediums, or links, it is not our job to question or interrogate the entities but simply to provide the means by which they can be released.

Most often this requires nothing more of us than sitting quietly and allowing the guides to do the work. To speak suddenly or at the wrong moment can cause a sharp change in vibrations which could cause the entity to slip away from us and become lost again. The largest part of the control's job is knowing when to remain silent and, if it is necessary to speak, what to say and how to say it.

The overall rule is to do nothing that could cause further shock for the entity. This is not only because the entity is shocked enough as it is, but because shock, like sudden noises or movements, can cause the guides to lose their grip on the entity.

Some entities can become talkative and it is not unusual to hear a stream of bad language but this need not go on for long if the control knows how to react. As a control I have been taught by David to remain placidly neutral, neither condoning nor condemning the behaviour of an entity.

I was once approached by a woman who suspected that her little girl had fallen victim to an astral entity. The child was constantly sick with minor ailments, suffered from regular nightmares and had totally lost concentration and confidence at school. She was also becoming quite withdrawn at increasing intervals. All efforts to find a physical cause had produced a blank.

Consultation with David confirmed the mother's fears. There were in fact several entities in the child's aura.

This called for a special technique in which the entities are drawn into the aura of an adult without the child's knowledge. It is not considered advisable to have children present at rescue sittings because of the danger of emotional upset for the child. The mother volunteered to 'collect' the entities and was taught how to draw them into her aura. It took three sittings to get rid of them all and the last of these is worth relating. I will call the woman Janet as I do not have her permission to make her identity public.

212

The sitting began like the previous two, which had simply involved sitting quietly while David did all the work. It was not to remain that way for long. Roland's eyes opened and I found myself subjected to a basilisk stare. I smiled slightly to show that my attitude was friendly and the entity spoke.

'What're you bloody-well laughing at?' it demanded, glaring at me belligerently.

'I'm not *laughing* at anything,' I responded, 'I'm smiling. People smile for all sorts of reasons, sometimes simply because they feel good. Don't you ever feel like smiling?'

'. . .Smile when I'm ready!' grunted our guest.

'Okay,' I agreed, and we lapsed into a delicate silence.

Eventually the entity grew tired of inactivity and once more it spoke, peering at me suspiciously.

'You got a name?'

'My name is Dawn and this is Janet,' I replied. 'Would you care to tell us your name?'

'Name's Jack,' was the answer.

'I'm pleased to meet you, Jack,' I said, and Janet hesitantly echoed my words. Silence reigned for a few more minutes. Jack seemed to be considering how to find an opening for conversation. I allowed him time to think.

'You got a job?' he asked suddenly.

'Yes, I work at a hospital. What is your work?'

'I'm a shearer meself,' he answered.

This gave me an opening. It was apparently up to me to make Jack aware of his situation and it had to be done without causing too much shock. Once a conversation started, I hoped to direct it where it needed to go. That is, if Jack felt conversational and it seemed that he did.

'It's funny about shearing,' I ventured, 'I once read that a good shearer can get the fleece off a sheep in one piece and I can't see how that can be done unless you actually skin the creature.'

Jack smirked slightly.

'Easy,' he said. 'The fleece is full of grease. It sticks together.'

'Well, how about that!' I declared. 'You learn something new every day, don't you? Shearing must have been enjoyable work for you, Jack?'

'The pay's good,' he replied.

I noticed that he spoke in the present tense, which indicated that he was apparently unaware of his state of non-physical existence. I would have to choose my words carefully.

'That is always an advantage, especially if you have something worthwhile to spend the money on,' I ventured. Jack glanced sidelong at me and there was a hint of a grin twitching at the corners of his mouth.

'Thirsty work,' was his statement.

'I suppose it would be,' I commented agreeably. 'It would need a lot of muscle and I guess you'd get fairly hot. Still, it's in the country, which would be nice.'

'Yeah,' he agreed. 'Can't stand cities.'

'When were you last in a city?'

'Oh, that was Brisbane, about 1951.'

'I see, and what about Sydney, where we are now? When were you last here?'

He scratched his head. 'Jeez, you're going back a bit now, girl. That was before the war.'

I decided that it was time for a careful question.

'Jack, can you tell me what year it is now?'

I watched closely as he rubbed his chin.

'Aw, that will take some figurin' out,' he reflected. 'Let's see, after Queensland we worked through western New South Wales and on down to Victoria . . . ah . . . about 1952, '53?'

'Wrong, Jack,' I answered. 'It is now 1978.'

He gave a start. '*What*? You're havin' me on!'

I offered him a copy of that day's newspaper.

'Take a look at the paper, see the date?'

He looked abashed and peeped at me shyly.

'That won't do me no good, love,' he mumbled, with a crooked grin, 'I can't read.'

'Dear me!' I remarked. 'That might handicap us a little bit. I'm afraid you are just going to have to take my word for it—Jack, the date today is June 6th, 1978. Honest truth!'

'Where have I been all this time, then?' he asked in amazement.

'Ah, well now we are coming to the point,' I began. 'I can tell you, but it is going to be a bit of a shock. Can you remember having an accident in recent memory, or becoming ill?'

He shook his head.

'Well,' I continued, 'it's like this. Some time around 1952 or 1953, you may have had a sudden accident and it shocked you out of your body. Your body actually died at the time, and you have been caught between the physical and non-physical worlds ever since.'

Jack stared at me as though I had gone mad.

'I'm dead, but I'm not dead, is that what you're tryin' to tell me?' he demanded.

'Something like that. You see, when you were shocked out of your body . . .'

''Ere, hold on a minute!' he cautioned. 'You're telling me I haven't got a body? What do you call this, then?' He indicated Roland's body with a sweep of the hands.

'That body belongs to my husband,' I persisted. 'He is what we call a trance medium and he is allowing you to borrow his body for the time being, so that you can speak with me.'

'Rubbish!' was the prompt reply. 'This is my body. Look at them hands—they're mine.'

'Jack, there is a wedding ring on the left hand. Were you married?'

He ignored the question. 'They're my hands!' he insisted. 'Look at them callouses! They're mine, I'm telling you.'

'My husband works in an office, Jack. There are no callouses. It seems as though we are going to have to do this the hard way. Are you ready for a shock?'

'Yeah.' Jack's voice held a note of challenge. 'Go on, what are you going to tell me now?'

'Nothing. I'm going to show you something.' I handed him a small hand mirror. 'Look into that and tell me what you see. Is that your face?'

With a resigned expression, as though humouring a lunatic, Jack took the mirror and glanced into it. Then he stared. The effect upon him was electric: he examined Roland's face from every possible angle. Realisation hit him and with a trembling hand, he passed the mirror back to me. He indicated my pack of cigarettes and asked if he could have one. I lit one and gave it to him. He thanked me but said nothing more for some time. I did not speak either, allowing time for his mind to adjust to the unexpected turn of events.

When he next spoke, it was with a new note, of something like awe, in his voice.

'I'm dead, you say?' he asked. I nodded sympathetically.

'. . .And that cove in the mirror, he's your husband? Jeez!' he breathed, absentmindedly flicking ash from his cigarette. The ash fell to the carpet and he was instantly contrite.

'Oh Gawd, look what I've done to your floor! Jeez, love, I'm sorry. I've just got no bloody manners in houses.'

I hastened to assure him that the carpet could be cleaned.

'Take your time,' I added, 'I realise what a shock this must be for you.'

'Listen love,' he said in a confiding tone, 'I think you better give me this "dead" lot again—from the beginning.'

While he sat silently smoking the cigarette, I filled him in on the details. I explained how the soul leaves the body at the time of death and under normal circumstances gravitates gently to the level of spiritual existence to which it is attuned. Since he had no recollection of any events which could have led to his death, I suggested that perhaps it had been caused by a sudden accident and that he had simply failed to see it coming. That would explain his earth-bound condition, since he was totally unaware of the fact that he should have been somewhere else.

'Well!' he considered aloud. 'What's a bloke supposed to do now?'

He looked at me, obviously expecting me to supply him with the answer to his dilemma.

'There are other beings here,' I told him. 'Spirits, like yourself. One of them will come and take you to your new home. . .' I was silenced by a movement from him and saw him staring over my shoulder. On his face was an enraptured expression, like a child seeing its first Christmas tree.

'That bloke there!' he exclaimed in excitement, 'is that him?'

216

I guessed that David had made himself visible to the shearer.

'That's him,' I agreed.

'How do I get over there?' asked Jack, looking now in annoyance at the body which must have seemed to be holding him down.

'All you have to do is close your eyes and let yourself drift. You will leave that body easily, there is nothing to hold you here now. Goodbye, Jack'

'Goodbye,' he replied. The eyes closed, then flew open again. He gazed at me as though I were an angel.

'And. . .thanks, love,' he whispered gently.

Then he was gone.

The proof of a pudding is in the eating and Janet subsequently contacted me to say that her little girl had improved dramatically and was catching up with her classmates in school. I have since lost touch with Janet, but at the last report the child was still doing well. Janet confessed that once we had got the conversation under way with Jack, she had actually grown quite fond of him and she had felt regretful that it had been necessary to part with him. I felt the same way but we had to remember that for the sake of Jack himself and those people with whom he may have come in contact, it was far better that he be escorted to his new home in the spiritual spheres, where he would undoubtedly be utterly contented.

I had not told Jack about the little girl or the effects he had caused through his entanglement in her aura because he would have been thoroughly dismayed and horrified had he known. Perhaps he was told later, when the full details of his condition were made known to him, but I felt quite strongly that such information was not for me to lay upon him. Whilst his manners may have been rough, he was a good-hearted fellow and meant no harm to anyone.

If all astral entities were like Jack, psychic rescue would be an easy and enjoyable task. Regrettably, there are many who know full well what they are doing and have no intention of stopping. Some of them are frighteningly powerful and, being full of hatred and bitterness, they use their power to do harm, even to the point of causing

217

death. One of these was an entity we christened 'The Dark Lady'. Her tale may provide a useful deterrent to those people who feel tempted to become too deeply involved in psychic activity, too soon.

Anne and Bernadette were university students and were friendly with my younger sister. Their experience began when Bernadette had an unsettling dream which began with a vision of her uncle lying on his bed.

As the dream progressed Bernadette saw a dark-haired woman, dressed entirely in black, enter the room and stoop over the bed. She appeared to be caressing the man's neck but when she stepped back and disappeared, Bernadette could see a length of wire twisted tightly around her uncle's neck. When she awoke she told herself sternly that her imagination was becoming morbid as a result of her concern for her uncle, who had been ill for some time. Two days later, the uncle hanged himself—with piano wire. Although she was stunned by the coincidence, Bernadette ascribed it to a possible premonitory awareness and tried to forget it.

A few days later, when Bernadette looked into a mirror, she saw the face of the Dark Lady leering back at her. She told herself that she was becoming morbid and the effects were being produced by a warped imagination. Nevertheless, she kept seeing the sinister figure reflected in shop windows and mirrors as the days passed and she began to wonder if she might not be going insane.

One day as she was talking with her friend Anne, she was horrified to see the form of the Dark Lady appear behind Anne. The threatening figure held a knife in one hand and walked forward, passing through Anne's body before disappearing.

The following day, mysterious bruises appeared on Anne's chest and back, at roughly the level at which the Dark Lady had held the knife. Anne now began to see the formidable figure herself and she became subject to sudden, dramatic changes of mood. At one moment she would be depressed and full of talk about suicide, then abruptly seething with hatred, she would spit abusive language at her companions and rave about getting revenge and killing people.

Both Anne and Bernadette were by now thoroughly

218

terrified and both held grave fears for their sanity but did not know where to turn for help. Their strange behaviour caused talk at the university and the general concensus of opinion there was that the two girls were taking drugs.

My sister Amanda had other ideas. She is clairvoyant and although she did not actually see the entity, she frequently saw a murky dark mass billowing through Anne's aura at the times when the other girl became most disturbed. Amanda suspected spirit possession and rang me for advice. I agreed with her opinion and suggested that if the girls cared to come and see me, I would do my best to help. A sitting was subsequently arranged for the following Friday, a week away.

During that week a lot of strange things began to happen. My son Darryl had been in hospital with influenza at the time of Amanda's first call and he suddenly began to get worse. He developed lobar pneumonia and could not keep anything down, vomiting even when he tried to swallow water. He began to dehydrate and the hospital staff started intravenous feeding. The doctors ran tests, altered his medication and dolefully shook their heads. They could find no cause for his sudden deterioration.

I began to be plagued by nightmares every night and Roland had a number of freakish close calls while driving his car. Other drivers made sudden, deliberate moves which placed him in danger. One driver actually forced him onto the wrong side of the road and into the path of oncoming traffic. When Roland frantically blew his horn, the other driver sneered and made a rude gesture. Roland avoided an accident by a very narrow margin and some skilful driving.

Darryl's condition became worse. On the Friday morning when I went to see him, he was a pale shade of his former self. His tongue and lips were black and swollen, his hands twitched restlessly on the covers and he hardly knew I was there. The ward sister gave me a pitying look as I left his room. She had already told me that unless the cause of Darryl's condition was found soon, the hospital would hold grave fears for his future.

Roland put his arms around me and asked if I felt that

we should cancel the sitting. I shook my head.

'It's possible that the entity is the cause of all this,' I said. 'If she is, the only way to help Darryl is to get rid of her. If I stop now, her triumph would be to see him die. I only hope, in a way, that she *is* behind it, because then I can do something about it. If she isn't. . .'

Both of us fell silent, not daring to pursue the subject any further.

When the girls arrived that evening they were not told of Darryl's condition or of the grave news that the hospital staff had given us. We simply went ahead with the sitting as planned. As I sat watching Roland sink into his trance, the air seemed to become suffocatingly heavy. The girls fidgeted nervously in their seats behind me and I heard Amanda's soft movements as she tried to calm them. Roland's lips curled into a sneer and his eyes opened. Meeting them with mine, I found myself looking into twin pits of the blackest malice I had ever seen.

We stared at each other for several long minutes, then Roland's hands moved upwards, palms out towards me. Psychic energy is transmitted physically through the palms of the hands as well as the eyes and I knew what was coming. The entity was trying to make me fight and that was the one thing I must not do.

I concentrated my thoughts on David, visualising him standing protectively behind me. When the wall of psychic energy coming from the dark being hit me, I raised my own hands—not to push back but to absorb. I felt my body tremble as a wave of rage and hatred surged through it, then it was over and I felt empty. Again the Dark Lady threw her destructive energy at me and again I took it, knowing that David was drawing it through me, to be dissipated where it could harm no one.

I cannot recall how many times I physically absorbed those waves of evil, but just as I was beginning to feel that I would soon be exhausted, the change came. The strategy had worked; the Dark Lady was weakened and she knew it. I watched, feeling a strange sense of detachment, as my husband's body crumpled in a fit of hysterical feminine weeping.

The rasping sobs continued for several minutes, then eased. Slowly, the figure in the chair straightened, the glittering eyes now fixed on Bernadette, who hid her face on my sister's shoulder.

'This is your fault, you filthy bitch!' shouted the enraged entity.

I moved so that I stood in front of Bernadette, hiding her from the entity's view.

'No,' I said quietly, 'it isn't her fault, it's mine.' She ignored me and switched her gaze to Anne.

'You!' she grated. 'Why did you listen to them?'

I moved again, once more placing myself as a barrier before her.

'Get out of my way!' she spat.

'No.'

'*Move*—or I'll go straight through you!'

I smiled grimly. 'You've already tried that, haven't you?'

The eyes dilated slightly and the entity fell silent. She would not look directly at me for some time, but occupied herself by gazing around the room as though trying to make herself familiar with her surroundings. When she finally looked at me again, it was with an altered manner, as though she recognized an equal in strength but could not gauge the intentions of her adversary. When she spoke it was in a tone that was resigned but speculative.

'Who *are* you?'

'My name is Dawn,' I replied.

Her eyes at last focused on the familiar point beyond my shoulder. Something akin to fear or defiance came into her expression and her eyes narrowed.

'And who is *he*?'

'His name is David. He will not harm you.'

Roland's body jerked slightly and lapsed into what appeared to be normal sleep. After a long wait, he spoke.

'My daughter, I am David. It is done.'

I felt close to tears with relief but David's task was not yet concluded. One by one, he called the girls to him, taking their hands and filling their auras with his own energy. The damage done by the Dark Lady was being healed. Even Amanda was given this treatment for she, too, had borne some of the strain exerted by the entity's influence on the others. For myself, I knew that it would take something more than a gift of energy to ease my

221

inner tension. After David had finished with the girls, Roland woke, as usual quite unaware of the evening's events.

Only then did we tell the girls about Darryl's condition and our fears for him. Bernadette and Anne were struck with horror.

'We wouldn't have come, if we'd known!' cried Bernadette.

'I know,' I replied, 'and if the entity has been causing his illness, he would certainly have died if tonight hadn't happened. The question is, *did* she cause it? We won't know until we see him tomorrow.'

Amanda bit her lip in distress and the two other girls came to me and gently touched my hands.

'We'll pray for him,' said Anne.

The final test came the following morning. Roland and I avoided each other's gaze and I felt my hand like ice resting in his as we walked the long hospital corridor to Darryl's room. We entered and I looked at his bed. A merry, rosy-cheeked youngster bounced up and greeted me with a grin. He waved a bandaged hand, still dangling the intravenous drip tube.

'Look Mum!' he chirruped. 'I've got a sore paw!'

Roland choked and muttered something about going outside for a cigarette. I turned to hide my misting eyes from Darryl and found myself face to face with the smiling ward sister.

'That imp,' she said, indicating Darryl with a wave of the hand, 'sat up and demanded breakfast this morn-ing—*and* ate it all. It stayed down, too.'

'Thank God!' I whispered. David had been here.

Before we left the hospital, Roland spoke with the ward sister, asking her what the doctors had done, what new medication had brought about such a change in Darryl.

'Nothing,' was the reply. 'The same medication as before.'

'But Sister, you saw him yesterday, how do you account for such a change?' asked Roland.

'Mr Hill, I am at a loss. I cannot explain it, I do not know.'

David usually tells us very little about the circumstances which caused a particular entity to become earthbound unless we need to know some details in order to help. Even then, only a bare minimum of information is given. The reason seems to lie in some code of professional conduct which preserves the privacy of all concerned. However, possibly because of the horrific effect that she had caused in our lives, we were later told a little about the Dark Lady, enough to help us understand why she had developed such a malicious personality.

The reasons lay in the spirit's two previous physical incarnations. In the first she had been born into a culture that treated its lower classes with indifferent cruelty. She was too immature spiritually to sense that this was wrong and there was nothing in her culture that was capable of teaching her. Privilege and power were hers by birth and she used both without conscience or mercy, simply because she knew no better.

In her next life, the scales were balanced and she was born into a lower-class family which suffered under the heel of its aristocratic oppressors. During that life she was subjected to the pitiless cruelty that she herself had wielded in her former existence.

She was incapable of understanding the reasons why she had to suffer and she developed only hatred for those who oppressed her, along with a burning desire to repay the misery she was being caused to bear. Once she departed the physical she discovered a way in which she could satisfy her lust for revenge. She found that she could prey on those still living by invading their auras. She could torment them until they were driven to suicide, suck energy away from them so that they became deadly ill, and influence them to torment others for her purposes.

I do not know how long she spent in the Astral, engaged in these horrifying pursuits, nor do I know how many people died as a result of her activities. I only know now, as I knew then, that I had been called upon to confront her and be the means by which she could be removed to a place where she could cause no further harm.

When she became aware of Roland and me, she sensed the power that surrounded us and the fact that we intended to curtail her activities. The only method of defence that she knew lay in attacking first and this is what she did, but she was confounded by our reaction. We neither crumpled under the onslaught nor made any attempt to fight back.

Have you ever played a game of push and tug, in which someone else tries to hold a door closed while you exert all of your energy in an effort to force it open? If your opponent steps away from the door at the very moment when you are pressing all of your force against it, the most likely result will be that you fall flat on your face.

If I had made any attempt to counter the Dark Lady with force I would have lost the contest, for she understood the use of violence far better than I ever could. It was a far greater power which defeated her: the force of compassion. She could not comprehend how anyone could possess power and yet refuse to use it in combat. When she hurled all of her force at me, she did not realise that her own momentum would be her downfall.

Her defeat at our hands may ultimately prove to be the means of her salvation. In the spiritual spheres malcontents are not punished, they are simply disarmed and confined in a region where they can cause no further damage. This is the spiritual equivalent to a hospital and there they are eventually healed, whereupon they can once more venture forth to take up the round of reincarnation and evolution.

As for the next entity, I know nothing of its origins, nor do I wish to for I am certain that I would find them distasteful. This was another which fully understood what it was doing and it persecuted a young woman for years before she was brought to us for help.

Her name is Kerry and she was brought to us by her doctor, who for ethical reasons would prefer to remain anonymous, so I will call him Doctor G. She had suffered from constant migraine headaches for a number of years; even the strongest medications only brought partial relief from the pain. Not surprisingly, she was also profoundly depressed, confused, and neurotic. She had been admitted to a mental hospital for a time and had been dismissed as a hopeless personality disorder or, to put it in Kerry's words: 'The psychiatrist said that I'm nuts.'

When Kerry first walked through our door with Doctor G. Roland's immediate reaction was startling, to say the least. He made a dive for the bath-room where he stayed for several minutes, vomiting violently. When he emerged, pale-faced, to join us, he rocked everybody with his opening words to our visitor: 'Kerry, I'm sorry to say this, but you make me sick!'

I expected the young lady to make an indignant exit but she only looked thoughtful as Roland explained that a feeling of nausea had swept over him from the moment he first looked directly at her. After listening to this explanation Kerry turned to Doctor G. with a question:

'Did you tell them that I've been vomiting all day?'

The doctor shook his head. He had told us only that Kerry was suffering from a migraine headache.

Something in Kerry's attitude was beginning to make me feel distinctly uneasy. She did not appear to question our ability as psychics, but I could feel distrust oozing from her, almost tangible in its intensity. I began to explain our role as psychics, hoping to dispel whatever it was that engendered the distrust within her. Despite my efforts, I felt that there were several firmly locked doors in the girl's mind and I could only guess what lay behind them. Meanwhile, Roland began to nod slightly—a sign that he was entering the first stage of a trance.

Keeping an eye on Roland's progress, I continued talking to Kerry, trying to dispel the aura of suspicion that hung about her like a cloud. Try as I might, I could not penetrate far enough to discover the cause of her attitude. Whatever it was, she wanted to keep it to herself. Eventually it became clear that she was only half listening to me and that she was beginning to feel disturbed about Roland's trance. She kept casting sidelong glances at him and each time it seemed as though she was making a physical effort to drag her eyes back to me. It was obvious that she was acutely uncomfortable and her eyes turned unwillingly towards Roland as though propelled by some irresistible force.

'Are you afraid?' I asked. She nodded, covering her face with her hands.

'Those eyes!' she whispered harshly. 'I can't bear to look.'

I turned my full attention to Roland. He was now completely in trance, his body rigid under the influence of the entity he had drawn into his aura. He stared fixedly at Kerry, his lip curling into a sneer. His eyes seemed to burn with diabolical intent but when he spoke, his voice was soft and persuasive.

'Look at me, Kerry.'

She kept her eyes covered and shook her head.

'Look at me Kerry, and I'll take your pain away,' he coaxed.

Deciding that the time for intervention had come, I spoke up firmly.

'The sitting cannot proceed until you have identified yourself. Will you tell us your name please?' I was dismissed with a contemptuous gesture. The entity spoke again to Kerry, a hard note now evident in the voice as it demanded that she look into Roland's eyes. She did not need me to tell her not to obey; her eyes remained firmly covered.

'Kerry!' the voice had become harsh and ugly. 'You know who I am. You have had instruction and you know the consequences. *Look at me*!' The terrified girl huddled in the seat and moaned softly, reaching in mute appeal for me. I took her hand in mine and spoke severely to the entity.

'Kerry is not yours to command! I am controlling this sitting and you have still given us no identification.'

The response was a grim chuckle.

'*Not* mine? She is more mine than yours and I shall prove it to you. Kerry, unless you obey, I shall make your pain unbearable!'

'You can't do that!' I exclaimed.

'Can't? On the count of twenty. One, two, three . . .' A tremor ran through Kerry's body. '. . . four, five . . .'

The hand that had been clutching mine was abruptly withdrawn. Kerry now clutched her temples.

'. . .sixteen . . .' She rocked from side to side, sobbing aloud and tearing at her hair.

'. . .nineteen, *twenty*.'

Kerry screamed and pitched forward, falling from the chair. She crawled towards me like a terrified animal seeking shelter, her tear-streaked face contorted with pain and fear. She was screaming continuously. I reached out and gathered her into my arms.

'Demonstration over,' declared the satisfied voice.

Kerry slumped, dropping her head onto my knees and I stroked her hair as I watched the painful shuddering subside. I was aware that Roland was awaking from his trance, but I concentrated my attention on Kerry. I was beginning to suspect a reason for her show of distrust earlier in the evening.

'That was no ordinary earthbound entity,' I commented. 'Kerry, there is something that you haven't told me and I think it is something I need to know. What is it?'

She raised her head and opened her eyes, then her face crumpled in horror and she cried aloud.

'I'm blind!'

Doctor G. jerked forward and stared intently at Kerry. The terror-stricken girl wept openly, tears coursing down her face from eyes that stared unseeingly towards me.

'It's all dark!' she panicked. 'I can't see.'

I placed a hand firmly on either side of her face. 'Close your eyes Kerry,' I ordered. The eyelids fluttered down and I continued to speak, calmly but insistently.

'Listen to me. As your fear subsides, your sight will return to you. Your eyes and your mind are connected by a pathway that cannot be broken easily. Your eyes are undamaged, it is your mind that is clouded. I will see to it that you are not harmed, there is no need to be afraid. Calm down, take a deep breath. Now open your eyes and see me.'

She opened her eyes, blinked for a moment or two, then looked at me with recognition.

'I really was blind,' she said in a little-girl voice.

'Hysterical reaction, it can happen sometimes,' I replied in a matter of fact tone. 'Now, tell me what I need to know.'

She muttered something and hung her head. I asked her to repeat herself and without lifting her head or meeting my eyes, she answered. 'I used to be involved in witchcraft.'

'Black Magic?' I asked remorselessly. She nodded.

'How long ago?'

She held up five fingers.

'Years? Months? I have to know all about it if you want us to help you, Kerry.'

Hesitantly at first, Kerry told us her story. During her early teens she had become disenchanted with the traditional churches because their teachings failed to answer the questions that teemed in her mind. Looking for an alternative, she found some books on Satanism and they fascinated her. At the age of sixteen, she formed an association with a young man who belonged to a coven known as the Sons of Satan. Little persuasion was needed to induce the curious teenager to join.

She stayed with the coven for a number of months but eventually her revulsion at their practices became too much for her. At the same time, she married and fell pregnant and she felt that the time had come when she should sever her association with the cult. Informed of her intention to leave, the coven leader told her that it was impossible and that her unborn child was now the property of Satan. Terrified, she took to her heels. The headaches commenced a few weeks later.

In the years that followed, ill fortune seemed to dog her footsteps. Her marriage disintegrated and she began to drift aimlessly, always plagued by the agonising headaches and a deep-seated fear for her little daughter. When she had finished speaking Kerry looked at me, patently expecting an angry, critical reaction. It was not forthcoming.

I explained the function of vibrations, pointing out how the involvement with black magic can attract lower astral entities. She had been taught how to invite these beings into her aura but not how to drive them out.

'We can teach you,' I promised, 'but it will take more sittings and you can expect the headaches to get worse in the meantime. The entity you have attracted is powerful and has a strong hold within your aura. It will fight us but it can be defeated with your co-operation. Can you face it?'

She nodded vigorously, promising at the same time that she would do everything that we asked. She also explained her earlier distrust of us.

'The only other so-called psychics I've ever known were

all in the coven. I thought you might be witches too.'

I laughed and told her that there are still a few people who cannot tell the difference, but Roland and I have never had anything to do with witchcraft—black or white.

It took three more sittings before Kerry's aura was cleared. The last is worth relating if only because it was during this sitting that Kerry made the mistake of panicking, almost causing a tragedy as a result.

It began like the sittings which preceded it, none of which had been pleasant. I was on guard as I watched Roland beginning to slip into his trance. I stood in front of him, the doctor sat on his right and Kerry's boyfriend was seated on his left. Kerry herself was sitting behind me, slightly to my right and facing Roland.

Roland's glittering eyes were fixed on Kerry, who fidgeted nervously in her chair, afraid to look at him. The air was crackling with tension. Suddenly Roland's body moved as though he were about to stand up. This sometimes happens during a sitting of this kind but while everyone in the room remains calm, David is able to keep a firm grip on the proceedings and prevent the entity from gaining full control of Roland's body. I stood quietly, waiting for the entity to give up the effort and slump back into the chair again.

But the movement had terrified Kerry and she gave a shriek, throwing herself to the floor and scrambling for cover behind me. This had the effect of disrupting the vibrations in the room and I watched in horror as Roland's set features were turned on me and he stood up. I took a step backwards and Kerry scuttled across the floor towards Doctor G., keeping her back turned to Roland all the while, afraid to see what was about to happen.

Petrified, I watched as the figure shuffled forward, clawed hands outstretched towards my throat. The sitting was out of control. As I tried frantically to think of a course of action, I thought absurdly that Roland's movements resembled nothing more closely than the gait of a Frankenstein monster. However this was no fantasy situation and if that entity were to reach me physically I would have to call on Doctor G. and Kerry's boyfriend to bring the body down, but that could mean serious injury for Roland. The prospects before me were ominous. One step, two. . .the looming figure drew nearer. In desperation, I cried out loudly:

'David! In the name of Christ, *stop him*!'

The approaching figure lurched to a halt and abruptly pitched forward, falling heavily to the floor. I had unthinkingly created another disturbance, this time causing the entity to lose its grip on the physical body and allowing David the opportunity to take over. Now, however, it was necessary for David to use force in order to overcome the other entity. I watched in awe as the two spirits battled for control of Roland's body and I wondered how long the frail physical vehicle would be able to withstand the psychic battering.

Roland's body jerked repeatedly, to such an extent that it was possible for me to tell which spirit had the upper hand at any given moment. Even though Kerry was crouching with her back to Roland and covering her face with her hands, she screamed with pain and clutched at her head every time the dark entity tried to raise Roland's body up from the floor. David's power was the greater however, and the body was firmly thrust back into a prone position each time. Eventually the body relaxed and I sighed with relief when I heard David's infinitely welcome voice.

'My daughter, I am David. It is over.'

I could not be annoyed with Kerry even though she had been warned against making any sudden moves or noises. She had been under tremendous strain and her fear had become so great that she was unable to control it. We were all fortunate that David is so highly developed, because anyone with less ability would have been unable to control the situation so quickly and I do not care to imagine the results. As it was, Kerry's muscular boyfriend later commented that he was glad it was me, and not himself, who had faced the entity during those few heartstopping moments.

All of that happened over a year ago. Since then, Kerry has had two or three headaches, but so has almost everybody else—the occasional headache is a fact of life for most of us. The intense, continuous pain that had brought her to us is another matter entirely—that has completely disappeared. Kerry herself is not out of the woods yet. Her original restlessness and dissatisfaction with life in general were the cause of her involvement with the unhealthy side of the supernatural and that attitude was caused by emotional problems that had been suffered during her childhood.

Roland and I are psychics; we deal with personal problems only when they relate to a psychic disturbance. We do not pretend to be qualified psychologists and we would not attempt to deal with personality problems that do not originate in the psychic spheres. Psychologists and psychiatrists had failed to reach Kerry when her problems became acute only because the psychic problem was in the way. Once that was removed, there was nothing to stop them from helping her and she is now happily attending counselling sessions with a psychologist who is helping her to understand and overcome her original emotional problems. We have maintained contact with her and at last report she was making satisfactory progress.

Kerry's future now lies in her own hands. If at some future date she decides to turn her back on the world and again join a black magic coven, that is her decision to make. Knowing Kerry, however, I sincerely doubt that she would make any such choice; she is far too intelligent and not nearly warped enough.

Kerry fell victim to one of the more potent dangers of the supernatural when she joined the coven. Because the supernatural is different and offers exciting alternatives to those which apply in everyday life, it attracts people who are psychologically disturbed. These people are out of balance within themselves and while ever they remain in that condition, no reputable psychic with an ounce of common sense would attempt to train them psychically. The risks are far too great, both for the would-be psychic and for the rest of humanity in general.

An unbalanced person is unlikely to comprehend the principles behind spiritual development. Being out of balance himself, he cannot understand or relate to the harmonics of the universe any more than he can fit into the physical system in which we all reside. Because this type of person frequently feels misunderstood and socially inferior, psychic energy in such hands could be a lethal weapon. In fact, this principle is the motive force behind black magic.

Most of the people who become involved in black witchcraft or satanism are simply colourful charlatans who do little more than make a nuisance of themselves. However an unbalanced psychic who pursues such a course can present a very real threat to other people.

It is easy for a highly psychic person to get out of balance if he has no understanding of spiritual principles because he may also be unable to adjust to reality in terms of fitting himself into the physical system of life. If he is intuitive enough he will become aware of the super-natural. If he is sufficiently unbalanced he will seek to use it in order to satisfy his own whims. Unfortunately, there are people who have learned how to manipulate psychic energy in this way. Because it is in their nature to seek an audience, their tendency will be to form cult groups or black magic covens, into which they entice other misfits like themselves who are also seeking something 'special'.

A classic example of this kind of psychic would be Charles Manson. The hideous deeds wrought by him and his followers should be enough to convince most people that psychic energy in the wrong hands is utterly perilous. Manson is not only unbalanced, he is a powerful psychic who is capable of controlling the minds of other people. There are others, more subtle than he and therefore potentially more dangerous because they are cunning enough to camouflage themselves under a plausible guise.

The comforting point in all of this is that a negative psychic has no chance of penetrating the Void. Their power may be formidable but it comes only from the lower regions of the Astral. The *real* power lies beyond the Void and those who can tap into it have nothing to fear from sorcerers, nor would they ever use their own power to harm anyone, for any reason. It is this principle and power which defeated the Dark Lady, despite the fact that she was an extremely powerful opponent. It has also been used by us on occasions to frustrate the efforts of unscrupulous psychics to hurt other people.

It is wise to bear in mind that there are sinister forces at work within the supernatural, just as there are in the physical and it is equally wise to be constantly on guard against them. This is the reason why I have always encouraged my students to test everything they are told and that includes everything that I say.

The most astute students have immediately responded to that instruction by subjecting me to a thorough interrogation and are continuing to do so whenever they suspect that they can catch me off guard. Far from annoying me, this proves their ability to comprehend the subject and it delights me to see them do it. Besides, it keeps me on my toes. I am only a psychic, not a superhuman, and being only human, I too can slip at times and develop a rather negative attitude towards life. My students are always ready and waiting to catch me out if I do and that knowledge serves as a reminder for me to practice what I preach.

I repeat here what I have said elsewhere in this book. No reputable psychic or spirit has any reason to fear investigation of their knowledge or methods. If anyone claims to possess spiritual awareness yet resists or resents close investigation, it is well to avoid them for it may be that they have something to hide. I am not suggesting that their private lives should be open to invasion; personal privacy is a precious thing. However, they should be prepared to allow their psychic activities and practices to be thoroughly scrutinized. If they are unwilling to do this, you have every reason to be suspicious of them. After all, it is your own welfare that you are protecting.

There is no absolute guarantee of protection against psychic infestation or attack. It can happen to anyone at any time, whether or not they are actively involved with the paranormal. Unless the victim is acquainted with a psychic who can assess the trouble, the likelihood is that the problem will remain unchecked. This need not always result in tragedy but the potential does exist. Most often it causes a series of minor ailments and troublesome emotional problems. The victim may begin to suffer from nightmares and/or neurotic disturbances.

Cases of this nature should never be tackled by an inexperienced enthusiast. Psychic rescue is a technique which requires steady nerves, concentration and above all, a thorough training along with powerful backup from the spirit helpers. Four years of intensive training have gone into my involvement with this work and even now I would not attempt it if I were not sure that David was right there with me. Even so, I have on one or two occasions made small mistakes which could have caused an eruption of violence had they not been checked in time. In fact, I once bore a black eye as testimony to a particularly careless move on my part. Needless to say, my precautions have become even more stringent since then.

It should be remembered that the technique of psychic rescue requires the medium to draw an entity into his own aura. It is, if you like, a form of carefully controlled possession. While the medium is in a trance he is dependent upon the expertise of the control, who works in conjunction with the spirit guides to ease the entity through his aura and into the spiritual sphere to which it belongs. A mistake on the part of the control can break the spiritual contact, leaving the entity enmeshed in the medium's aura and capable of controlling the entranced physical body. Since some of these entities are malicious and violent, the results could be tragic.

It is unfortunate that psychic research continues to be regarded as a novelty, unrelated to 'real' life as most people understand it. The average man in the street would be astonished to discover just how much of his daily life is subject to psychic influences. The rules which govern psychic activity prevent reputable psychics from forcing their knowledge upon anyone who chooses not to become involved and for that reason I have often had to ignore a case of psychic infestation simply because the victim wished to know nothing about the paranormal.

Of particular interest to me are the number of cases in which a person carries out an act of violence, or even murder, and later attempts to explain his actions by saying that 'something came over him' and he was unable to control his actions. There is, of course, no evidence to suggest a psychic influence in these cases, but I suspect that if psychics were permitted to investigate they would find that many of these unfortunate episodes were in fact the result of psychic infestation. Of course, this would raise some interesting legal problems concerning the guilt of the hapless defendant, since it would tend to lay the blame on a being who could not be apprehended and punished in the accepted manner.

One case which aroused my interest in this respect was the series of murders carried out by the 'Son of Sam' killer in the United States. When apprehended, he claimed to have been instructed to kill by a voice which could only be heard by him. Not all 'voices from nowhere' are malicious of course. I recently read a biography of Florence Nightingale in which it was stated that on occasions the great lady heard a voice which guided her in the pioneering of the nursing profession. Another obvious case is Joan of Arc, who is mentioned elsewhere in this book.

Whether unseen voices cause mayhem or blessings is entirely dependent on the purity of the channel through which they manifest. As I have already stated, psychic energy is mindless and the type of energy you attract is entirely dependent upon the type of radiations you emit.

For the student of psychic phenomena, the risk of interference should be borne in mind and careless or lighthearted experiments should be avoided. It is far better to gain as much knowledge as possible and allow your abilities to develop naturally than to experiment with forces that you do not fully understand and cannot control. If you are truly seeking spiritual understanding, it will come when you are ready for it. The Eastern mystics have a saying: 'When the pupil is ready, the teacher will come'. This is roughly equivalent to the Christian adage: 'Seek and ye shall find'. I have often been impressed by the number of people who have 'just happened' to come into contact with me at precisely the time when they were seeking someone who could explain their psychic experiences. It seems fairly obvious that our friends on the 'other side' have a very real influence in this respect.

Just as the higher spirits respect and acknowledge your free will and your right to make your own decisions in life, it is necessary for you to understand the responsibility that goes with that right. Your welfare is entirely your own concern and it is up to you to make sure that you do not expose yourself to danger while you pursue your search for understanding.

There are a number of techniques that can help you to protect yourself. Whenever you are meditating or carrying out some activity of a psychic nature, visualise your whole being suffused with a clear, white light. This will have the effect of clearing your aura of negative radiations and it will also help to raise your vibrations.

Also, begin each meditation or practice period with a prayer of some kind for protection. It does not matter which religious philosophy you embrace, or even whether you follow a religion at all. Direct your thoughts to the essence that you feel to be the highest and the most pure and request that presence to surround you with love and protection. This will draw guides and protectors into your vicinity and once having been requested to provide protection, they will happily respond. It is advisable also to spend a few minutes prior to your meditation sessions 'feeling out' the atmosphere that surrounds you. If you feel warm, secure and comfortable, go ahead with your psychic activity. If, however, you feel cold and uneasy, it might be better to postpone your session until the atmosphere is more conducive to what you are trying to achieve. Your own senses are usually the best indicators you can have, and even though you may not be able to see the spirits who surround you, it is possible for you to be aware of them and any suggestion of uneasiness or discomfort may indicate the presence of undesirable entities.

At all times, strive for increased understanding of the spiritual worlds. David consistently reminds me that knowledge is growth and if you are seeking to develop your psychic abilities, no knowledge is superfluous.

I have devoted this chapter to making you aware that there are strong negative forces within the supernatural, just as there are in the physical, and it will benefit you very little to invite such things into your aura. Knowing that these things exist and understanding something about them can help you to avoid making any mistakes that could lead you into trouble. Remember that like does attract like and if you devote your time to raising your

vibrations you are less likely to attract low or coarse
entities. The higher beings are there to help you; seek
them out.

CHAPTER TWENTY
Psychic healing

No book on the Psychic would be complete without some
space being dedicated to the phenomenon of psychic
healing. For us it has become one of the most intriguing
areas to which we have been led by our Guide and it is the
area where we are most aware that an agency far beyond
the limitations of man's capabilities is at work.

Although many people have visited us for the purpose
of healing, it must be clearly understood that we lay no
claims to supernatural powers within ourselves. We
recognise only that we are the instruments, or channels,
through which these healings may take place.

Psychic healing is a phenomenon quite distinct from
'faith' healing. In the latter, it is the patient's own faith
that healing will occur which produces an improvement.
In psychic healing no such belief is necessary and we have
found through personal experience that healing is not
limited to the 'faithful' or the 'believer' but is equally
possible with a person of the most stubborn sceptical
nature.

An interesting facet of human nature has been
highlighted during our investigations into the area of
healing and it shows just how stubborn we humans can be
when we choose. We can be witness first-hand to a healing
and yet come away unconvinced. We can talk to the
person who has been treated and ask him 'Has it really
happened, are you really better?' We can examine the
once afflicted area and see for ourselves the results of the
healing that we watched and then dismiss the matter with
a simple 'I don't believe you'. Let me give you an example:

We were expecting a visitor who had previously
contacted us with regard to a healing session for himself.

237

This man was in his late thirties and was a keen physical fitness exponent, but for reasons unknown had developed a rather nasty blood disorder. He had heard about us from an acquaintance and, while sceptical himself, had asked if we could help. We told him that we could only try, and arranged for him to come and see us at our home. On the same day we were visited by my ex-husband, Dennis, who had come to spend the day with our son.

Shortly before our visitor was due to arrive, Roland, who was in the garden, decided to make some tea. As he came into the house however, he tripped and fell heavily against the back step, his right knee taking most of the impact on the edge of the concrete tread. He tried to rise but found that he could not—the pain from his knee was too severe.

Dennis and I virtually carried him inside and sat him on the sofa, whereupon he pulled up the leg of his trousers and exposed the knee. It was horribly indented; the kneecap, having been displaced sideways, was bulging unnaturally from the side of his leg and blood oozed from a three-inch cut across the face of the indentation.

Dennis immediately offered to drive us to the hospital but Roland asked to sit for a while in order to get over the shock. He looked very pale, the knee was already swelling and taking on a purplish hue. I did not think it advisable to delay but Roland can be very obstinate at times. When he asked for a cup of tea, I was astonished. How anyone could sit and drink tea with a knee in that condition was beyond me. I demurred, he insisted.

While I was in the kitchen, I heard a startled exclamation from Dennis. Not knowing what to expect, I hurried into the lounge room. Roland was still on the sofa, but was looking dazed—his knee was now twice its normal size and turning an ugly shade of blue. Blood from the cut had run down his shin and was reaching towards his ankle. The kneecap itself, however, no longer bulged from the side of his leg. Dennis explained:

'He just grabbed his kneecap and pushed back into place!'

To say that I was flabbergasted would be underestimating the situation somewhat, as I knew perfectly well that a procedure of that magnitude is normally performed in hospital under a general anaesthetic because it is so painful.

A sudden knocking at the front door made me jump and stopped Dennis before he could explain any further. In my concern for Roland I had completely forgotten that we were to have a visitor. I let him in and quickly explained what had happened adding, needlessly, that the sitting would have to be postponed. However, as we were about to have the tea that Roland had insisted upon, I asked our visitor if he would care to join us.

We were all soon ensconced in the lounge room, tea cups in hand. Dennis was about to enlarge on his story when Roland's actions stopped us cold. His eyes closed and he took on the appearance of a trance. His hands closed over the grossly swollen knee, his fingers interlaced over the open cut and he began to sway back and forth. There was complete silence in the room for about thirty seconds after which Roland opened his eyes and looked at his hands with some surprise. When he took them from his knee we were all stunned. The swelling and discolouration had disappeared. So had the cut! All that remained was the blood on his leg and that was still fresh, still moist. He excused himself to the bathroom and came back a few moments later, after washing the blood from his shin. No trace of the accident remained—not a mark!

The effect on the men was stupefying: their faces showed their incredulity, their sheer and utter disbelief that such a thing could happen. Our visitor gave Roland a long and searching look and then in a voice that was none too steady announced that he felt the need for some air—outside.

Dennis, confirmed sceptic that he is, reacted by saying: 'I didn't see that—and I don't want anybody to tell me that I did. I know that I saw it, but I'm having trouble believing it'. He now prefers not to discuss the matter at all.

For an explanation of how such healing is possible we need to look to another case. This one involved a woman in her early thirties who was brought to us by Doctor G.

He explained that she had a double set of kidneys and was subject to recurring infections in that part of her body. In the past the most effective remedy had been to admit her to hospital and treat her with intravenous antibiotics; a process that usually required some three weeks hospitalization and nursing care.

The lady looked obviously ill. Her complexion was a dull grey under her make-up and her eyes lacked the lustre of a person in good health. Doctor G. explained that pathology tests indicated the return of her renal infection. He had spoken to her about us and she had agreed to try psychic healing, but voiced her reservations not only to him at the time but also to us when we were introduced.

Roland countered by explaining that it was not us who would do the healing, if indeed a healing were to take place, but rather her relief would come from a hand far mightier than that of any man. The sitting began. Roland tranced and David arrived. He placed Roland's hands in position, one in front and one behind the kidney area on the left side of her body and then again over the right. All in all this process took some ten minutes, during which Doctor G. questioned his patient as to what, if any, sensations she was feeling.

She replied that the first sensation was of heat coming from my husband's hands; heat that built up and then began to suffuse inwards. There was an increase in the pain from her kidneys that rapidly increased to the point where she felt that if it grew any more she would not be able to bear it. At that point David moved the hands to the other side of her body and repeated the process, once more bringing the heat to just below her tolerance level.

When the sitting had finished and while Roland was still coming out of his trance state, the lady surprised Doctor G. by asking him if it were possible for pain to travel.

When the doctor asked her to elaborate she said that it felt as though the pain was moving towards her solar plexus; contracting. Then she announced in a startled voice that the pain had gone!

Doctor G. was intrigued and his medical curiosity aroused. He could accept the removal of pain as a subsconscious conditioned reflex. Because she was expecting something to happen his patient could have subconsciously initiated a blocking mechanism such as would be induced by a hypnotherapist in a patient who is about to undergo a tooth extraction. With this in mind, the doctor took her back to his surgery for a detailed examination and further pathology tests. He rang us the following day with the news that the path. tests were clear: there was no trace of the infection to be found.

David explained that in this case he had merely accelerated the body's natural healing abilities, compressing into minutes what would normally have taken much, much longer. From that point of view it explains the increase of pain, controlled as it was, as the infection ran its course through an accelerated time span.

Many people today are beginning to explore alternative avenues of healing such as chiropractic and naturopathic healing and acupuncture—methods which have been regarded as suspect until recent times. Traditional medical science is slowly accepting the validity of these alternative sources of healing and it is possible that at some time in the future, psychic healing will also gain acceptance. This will only come about if the results produced by this method are published and if the medical profession becomes willing to examine the results produced and make objective judgements, unclouded by dogma or scepticism.

It is common for people to make the mistake of equating Psychic healing with Faith healing, but in fact they are quite different. Faith healing requires that the sufferer believe that a cure will take place once certain rites are performed. It is actually the sufferer's faith which generates the cure. It works because the solid faith required in this method generates positive energy within the aura and reverses the negative trend which gave rise to the illness.

Psychic healing is different for the simple reason that faith on the part of the sufferer is not required. It does not matter whether the patient believes or not; the healing energy flows through an independent channel—the medium. A few of the people who have approached us for healing did so only at the urging of

241

someone else. They would always inform us that they 'don't really believe in all this stuff, but it can do no harm to give it a try'.

With those people we make a point of telling them that we have no particular wish to proselytize anyone. We simply do what we do. As to whether or not the 'treatment' will work, that is not in our hands. We are simply channels through which an unseen force can flow.

'Whether or not you believe in it, the force is there,' we say. 'It will not go away just because you don't believe. Your beliefs, before and after you come here, are none of our concern. That is a matter that you alone can decide.'

We spoke this way to a young man named Michael who had grudgingly agreed to try psychic healing at the urging of his wife Sue, who was herself seeking healing for a spinal complaint. He suffered from continuous 'pins and needles' in his right arm, which medical treatment had been unable to relieve. He was not aggressively sceptical but nor did he see any particular reason for believing in supernatural forces. He simply wanted to make his position quite clear to us.

Having spoken his mind, Michael calmly allowed himself to be treated by our guides in two sittings a week apart. He asked a number of astute questions and spent some time discussing the supernatural with us and when his annoying complaint disappeared he did not seem unduly surprised. He still reserves his opinion as to what it was that brought about his relief; there has been no enthusiastic 'conversion' in him, nor would we expect one. The only important thing is that his condition was healed and he no longer suffers from the continual irritation that plagued him before.

Several years ago, when Roland and I had only been training with David for a few months, I received the benefit of psychic healing myself. It was necessary for me to undergo an operation for the removal of my gallbladder and before the surgery was performed, the doctor told us that I was almost certain to develop pneumonia as a post-operative complication. This, said the doctor, was due to the fact that I am a smoker and also because the operation is performed just below the diaphragm. He assured us that there would be no real cause for alarm as it is a common complication with this type of operation and the staff were well prepared to handle the situation. Sure enough, a couple of days after the operation I began to have trouble breathing and felt severe pain in my chest. The doctor informed me that I had developed pneumonia, just as he had predicted.

What I was not told was that my right lung had collapsed, my left lung was half filled with fluid and I had blood clots in both lungs. It was the blood clots which caused the greatest concern since if they moved they could block vital coronary blood vessels, causing rapid death. It was Roland who heard this news and was informed that I had been placed on the 'Dangerously Ill' list. When he asked about my chances of recovery, the doctor looked thoughtful, then said, 'Well, we'll see how she goes through the next forty-eight hours'.

Not surprisingly, Roland was utterly distraught. He knew that the hospital staff would do everything medically possible but he could not simply sit by and wait out the next two days without doing something himself.

He knew that one of his workmates was associated with a psychic group and, although still inclined to be sceptical himself, he asked his friend for help. He was told that the group would be meeting that evening and they would do what they could for me. No contact was made with me; the method that was used is known as absent healing. The members of the group simply contacted their spirit friends and asked them to go to work.

When Roland left me I was propped up on a pile of pillows, semi-conscious and connected to drip tubes and an oxygen mask. I was in considerable pain and powerful analgesics were given to me every four hours for pain relief. The combined effect was to make me hardly aware of my surroundings and I seemed to drift in and out of a mist of unconsciousness.

The following morning I sat up, removed the oxygen mask and calmly manoeuvred myself out of bed. Pneumonia or no pneumonia, my hair was dirty and I was going to wash it. Trailing the drip stand behind me, I made my way to the bathroom and proceeded to give my hair a thorough wash; I was just wrapping a towel around my head when a horrified nurse dashed in and remoniously bustled me back to bed, informing me that I must not get up again without the doctor's express permission.

As an ex-nurse, I understood hospital routine and made no objection to remaining in bed, but I was a little puzzled by the degree of consternation that had been caused by my escapade. Roland arrived at visiting time to find me sitting up brightly, brushing my hair and wearing a happy smile. An expression of blessed relief crossed his face. I wondered why eveybody seemed to be making such a big deal out of a simple gallbladder operation; surely, I thought, a touch of pneumonia could hardly be sufficient reason for the fuss everyone was making.

It was not until I had been out of hospital for a week that Roland told me the full extent of my complications. He added that he had never expected his approach to our psychic friend to yield such dramatic results. There is, of course, no way of proving that the psychic healing *was* responsible in this instance for my rapid recovery, but it does seem unlikely that medical science alone could claim the credit, particularly in view of the gloomy prognosis given by the doctor.

Although Roland and I have had a number of experiences with psychic healing during the course of our training with David, we are not being trained as healers but as teachers. Although we are fascinated with the healing process as explained by David, it is only a part of our studies.

We are well aware, however, that it constitutes a fascinating field on its own and we would be only too happy to work with people who are interested in exploring the possibilities for themselves. We speak of healing only in the psychic terms that we understand, however we both feel very strongly that psychic healing has a great deal to offer in terms of relief from human suffering. We have seen and experienced for ourselves the benefits of psychic healing and our friend Doctor G. has been impressed enough to bring several of his patients to us for help. At the time of this writing, some four and a half years after beginning our psychic training, we have not had a failure.

One thing that really saddens me is the widely held

244

opinion that sickness and suffering were introduced into the world as a punishment for human sin. Nothing could be further from the truth nor give a more derogatory impression of the Creator who blessed us with life. Disease is produced when something goes wrong with your life mechanism. It can happen through injury or infection or it can result from some other cause: whatever the reason, it has happened because of a malfunction, not because you are unworthy of good health and happiness.

Today we smile at our superstitious ancestors, who believed that every calamity which befell them was visited upon them by vengeful gods, yet in the belief that sickness is God's punishment for sin, we are not very far removed from our credulous forebears. There are certain natural laws which are designed to maintain the balance of harmony within the universe. They are laws of nature and are utterly oblivious to the vagaries of human nature—they simply function as they are intended to do regardless, or perhaps in spite of, our activities.

It is not a sin to stand on a railway line, but if you happen to be doing it when the 8.05 comes roaring through, a certain natural law dictates that unless you get out of the way very quickly you will discover the effects of a collision with a heavy object moving at high speed. It would, however, be totally unrealistic of you to blame a heavenly power for sending the train along at that particular time.

With healing, as with any other aspect of psychic development, understanding is the key to progress. It is necessary to understand the human being as a complete entity, body and soul, before you can hope to ease any of the problems that person may be caused to suffer in life.

To reiterate what I have said elsewhere in this book, you are a spirit—your eternal existence is not dependent upon physical substance. For the time being you possess a physical vehicle through which you manifest yourself in this world. When your time here is finished, you will discard that body and progress onwards. In the meantime, it is in your own interests to keep your body functioning at optimum efficiency, if only because it better enables you to carry out the roles that you undertook when you came here. As a spirit, you exist

245

within the aura which surrounds and permeates your physical body and you control the body by directing your will through it.

The receptor centres in your body through which emotional messages are received or transmitted are known as chakras. The chakras also play a vital part in the maintenance of body functions and it is not by accident that they are located in the region of the body's endocrine glands. Let us use one example of an instinctive triggered response: adrenalin, the 'fight or flight' hormone that is produced by the adrenal gland, located on your kidney. What originates the bolt of emotion which triggers the gland to produce that vital hormone?

Can you recall the last time that you had a fright or a shock which left you trembling and ashen-faced? If you can, try to recall where you actually felt the bolt of emotion in your body. Wasn't it somewhere in the region of your solar plexus? This is where one of your chakras is located. The emotion which actually triggered the gland came *through* the chakra. From where?

The adrenalin which is released into your bloodstream stimulates the body to carry out feats which would be impossible under normal circumstances. You may temporarily develop superhuman strength in order to save someone else's life, for instance. But can you imagine what the effect would be if adrenalin were continuously being fed into your system when no such activity was required? It would be rather like continuously revving the engine of a car—the wear and tear would be astonishing.

Thought and emotion are not physical energy forms—they are psychic emanations which originate within your soul or spirit. Their effects on your body can be traced and measured but they themselves cannot. If your thoughts and emotions are operating smoothly and are not unduly disturbed, you function efficiently as a person.

If you are constantly being disturbed or upset, your ability to fulfil your potential will be severely diminished. It is not for nothing that we advise you to cultivate tranquillity within yourself.

So much for your own thoughts and emotions, but

what of those being transmitted by other people? Can they have an effect on your health also?

How often have you heard someone describing the 'instant chemistry' that took place when he or she met a member of the opposite sex? Why does it happen with some people and not with others? On the other end of the scale you have probably felt an instant surge of dislike for a person you have just met for the first time. There may have been nothing in that person's words or manner to provoke this reaction in you yet it was there all the same.

Spend some time in the company of a person who persists in taking a gloomy, pessimistic outlook on life and you will find before long that you begin to feel depressed and it is an immense relief when you part company with that person. You were picking up their vibrations and unless you learn to screen them out, they will continue to affect you each time you come into contact with the person concerned.

On the other hand, some people can make you feel cheered and vitalised because they seem to radiate exuberance and charm. You are constantly being bombarded by the thoughts and emotions of other people. The person that you know as a psychic is simply someone who knows how to analyse and interpret the signals he or she is receiving. A psychic does not produce something magical out of thin air—he is simply using a wider range of senses and perceptions than most people are accustomed to using.

You cannot retire to a desert island and spend the rest of your life in solitary contemplation of your navel; that is not the purpose for which you entered this world. Neither can you permit yourself to remain at the mercy of the tumultuous flood of psychic currents which surround you in the everyday world. You must be able to function without undue interference. If you cannot, you will become subject to moods and depressions and possible illness because your own energy flow will be constantly disturbed.

There are, of course, other things which can and do cause illness. Your body can be invaded by microscopic organisms which produce sickness, or it can be accidentally injured. Most of these conditions can be alleviated by conventional medical techniques but some of them cannot. Psychic healing, however, possesses in itself the potential ability to cope with each and every one of them, provided that enough people spend the time and energy to develop it.

Whatever the cause of your ailment, what is happening is an interruption in the normal flow of energy through your body. If that vital energy is completely interrupted, your physical body will die. If it is partially blocked, there will be some dysfunction, which will be mild or severe, depending on the extent of the blockage.

Sometimes the messages that you are sending to your body will be distorted. You may, for instance, be trying to make your arm bend but the arm receives instead a signal to stiffen. At the same time you are likely to feel pain, for this is the body's signal that something is going wrong. No matter how hard you try to force that arm to move, it will only stiffen more because your signal will continue to be distorted.

The obvious solution would be to locate the point at which the signal is being distorted and correct the energy flow. This may be possible with conventional medical techniques or it may not. A psychic healer would attempt to correct the situation by taking hold of the afflicted part or placing his hands over it, then placing himself in communication with the guides who carry out the actual work of healing. Roland does this by placing himself in a trance state and allowing the spirit healer to take control of his body, but it is not necessary to go to that extreme; Roland does it simply because he is a trance medium.

It is the spirit guides who carry out the healing work and they tell us that they do it by using the energy at their disposal to correct the energy flow within the recipient.

Have you ever watched a hospital drama on television and heard the doctor announce in an urgent voice that his patient is 'fibrillating'? If so, you will know that this always produces a flurry of frantic activity, usually the high point of the programme. Fibrillation occurs when the heart muscle ceases to pump strongly and instead flutters uselessly; if the situation is not quickly corrected the patient goes into heart failure and dies.

At such dramatic moments the doctor usually reaches

for a machine called, appropriately enough, a defibrillator. Taking two paddle-shaped conductors, he places them on the patient's chest and a powerful surge of electricity (energy) is then pulsed through them. The object is to overcome the malfunction within the heart muscle by stimulating it to resume its normal beat.

In a gentler form, this is the underlying principle in psychic healing. We can liken the hands of the psychic to the defibrillator paddles, because healing energy is propelled through them by the guides. The similarity ends there however, because the psychic also functions as a diagnostic instrument for the healers. Before it is possible to correct a malfunction the condition must be assessed. To this end, the healing medium allows the patient's vibrations to flow through himself so that the spirits can make their analysis and decide upon the appropriate form of energy transmission.

This method of healing can be very effective in cases of intractable pain such as migraine. As a case in point: Doctor G. brought to us a lady who had suffered from chronic migraine headaches for around twelve years. He had referred her to five different neurologists, the Sydney Headache Clinic and the Human Performance Laboratory in attempts to isolate and treat the cause of the ailment.

All of these efforts had proved unsuccessful. In the meantime, Doctor G. was forced to administer powerful pain-killing drugs with increasing strength and frequency; a situation that he regarded as very unhealthy.

When they arrived on our doorstep the lady looked very ill. Her face was grey and her features were drawn and tense. She moved like a robot in an obvious effort to cushion her body against all unnecessary motion. When she sat down it was on the edge of a chair, eyes half-closed. She spoke in a whisper through clenched lips and it was apparent from the start that she expected very little from the visit. She admitted to being highly sceptical about psychics of any description and it was evident that she had come to us only as a last resort.

Roland startled her somewhat by stating quite plainly that if she was expecting *him* to heal her, she could forget it. He told her that if relief was forthcoming it would be delivered by those who worked through him. His function was simply to make himself available as a channel. This information seemed to reassure her a little and she declared herself quite willing to let us do what we could, on the basis that we could offer no guarantees of success.

Roland settled himself into a chair and it was not long before his breathing altered to the now-familiar pattern which heralds the approach of the guides. Our lady visitor eyed my 'sleeping' husband dubiously and kept glancing towards Doctor G. for reassurance.

One of our healing guides, a tersely humorous character named William, arrived quite soon and his no-nonsense manner rapidly dispelled our visitor's uneasiness. It seemed to me that his presence alone brought comfort to her and she relaxed slightly as Roland's hands skimmed along, some two inches above her hair, 'scanning' the top of her head.

As he worked, William explained his method to us. He was scanning in order to detect heat emanations and thus pinpoint the pain centre. Once he was satisfied that he had located the source of the pain, he moved in for a closer examination, his fingers running lightly over the base of her skull. He was feeling for a small indentation. This, he told us, would be located on the other side of the head, opposite the centre of the pain. Doctor G. asked how William knew this and was told that these indentations can always be found when migraine is present.

William made a satisfied noise and rested Roland's right hand against the patient's head at a point on the right-hand side of the skull, quite close to the temple. He explored the area at the base of her skull, slightly to the left of the spinal column; it did not take him long to locate the indentation, over which he rested the left hand.

He explained that his next step would be to pour energy through one of the hands and remove it with the other, hopefully taking the pain with it. After telling the patient that she would probably feel nothing more than a sensation of heat, he asked her to let him know immediately if the level of heat became uncomfortable.

In right-handed people, the right hand is usually the

energy 'transmitter' while the left functions as a receptor. Roland, however, is left-handed so in his case the reverse is true. Our patient confirmed that she could feel a slight warmth radiating from the left hand and we sat quietly waiting for William to complete his task. After about five minutes had passed, he removed the hands and told the patient that her headache would completely dissipate within another five minutes or so. On that note, William departed, leaving Roland to sleep peacefully for a few minutes.

By the time Roland was fully awake, the lady had seated herself comfortably on the sofa and was busily plying me with questions about our experiences with the guides. All traces of pain had disappeared and she was smiling happily. The contrast between this vivacious woman and the pain-wracked creature who had stepped through our door was almost too much for Roland who, as usual, could remember nothing of the trance proceedings.

In the twelve months that followed, this patient consulted Doctor G. only twice with headaches. This was a marked comparison to the constant pain that had plagued her for years prior to her visit to us.

The technique described above has worked in every instance where it has been applied in our sittings. It was also taught to Doctor G. as a method of drug-free pain relief by David, who told the doctor to go away and try it for himself over the next week or so. Ten days later, Doctor G. was back, claiming that he had a complaint to make about 'this psychic healing business'. When we questioned him, he said, 'Well, I've tried it on eighty-four patients—and on four of them it didn't work!' A 95 per cent success rate of drug-free therapy in the first week and he complains! Fortunately (perhaps for him!) the good doctor was merely having a little joke at our expense.

It is important to understand that there is a distinction between psychic healing and miraculous cures. Although we have seen some dramatic demonstrations of instant healing, it is more common for the process to be slower. Some complaints may only require one sitting but a severe or chronic condition may require several. Part of the reason for this lies in the fact that Roland and I do not

251

habitually work as healers and we are therefore not developed to full capacity in that respect. There is also a correlation between the medium's level of vitality and the capacity for energy transference. After a long and strenuous day at work it is not as easy for Roland to produce remarkable results as it is when he is fresh and full of vim. Equally, if he is tense or irritable, the energy flow is severely restricted.

One patient who required more than one visit was a friend of mine named Chris. In childhood she had suffered a serious fall and some ten years ago she fell victim to rheumatoid arthritis. Her condition was so severe that she was not expected to recover but the doctors had not reckoned on her remarkable determination. She did eventually get the better of the disease but it was some time before she was able to walk, much less carry out any strenuous activity.

She consulted doctors and chiropractors many times over a number of years and her back, which had been the site of most of her troubles, improved greatly under treatment. However, there was some residual damage that resisted all treatment and she resigned herself to the prospect of living with the nagging pain for the rest of her life.

Chris is psychic herself but she does not work in the field of psychic healing. When she got to know us and discovered that we do, she asked if we would allow her to consult the guides. We agreed readily and the first sitting was held almost immediately. She chatted amiably with William as he examined her back thoroughly: she seemed quite impressed when he indicated three points at which he said that her spinal column had fused. These were indeed the points at which she felt the most pain. William instructed me to examine the spine under his guidance and I could clearly feel three hard protuberances at the points indicated by him.

The healer told us that he could cope with one fusion at a time and asked Chris if she would return twice more for further treatment. She agreed and he set to work on the first healing session. I watched in fascination as he vigorously manipulated her spine for a period of about fifteen minutes, after which he called me over to examine the spot myself. Where before there had been three unmistakable lumps, I could now find only two.

In the two sittings which followed, the remaining lumps were removed from Chris's spine. All in all, the three sittings had taken place over a total period of two weeks. To say that Chris was delighted to be able to move freely for the first time in memory, free of pain, would be a considerable understatement.

You will by now have noticed that all the cases I have cited (except for Roland's knee) involved physically tangible illnesses or ailments that had proven unresponsive to modern day medical technology and practices. Yet these same ailments responded dramatically, even instantly in some cases, to the healing energies produced by the guides. That should tell us something.

Whether or not the patient believes in psychic phenomena, psychic healing *works*. Whether or not you believe in them, the psychic spheres exist and so do the beings who populate them. Whether you know it or not, you are an immortal spirit, following a process of growth and evolution which will ultimately take you far beyond the physical and into dimensions of existence that the human mind is barely capable of imagining. Throughout this book, we have not asked that you believe what we tell you, nor have we tried to present any proof that the psychic worlds exist. Nor have we attempted to argue any doctrines, for that is not our purpose.

Our purpose in this book and in the ones which are to follow it, is simply to make available the information that we have accumulated during our own pursuit of psychic understanding. Roland and I feel that there is much in what we have encountered that can be of value to others who, like us, seek an understanding of the realms which lie beyond the physical.

In spiritual terms, understanding is the key to growth and happiness. If by sharing our knowledge and experience with you, our readers, we have helped you to understand a little more about your purpose for being here and the direction that your life is taking, this book has achieved its purpose. If a little more light has entered your life through its pages, Roland and I are fulfilled also.

CHAPTER TWENTY ONE
Hauntings

Whenever the subject of haunted houses comes under discussion the imagination naturally turns to visions of crumbling mansions and stately English abbeys. The British Isles reputedly teem with the shades of grey monks and melancholy Gothic ladies, all lovingly catalogued in countless books on the subject. The whole world knows that Anne Boleyn was reported to walk the Tower of London with her head disconcertingly tucked underneath her arm. Her cousin Katherine Howard, King Henry's equally luckless fifth wife, has been heard screaming with terror in a corridor of Hampton Court, the scene of her last desperate attempt to plead for her husband's non-existent mercy.

Much controversy has surrounded the story of Borley Rectory, once known as the most haunted house in England. It was claimed to be the site of an assortment of supernatural occurrences which included savage poltergeist phenomena and the sudden disappearance of objects which would reappear inexplicably somewhere else. Barely legible writing appeared on the walls and several people claimed to have seen the ghostly figure of a nun moving through the grounds. A number of attempts were made to penetrate the mystery of Borley Rectory and find the source of the strange manifestations.

Harry Price, the famed ghost-hunter, spent a great deal of time in the place, trying to isolate the source of the phenomena and he even wrote a book about his investigations. But like everyone else, he failed to unravel the puzzle and eventually the old place put an end to the speculation by burning to the ground (apparently by spontaneous combustion).

It is traditional for hauntings to be surrounded by rumours of woeful events. Rarely, if ever, do we hear anything about a happy ghost. The pages of supernatural legend are populated by walled-up nuns, murder victims, dolourous ladies pining for lost lovers and frustrated souls seeking redress for untold wrongs.

Ghost stories have always been a popular source of entertainment, all the more so when they are reputed to be factual. These stories might not find such a ready audience if the hearers did not, deep down inside themselves, acknowledge that such things might actually happen. All the same, it is much more entertaining to hear about the ghost that appeared to somebody else. Nobody really wants to go home one evening and discover that a spectre has taken up residence during their absence. How would *you* feel if you were woken each night at midnight by the sounds of female sobbing coming from somewhere in your house?

There are many stories told about real cases in which precisely that kind of thing happened—to ordinary, down-to-earth people like you. For instance, the unsuspecting couple who moved into their new home in the Sydney suburb of Surry Hills about fifty years ago. Every night for weeks they were disturbed by the sound of infants crying. Eventually, while digging in the garden, the husband unearthed the badly decomposed body of a small child. Subsequent police investigations revealed the bodies of numerous small children interred there.

A previous tenant had decided to supplement her income by taking foster children into her care. However, she did not feel inclined to spend the proceeds on her small charges, so she calmly murdered them.

I have read that story more than once in the local press and each time I have wondered what that couple felt when they realised that the spirit of a dead child had deliberately sought their aid.

Something haunted a house in which I once lived with my ex-husband but to this day I do not know what it was and, as far as I know, it is still there. Whatever it was, it certainly wasn't benevolent. Several visitors who came to the house claimed to hear footsteps climbing the steps to the front door and they always expressed surprise when I informed them that not only could I hear nothing, but I had no intention of opening the door.

Footsteps were often heard in and around that house,

although I never heard them myself. One night, Dennis lay awake for over an hour, listening to stealthy footsteps pacing to and fro on the path outside our bedroom window. Several times he crept to the window and peered out but although the footsteps could still be heard, there was nothing to be seen. Nor were the disturbances confined to the dark hours: one morning I got up to drive Darryl to school, leaving Dennis comfortably reading in bed. He heard the car when I returned and heard the front door latch, followed by the rapid click of high heels across the floor. It occurred to him that I must have moved quickly to get inside so soon, but then he heard a sound that made his blood freeze—the sound I made as I closed the car door.

When I entered the house, he asked if I had come in earlier. As he related what he had heard, I shook my head and pointed silently at my flat-heeled, rubber-soled shoes.

Although I was interested in psychic phenomena at the time, I never heard any inexplicable sounds, nor was I particularly aware of a presence. I simply found the house cold and depressing. I could not feel contented there and I frequently lapsed into periods of mindless lethargy during which my body felt like a lump of lead and the mental effort of answering the telephone could take on the proportions of a major operation.

Darryl suffered from frequent nightmares; hardly a night passed without his terrified screams piercing the air in the middle of the night. He was also constantly ill with asthma and strung out with nervous tension.

My marriage finally ground to a halt in that house, although I don't lay the blame for that on the supernatural. The signs of decay were evident long before we went to live there, but I suppose it is possible that the house may have accelerated matters.

After I left, Dennis remained in the house for a while and the disturbances increased. Now there were heavy, menacing footsteps in the hall and the sounds of furniture being moved. Dennis lost count of the number of times he went to check after hearing a chair scraping across the floor, only to find everything as he he had left it. Several times, he heard a voice that sounded like mine, calling his name. I recall other occasions when he had come to ask me what I wanted, saying that I had called him. I assumed that he had mistaken a neighbour's voice for mine but he was adamant that he had distinctly heard me call. All of these things happened during broad daylight.

It was worse at night. The noises would stop and the house become heavy with silent foreboding. No one could ever identify the cause of this feeling.

There were no sounds, nothing moved and there was nothing to see, yet quite a few of the people who slept in that house claimed to feel a nameless threatening uneasiness. My sister Amanda could never bear her bedroom to be in darkness; she slept with the light on all night. My other sister, Jacqui, sensed a heavy presence so tangibly that she could almost touch it. Dennis told me that it got worse after I left, often waking him at night. He always awoke suddenly, panting with fear, and could not go back to sleep because of the overwhelming sensation that something was brooding over him, waiting, watching.

The neighbours regarded the house as unlucky. They told me that no couple who went to live in that house had ever stayed happy. Several marriages broke up there and one happy couple were parted when the husband was killed in an accident.

As to what it was or why it seemed to weaken in my presence, I cannot be sure. Perhaps it was the lost soul that later followed Roland and me to North Sydney or maybe it was something else. Whatever it was, it made its presence known to a number of people. Perhaps it is lurking there still.

Not all hauntings are ominous, some are simply pathetic. My mother once told me of an apparition that she saw while still in her teens. She was staying with friends of the family in a Tasmanian coastal town and she awoke in the middle of the night to see a woman in a long nightgown standing at her door. At first she thought it was her hostess but then the translucent figure glided forward and was revealed as a wraith. Rigid with fear, Mum lay stiffly in the bed while the ethereal being bent to tuck in the blankets around her. The figure then drifted back to the door and was gone.

At breakfast, Mum told her hosts about the nocturnal visitor. To her amazement, they only smiled. 'Don't worry, she won't hurt you,' they assured her. 'She is only looking for her baby. Apparently it died and she went out of her mind with grief. She used to wander all over the place searching for it. Never recovered her wits, poor thing. She always appears when a young person is in the house but she only wants to take care of them. I suppose she still misses her baby. Sad, isn't it? Have some more toast.'

Hauntings differ from possession only in the nature of attachment. Instead of being enmeshed in the aura of a living person, the spirit is tied to a particular house or location. Always there is some emotional bond at work—an entity might remain in a house where it once lived, or revisit the scene of a traumatic event, because of some powerful emotional attraction towards the place.

Graveyards are almost *never* haunted. A spirit will be drawn to a place that figured prominently in its life, but very few of us form powerful emotional links with a cemetery. It is far more likely that you will find a ghost in an airy suburban home than in the peaceful stillness of a graveyard. As a child I was instinctively drawn towards cemeteries and my mother feared that I might be developing a morbid preoccupation with death but it was not so. In the light of my present knowledge I can easily understand what it was that attracted me. It was the peace and solitude.

I used to love visiting my Aunty Dorrie, who lived in Launceston, because her house was only a few doors away from the city cemetery. As soon as I could politely excuse myself, I would hurry off to the cemetery gates and walk in reverently, shoes crunching on the crisp gravel underfoot. My steps carried me swiftly away from the new part of the graveyard, although sometimes I might pause to look at a neatly lettered granite memorial. My target was always the same—the old section. Here bleached white headstones stood silent sentinel over the graves they had guarded for years. Faded china flowers, topped with glass domes nestled on the neat gravel surfaces of the tombs. Here and there gleaming evergreens threw cool shadows across the path and the breeze murmured softly through their branches.

I was alone, and in the solitude I could walk with my unseen friends and ponder about the things that they silently whispered in my mind. They told me things for which my youthful mind could find no words, only feelings. In the organised bustle of the adult world outside, there was no time for meditation—indeed, what adult would have imagined that a child would need to meditate in any case? In the cemetery all was still and quiet and there was nothing to disturb my mood of contemplation. No jibbering demons assailed me, nor any wailing spectres. I knew I was safe there, and I was only a child.

If the spirits of the dead remain close to the physical world, it is amongst the living that they will be found. Just as with cases of possession, there is always a reason why the spirit becomes earthbound and that reason is usually an unhappy one. A person who has lived a rich and fulfilling life is not likely to be earthbound. The low vibrations of negative emotion are what tie a spirit to the earth plane, and that is why the themes of ghost stories are full of sorrow and despair.

The very first time that Roland and I were asked to use our psychic abilities to help anyone, the problem was centred in a house where strange things were happening. Objects were vanishing only to reappear several days later, locked doors and windows were being mysteriously opened and the family car started running its motor all by itself in a locked garage. The woman who lived there began to wonder if she was losing her mind but her three children also commented on the inexplicable events. Nola confided in a friend at work, who advised her to ring the Psychic Research Centre.

By chance, she happened to speak to someone at the Research Centre who knew Roland and I. He gave her our telephone number and suggested that we might be able to help. Up until that time, we had only held our sittings with David alone in our own home. We had never investigated a psychic disturbance and had no idea of how to start, so we decided to play by ear and see what happened. We agreed to visit the house.

When we arrived Nola offered us coffee, which we

drank in the dining room. I felt uncomfortable; although the weather outside was sunny, the interior of the house was cold, almost clammy. Also, there was a strange air about the place. After a reasonable period of occupation, a house tends to absorb the vibrations of its tenants, to such a degree that it seems to take on a personality of its own. This house had absorbed nothing, it felt as though nobody lived there. Yet there was a personality present. I felt it and I could sense its emotions. They made me feel ineffably sad and I wanted to cry. I looked at Roland. He was half tranced and tears were pouring down his face.

After a few moments, Roland abruptly stood up and started pacing through the house. Nola went with him, telling him a little about each room but I had the impression that he was barely listening. Eventually he walked into the lounge room and sat down on the floor in a corner, knees drawn up under his chin, eyes flicking back and forth between Nola and I.

His gaze settled on Nola and he began to stare at her intently. I watched his features take on an expression of hostility, then he spoke.

'Get out!' he thundered at Nola.

'Do you want Nola to leave the room?' I asked.

'No, the house! I want her out!'

'But that's hardly fair. The house belongs to her.'

'It does not, it's *mine*.'

'How can that be?' I countered. 'Did you design it?'

'. . . and built it,' came the reply.

I looked at Nola. She nodded slightly but I could not read her expression. I turned back to my entranced husband to see tears glistening on his cheeks.

'I built it! I *built it*!' he declared with vehemence, then, almost as though talking to himself '. . . no one likes it but me, no one loves it.' His voice was strained with emotion.

'That's not true,' I stated, 'Nola likes it.'

'Then why isn't she happy here?' Again there was that icy vehemence.

'That has nothing to do with the house . . .' explained Nola. She was interrupted by an anguished cry.

'*She* didn't like it, she hated it!' the voice trailed off in a wail and Roland awoke from his trance.

I asked Nola if she knew the history of the house and

260

she nodded. It had been designed by the first owner and he had indeed helped to build it. It was built for his wife but she had never liked it and she finally committed suicide there. The house was sold several times after that but no one had ever been happy in it. Several marriages foundered and there was another suicide. Nola's marriage had also broken up while she was living there, and this was the reason for her unhappiness.

Now that we knew the problem the next step was to find a solution. I stood up and spoke to the invisible presence.

'I know that you will hear what I am saying, my friend. We understand why you are distressed, but your difficulties will not be solved with hostility. You are only creating an atmosphere that will drive happiness away. Let Nola be a friend; give her your friendship and offer her the freedom to love the house as you want it to be loved. Try it and see.'

I looked enquiringly at Roland, who shrugged and gave me his 'who knows?' look.

Nola offered us more coffee, which was gratefully accepted, but we had hardly begun to drink when Roland's attitude altered dramatically. He gazed steadily at me, a quizzical expression on his face.

'Who are you?' I asked.

'A friend.'

'Can I be sure of that?'

The grey eyes surveyed me speculatively.

'It was you who suggested that I make friends. I want to know more about your proposal.'

'Are you the person I was speaking to earlier?' I asked. The answer was a brief nod.

'I built this house,' he said. 'I built it for her but she hated it. I had put so much of myself into it. I created it, it's like a part of me. It was as though she was rejecting me too. Now there is just the house and it has never known happiness. I put so much of myself into it . . . I can't leave until it's happy.'

'Do you understand that you've been going the wrong way about it?' I queried. Nola leaned forward in her chair, looking first at me and then at the entranced figure of my husband. She was intently following the con-

261

versation, nodding her head slightly as I spoke.

'Your actions are all negative,' I continued. 'The house is filled with unhappiness so it attracts the same thing. Happy people find it cold and uninviting so they don't consider living in it. If you fill it with love and light instead of trying to chase people away you will create a happy atmosphere. Welcome those who want to live here and try to surround them with love. It may take time but you will succeed.'

Our companion agreed that my argument was logical. He thanked me and courteously assured Nola that he would cause no further trouble. Then he withdrew and Roland awoke.

We stayed in touch with Nola for about twelve months after that. She reported that there had been no further disturbances. As to her personal problems—we don't possess magic wands and the matter was not ours to pursue. But at least her situation was no longer complicated by the perambulations of a disgruntled ghost.

We made no attempt to move that spirit on because it was plain that he would have put up a vigorous resistance. He felt that he had a purpose which must be achieved before he could really feel free. I believed that the best thing to do was offer him the means of fulfilling his commitment so that he could move on naturally. Besides, he was very pleasant once we got through to him properly and he had, after all, been the one who had brought the house into existence. I saw no reason why he should not be allowed to give his love to his own creation.

Oddly enough, the next haunted house that was brought to our notice was also inhabited by a spirit who had played a part in its construction. This one, however, had been involved in building an addition onto the rear of the house.

We were approached by an acquaintance who had been lodging in the place. The owner had sold it and they were due to move out soon, but Tony was concerned. There was a history of broken marriages in the house and also the deaths of several small children. Tony insisted that there was an entity in the rumpus room. He had not seen it but he could feel its brooding presence.

He was uneasy because he had met the people who had bought the house. They were a young couple, expecting their first baby. Tony was convinced that unless the entity were removed, the child would suffer. He urged us to do what we could. We agreed and he obtained his landlady's permission for a sitting to be held in the house. She elected to stay the night with a friend.

When we entered the house my attention was immediately drawn to a room at the rear.

'Is that the rumpus room?' I asked. Tony nodded, looking gratified that my instincts aligned with his own feelings. I was dismayed by the room, chiefly because it was entirely painted in pillar-box red, a colour that signifies passionate emotions. The room had the atmosphere of a witches' den and although it was large and airy, I felt stifled.

The trance session was strange and unnerving. Roland paced restlessly back and forth, apparently oblivious to Tony and I; if we spoke, he would jerk his head up and gaze distractedly in our direction as though we had aroused him from some deep level of contemplation. He appeared to be confused and uncomfortable and although I guided him gently to a chair, he could not remain seated but resumed his uneasy pacing. Eventually he paused to rest, leaning against a pillar in the centre of the room. His head drooped a little and I was aghast to realise that he had fallen into a trance. I don't like to see him trance on his feet when we are dealing with an unknown entity. His body is temporarily controlled by the entity during a trance and should the being prove hostile, mobility could render it highly menacing.

However, it seemed that the entity was either uninterested or unaware of our presence. There was a bar in one corner of the room and it was towards this that the spirit made its way. As he shuffled slowly towards the bar, I followed close behind. When he reached his goal, the silent figure squatted beside a small refrigerator and reached for the electric cord. With a savage jerk he wrenched the plug from its socket, then sagged back against the wall. Moments later, Roland awoke.

We were undecided as to what should be done next. I felt that we had not really succeeded in releasing the spirit; we had merely observed while it pursued some mysterious course of its own. The room was still oppressive and Roland acted slightly dazed, as though some influence still hung within his aura. We tried again for a trance communication, to no avail. By then, Roland had become acutely uncomfortable and asked us to take him home, as he did not want to remain in the house any longer.

We gathered up our belongings and prepared to leave, but we were prevented. Roland could not step through the front door. He made three attempts and each time it appeared as though he had collided with an invisible barrier. Three times he halted and turned, to walk stiffly towards the rumpus room. Halfway across the floor he would stop and shake his head in perplexity, then turn his distressed gaze to me and ask what on earth he was doing there.

Finally, I decided something didn't want us to leave. It seemed that our job wasn't finished. I doubted that we would be able to leave until we did what was wanted and it seemed that *something* wanted Roland back in the rumpus room.

He shrugged his shoulders in irritation: 'All right, we'll see what the hell it wants!' He marched into the rumpus room, stood behind the bar and addressed the empty room while Tony and I hovered in the doorway.

'Okay, I'm here! What do you want?'

Silence reigned. Nothing moved and there was no sign of Roland entering a trance. He moved impatiently.

'Enough of this,' he declared. 'Let's see if we can get out of here now.'

This time nothing impeded our progress. Roland hesitated when we reached the front door but when he strode purposefully forward he passed through without incident.

'That's that,' he grinned. 'Let's go.'

We were somewhat thoughtful as we drove away. I was plagued by dissatisfaction: I dislike vague endings and much prefer to bring our activities to a neat and definite conclusion. Nothing definite had been achieved on this occasion and I wondered morosely if we had encountered our first failure. What had we left behind and how would it affect the new residents? I could muster no optimism—nothing was clearcut.

All at once I became uneasily aware that the back of my neck was prickling. I turned to look at Roland and saw that his eyes were wide open and staring blankly ahead. My heart sank: a moving car is not an ideal setting for a trance, especially when a disturbed entity is present. I motioned Tony to slow down and warned him to be prepared to stop quickly. I did not want the entity throwing my husband's body out of a moving vehicle.

I kept my eyes fixed on Roland and noticed a tear sliding down his face. His expression was dismal and I felt a wave of compassion. Softly, I spoke.

'Will you talk to me? I want to help.'

Eyes full of misery met mine and a rusty voice spoke. 'Where are you taking me?'

'To my home. We can talk there, if you like. I was sent to see if I could be of help to you, do you understand?'

'It doesn't matter,' was the flat response.

The entity lapsed into silence. Tony glanced at me and raised his eyebrows. I answered with a helpless shrug. I could not risk forcing the pace; the spirit would speak again when it was ready. At least we knew that we had not left it behind in the house.

'It was a saw, you know,' the voice startled me and it took a few moments for me to collect my wits. Suddenly I recalled the savage intensity with which the plug had been pulled from the electric socket in the bar.

'An *electric* saw?' I murmured gently. Roland's head nodded slowly and I heard his breath catch in a sob.

'I should never have left it plugged in. I never realised she'd pick it up and play with it.'

'She . . . your child?'

He nodded again. 'She came skipping out of the house and picked it up. By the time I got to her—I wasn't quick enough.'

He covered his face with his hands and sobbed desperately. I felt tears filling my eyes—I did not want to imagine the scene being described but the horror swept over me nonetheless. I, too, am a parent.

The harsh sobs subsided and those tragic eyes stared into mine once more.

'I can't face it,' he moaned, 'I have to live with that memory for the rest of my life. It's too much, I can't bear it!'

'Listen to me,' I urged. 'You may not understand this, but your daughter has been healed. She is whole now, and happy. I can have her brought to you if you like.'

His expression displayed his disbelief. There was a long, tense pause and then the eyes closed and I heard David's voice.

'My daughter, it is done. He is now with us.'

I let out a long sigh of relief.

We were not told whether the distraught father had suicided after the tragedy or had met his end by some other means. After witnessing his extreme state of distress, I tend to suspect the former, but it was obvious from his words that he did not know that he had passed out of this world. That is frequently the case with earthbound spirits; it seems that trauma or great mental distress may overshadow the effects of transition so that the spirit remains unaware of the great change that has taken place.

There is some controversy about whether 'ghosts' are in fact the souls of the departed. There is a school of thought which suggests that traumatic or emotionally charged events may cause a burst of energy to be released and absorbed by inanimate objects in the immediate vicinity. According to this line of belief, a sensitive person coming into contact with the charged objects would experience the emotions imprinted on them and may even 'see' the events which took place years before. I cannot entirely dispute this suggestion; it seems to be based quite soundly on the principle of psychometry, and there may be some hauntings where this is indeed the cause.

Nevertheless, psychometry does not account for the hauntings that involved Roland and me. Roland has often performed psychometry but it has never been necessary for him to trance in order to do so. He trances only when it is necessary to make his body available to another entity. Nor is the decision about whether or not he will trance made by him. He simply prepares himself and if a trance is needed it will be induced by the guides.

He cannot trance at will. Since he has tranced each time we have attended a haunting and since a personality has manifested through him on each occasion, we have satisfactory evidence for accepting that a definite presence existed in those cases.

That is not to say that an earthbound spirit is at work in every haunted house. Roland and I are both keenly aware of the pitfalls involved in making snap judgements. On the occasions when we have made assumptions, subsequent events have proven us wrong. Therefore we can only base our judgements on the facts that we already know. By that line of reasoning we can say that earthbound entities may prove to be responsible for a number of hauntings but there may be different factors at work in other cases.

The poltergeist presents another frequently observed form of psychic disturbance. It is accepted that the majority of poltergeist disturbances occur around pubescent children and there is a logical reason for this. Just as a disturbance within your aura can interrupt your bodily functions, physical disturbances can disrupt the aura. In puberty the body undergoes periods of rapid growth and major hormonal changes. A great deal of energy is produced and expended during this period of life. Poltergeist phenomena occurs when these bursts of energy break free from the body. Because a pubescent child is also subject to violent swings of emotion, the energy tends to manifest itself in violent ways, e.g. smashing crockery or upending furniture.

There is another factor which can emerge during a period of poltergeist activity. Free-floating psychic energy can attract disturbed spirits. If this happens, the disturbances can be greatly intensified because there are now two or more forces at work. The presence of earthbound entities can also have a detrimental effect on the sensitive teenage psyche, causing even greater depths of moodiness than normal. The answer to this would be the same as in cases of possession but it would take a trained psychic to determine whether or not an entity were present.

There are some cases of poltergeist phenomena where there are no teenagers involved. Remember that it is only necessary for there to be uncontrolled bursts of psychic energy to create this phenomenon. I once read an interview with Uri Geller in which the interviewer claimed to have witnessed manifestations of poltergeist phenomena in Geller's apartment. Geller is reported to have said that these disturbances are constantly occurring around him. Since he has also stated that he does not fully understand the source of his gift, it seems logical to assume that he does not know how to control the energy that flows through him.

Concerning our involvement with the supernatural, haunted houses et al, I am often asked 'Doesn't it scare you?' It is impossible to give a straight yes or no answer to that question. It would be untrue to claim that I never have any misgivings; indeed I would be extremely foolhardy to plunge into a confrontation with an unknown and possibly unstable entity without any reservations at all. On the other hand, if the prospect of facing up to the supernatural held any real terrors for me I simply wouldn't do it.

Anything is forbidding the first time it is experienced. When I took my car onto the road for the first time after getting my licence I crawled along so slowly that the poor little engine almost had an internal haemorrhage. I kept thinking about all the disastrous things that could possibly happen to me, but once I had gained a bit of practice those fears melted away. I developed some confidence and after taking every reasonable precaution against danger I actually started to enjoy myself.

It is never wise to allow familiarity to breed carelessness, because the backlash can be instantaneous and we are dealing with a very powerful form of energy. Properly channelled, the energy can be beneficial but it should always be treated with respect. The most sensible attitude is to always be aware of the need for caution and make sure that you are doing nothing that can upset the balance, but you need not creep around as though you were standing on top of a fully armed atomic missile.

Apart from all the possible physical precautions, there is one factor which should never be overlooked—the confidence that comes from knowing beyond a doubt that you are continually guarded by a being whose knowledge, strength and expertise are more than equal to anything you may have to face on your level of existence.

Remember when you first learned to ride a bicycle? As long as Dad kept a firm grip on the seat you rode steadily and you continued to do so even after he let go. Only when you realised that he wasn't holding you any more did you begin to wobble. However, before you could fall, he was there to steady your erratic progress. You only really started to ride alone when you developed enough skill to handle the bike by yourself.

Working with spirit guides in psychic development is a bit like riding a bike. As long as we progress steadily and in safety, the guides do not interfere. Should we veer towards danger or begin to show signs of fear, the steadying hand is always there to take over until we are again capable of fending for ourselves. With this awareness of protection is it any wonder that I am sometimes at a loss for an answer when someone asks me if I am not rather frightened of the supernatural?

It would be an entirely different story if I did not have the protection of my guide and I don't advise anyone to become involved in psychic activity until they have sought and gained the assistance of their own guide. That is why this book has been designed to tell you, as far as it is possible for one person to explain in words, how to go about establishing contact with your guide.

We are all individuals and your experiences will by no means exactly mirror mine or Roland's. However, if you are operating on a similar wavelength, you will experience many things which you will recognize as being in common with what we have described. We cannot bring you to where we are, we can only tell you how we got here.

On that final note, I think it is fitting that we close this book with some words of wisdom given to us by David himself:

'You are where you are, yet you are with me. I am where I am, yet I am with you. Neither of us has moved, yet we are together. We have traversed . . . do you understand?'

Afterword

Having completed our first book, we now look forward to producing the second and subsequent volumes until it is no longer possible for us to lift a pen.

The love and wisdom that has come to us from the spirit world has not only transfigured our lives, it has created within us a desire to share our good fortune with others. Among our readers there will be those who are seeking the kind of enlightenment that David has brought to us and it is to them that we address our work.

We do not intend to found a new religion, nor shall we permit any organisation to be formed in our name, for our interest does not lie in creating institutions but simply in passing on the knowledge that David has given to us.

A spiritual teacher should be just that: someone who awakens the spirit within you. Do not try to memorise our words—just open up your mind and see what awakens inside you. You may be able to experience something that you would like to share with us. This is how spiritual development happens, by the exchange of information between people who have had experiences of a spiritual nature.

Our books are being written for you so that you can share in the understanding that David has imparted to us. Consequently, we would like to hear from you. Write and tell us of your experiences with supernatural phenomena; under what conditions did they occur and how did you react to them? Tell us if you think there is an area of the supernatural that we have overlooked. Argue with us. If you think we are wrong tell us so, and why.

Understand that the feedback we receive from you will give us some idea of what you want to know about the spiritual and your letters may form the basis of some of our future works. There is some difficulty, however, which may arise if you wish to receive an answer from us. Please understand that there are only twenty-four hours in a day and if we receive as much mail as we would like, it may not be possible for us to answer each letter personally, although we promise to do our best. In addition, we must point out that we are not millionaires and postage in large lumps can be expensive. If you want an answer and you live in Australia, enclose a stamped envelope and we will do our best to reply to you, but please understand our limitations and forgive us if our answer is slow in coming or if we simply cannot find the time to reply. If you live overseas, you may need to obtain an international money order for the appropriate value of postage—an enquiry at your post office will give you the information you need in that respect.

One last thing, please, *please* do not send mail to us care of our publisher. He is a very busy man and I am sure he would not appreciate being required to operate as a mail exchange. If you wish to write to us, do so at the following address:

> C/- Post Office
> Mount Pleasant
> North Queensland 4740
> Australia